BUILDING A NEW WORLD ORDER
Sustainable Policies for the Future

This book is to be returned on or before the last date stamped below.

3 - DEC 2009

4 OCT 2011

1 8 DEC 2013

- 8 SEP 2014

- 3 JUL 2015

1 4 SEP 2015

2 8 SEP 2016

Campus Library Services Limited

41458

WARWICK SCHOOL

Our world is characterized by diverse values, cultures and ideologies, and diverging interests, beliefs, moral values, passions, and notions of good and evil. Democratization based on values and norms rooted in the Age of Reason in Europe stands in contrast to non-democratic countries. The call for 'global governance' which institutes worldwide measures for managing conflict and risk is becoming ever louder. This book shows why the success of global governance depends on the commitment of many, not just of a few heads of state, and shows how the prerequisites for formulating sustainable rules of such global governance can be established.

Born in 1949, Harald Müller is the Head of the Peace Research Institute, Frankfurt, (PRIF) and a professor of International Relations in Frankfurt am Main. For many years he was an adviser on disarmament to former UN Secretary-General Kofi Annan. His recent titles in English include: *Democratic Wars: Looking at the Dark Side of Democratic Peace* (ed., with Anna Geis/Lothar Brock, Palgrave Macmillan 2006) and *Democracy and Security: Preferences, Norms and Policy-making.* (ed., with Matthew Evangelista and Niklas Schörnig, Routledge 2008)

Our addresses on the Internet:
www.the-sustainability-project.com
www.forum-fuer-verantwortung.de
[English version available]

BUILDING A NEW WORLD ORDER
Sustainable Policies for the Future

HARALD MÜLLER

Translated by Matthew Harris

Klaus Wiegandt, General Editor

HAUS PUBLISHING

First published in Great Britain in 2009 by
Haus Publishing Ltd
70 Cadogan Place
London SW1X 9AH
www.hauspublishing.com

Originally published as: *Wie Kann eine Neue Weltordnung Aussehen?
Wege in eine Nachhaltige Politik* by Harald Müller

Copyright © 2007 Fischer Taschenbuch Verlag in der S. Fischer Verlag
GmbH, Frankfurt am Main

English translation copyright © Matthew Harris 2009

The moral right of the authors has been asserted

A CIP catalogue record for this book
is available from the British Library

ISBN 978-1-906598-16-7

Typeset in Sabon by MacGuru Ltd
Printed in Dubai by Oriental Press

CONDITIONS OF SALE
All rights reserved. No part of this publication may be reproduced,
stored in a retrieval system, or transmitted in any form or by any means,
electronic, mechanical, photocopying, recording or otherwise, without the
prior permission of the publisher.

This book is sold subject to the condition that it shall not, by way of trade
or otherwise, be lent, re-sold, hired out or otherwise circulated without
the publisher's prior consent in any form of binding or cover other than
that in which it is published and without a similar condition including this
condition being imposed on the subsequent purchaser.

Mixed Sources
Product group from well-managed
forests and other controlled sources
www.fsc.org Cert no. CU-COC-809367
© 1996 Forest Stewardship Council
FSC

Haus Publishing believes in the importance of a
sustainable future for our planet. This book is
printed on paper produced in accordance with the
standards of sustainability set out and monitored by
the FSC. The printer holds chain of custody.

For Piwi

Contents

Sales of the German-language edition of this series have exceeded all expectations. The positive media response has been encouraging, too. Both of these positive responses demonstrate that the series addresses the right topics in a language that is easily understood by the general reader. The combination of thematic breadth and scientifically astute, yet generally accessible writing, is particularly important as I believe it to be a vital prerequisite for smoothing the way to a sustainable society by turning knowledge into action. After all, I am not a scientist myself; my background is in business.

A few months ago, shortly after the first volumes had been published, we received suggestions from neighboring countries in Europe recommending that an English-language edition would reach a far larger readership. Books dealing with global challenges, they said, require global action brought about by informed debate amongst as large an audience as possible. When delegates from India, China, and Pakistan voiced similar concerns at an international conference my mind was made up. Dedicated individuals such as Lester R. Brown and Jonathan Porritt deserve credit for bringing the concept of sustainability to the attention of the general public; I am convinced that this series can give the discourse about sustainability something new.

Two years have passed since I wrote the foreword to the initial German edition. During this time, unsustainable developments on our planet have come to our attention in ever more dramatic ways. The price of oil has nearly tripled; the value of industrial metals has risen exponentially and, quite unexpectedly, the costs of staple foods such as corn, rice, and wheat have reached all-time highs. Around the globe, people are increasingly concerned that the pressure caused by these drastic price increases will lead to serious destabilization in China, India, Indonesia, Vietnam, and Malaysia, the world's key developing regions.

The frequency and intensity of natural disasters brought on by global warming has continued to increase. Many regions of our Earth are experiencing prolonged droughts, with subsequent shortages of drinking water and the destruction of entire harvests. In other parts of the world, typhoons and hurricanes are causing massive flooding and inflicting immeasurable suffering.

The turbulence in the world's financial markets, triggered by the US sub-prime mortgage crisis, has only added to these woes. It has affected every country and made clear just how unscrupulous and sometimes irresponsible speculation has become in today's financial world. The expectation of exorbitant short-term rates of return on capital investments led to complex and obscure financial engineering. Coupled with a reckless willingness to take risks everyone involved seemingly lost track of the situation. How else can blue chip companies incur multi-billion dollar losses? If central banks had not come to the rescue with dramatic steps to back up their currencies, the world's economy would have collapsed. It was only in these circumstances that the use of public monies could be justified. It is therefore imperative to prevent a repeat of speculation with short-term capital on such a gigantic scale.

Taken together, these developments have at least significantly improved the readiness for a debate on sustainability. Many more are now aware that our wasteful use of natural resources and energy have serious consequences, and not only for future generations.

Two years ago, who would have dared to hope that WalMart, the world's largest retailer, would initiate a dialog about sustainability with its customers and promise to put the results into practice? Who would have considered it possible that CNN would start a series "Going Green?" Every day, more and more businesses worldwide announce that they are putting the topic of sustainability at the core of their strategic considerations. Let us use this momentum to try and make sure that these positive developments are not a flash in the pan, but a solid part of our necessary discourse within civil society.

However, we cannot achieve sustainable development through a multitude of individual adjustments. We are facing the challenge of critical fundamental questioning of our lifestyle and consumption and patterns of production. We must grapple with the complexity of the entire earth system in a forward-looking and precautionary manner, and not focus solely on topics such as energy and climate change.

The authors of these twelve books examine the consequences of our destructive interference in the Earth ecosystem from different perspectives. They point out that we still have plenty of opportunities to shape a sustainable future. If we want to achieve this, however, it is imperative that we use the information we have as a basis for systematic action, guided by the principles of sustainable development. If the step from knowledge to action is not only to be taken, but also to succeed, we need to offer comprehensive education to all, with the foundation in early childhood. The central issues of the future must be anchored firmly in school curricula, and no university student should be permitted to graduate without having completed a general course on sustainable development. Everyday opportunities for action must be made clear to us all – young and old. Only then can we begin to think critically about our lifestyles and make positive changes in the direction of sustainability. We need to show the business community the way to sustainable development via a responsible attitude to consumption, and become active within our sphere of influence as opinion leaders.

For this reason, my foundation *Forum für Verantwortung*, the ASKO EUROPA-FOUNDATION, and the European Academy Otzenhausen have joined forces to produce educational materials on the future of the Earth to accompany the twelve books developed at the renowned Wuppertal Institute for Climate, Environment and Energy. We are setting up an extensive program of seminars, and the initial results are very promising. The success of our initiative "Encouraging Sustainability," which has now been awarded the status of an official project of the UN Decade "Education for Sustainable Development," confirms the public's great interest in, and demand for, well-founded information.

I would like to thank the authors for their additional effort to update all their information and put the contents of their original volumes in a more global context. My special thanks go to the translators, who submitted themselves to a strict timetable, and to Annette Maas for coordinating the Sustainability Project. I am grateful for the expert editorial advice of Amy Irvine and the Haus Publishing editorial team for not losing track of the "3600-page-work."

"We were on our way to becoming gods, supreme beings who could create a second world, using the natural world only as building blocks for our new creation."

This warning by the psychoanalyst and social philosopher Erich Fromm is to be found in *To Have or to Be?* (1976). It aptly expresses the dilemma in which we find ourselves as a result of our scientific-technical orientation.

The original intention of submitting to nature in order to make use of it ("knowledge is power") evolved into subjugating nature in order to exploit it. We have left the earlier successful path with its many advances and are now on the wrong track, a path of danger with incalculable risks. The greatest danger stems from the unshakable faith of the overwhelming majority of politicians and business leaders in unlimited economic growth which, together with limitless technological innovation, is supposed to provide solutions to all the challenges of the present and the future.

For decades now, scientists have been warning of this collision course with nature. As early as 1983, the United Nations founded the World Commission on Environment and Development which published the Brundtland Report in 1987. Under the title *Our Common Future*, it presented a concept that could save mankind from catastrophe and help to find the way back to a responsible way of life, the concept of long-term environmentally sustainable use of resources. "Sustainability," as used in the Brundtland Report, means "development that meets the needs of the present without compromising the ability of future generations to meet their own needs."

Despite many efforts, this guiding principle for ecologically, economically, and socially sustainable action has unfortunately not yet become the reality it can, indeed must, become. I believe the reason for this is that civil societies have not yet been sufficiently informed and mobilized.

Forum für Verantwortung

Against this background, and in the light of ever more warnings and scientific results, I decided to take on a societal responsibility with my foundation. I would like to contribute to the expansion of public discourse about sustainable development which is absolutely essential. It is my desire to provide a large number of people with facts and contextual knowledge on the subject of sustainability, and to show alternative options for future action.

After all, the principle of "sustainable development" alone is insufficient to change current patterns of living and economic practices. It does provide some orientation, but it has to be negotiated in concrete terms within society and then implemented in patterns of behavior. A democratic society seriously seeking to reorient itself towards future viability must rely on critical, creative individuals capable of both discussion and action. For this reason, life-long learning, from childhood to old age, is a necessary precondition for realizing sustainable development. The practical implementation of the ecological, economic, and social goals of a sustainability strategy in economic policy requires people able to reflect, innovate and recognize potentials for structural change and learn to use them in the best interests of society.

It is not enough for individuals to be merely "concerned." On the contrary, it is necessary to understand the scientific background and interconnections in order to have access to them and be able to develop them in discussions that lead in the right direction. Only in this way can the ability to make appropriate judgments emerge, and this is a prerequisite for responsible action.

The essential condition for this is presentation of both the facts and the theories within whose framework possible courses of action are visible in a manner that is both appropriate to the subject matter and comprehensible. Then, people will be able to use them to guide their personal behavior.

In order to move towards this goal, I asked renowned scientists to present in a generally understandable way the state of research and the possible options on twelve important topics in the area of sustainable development in the series "*Forum für Verantwortung*." All those involved in this project are in agreement that there is no alternative to a united path of all societies towards sustainability:

- *Our Planet: How Much More Can Earth Take?* (Jill Jäger)
- *Energy: The World's Race for Resources in the 21st Century* (Hermann-Joseph Wagner)
- *Our Threatened Oceans* (Stefan Rahmstorf and Katherine Richardson)
- *Water Resources: Efficient, Sustainable and Equitable Use* (Wolfram Mauser)
- *The Earth: Natural Resources and Human Intervention* (Friedrich Schmidt-Bleek)
- *Overcrowded World? Global Population and International Migration* (Rainer Münz and Albert F. Reiterer)
- *Feeding the Planet: Environmental Protection through Sustainable Agriculture* (Klaus Hahlbrock)
- *Costing the Earth? Perspectives on Sustainable Development* (Bernd Meyer)
- *The New Plagues: Pandemics and Poverty in a Globalized World* (Stefan Kaufmann)

- *Climate Change: The Point of No Return* (Mojib Latif)
- *The Demise of Diversity: Loss and Extinction* (Josef H Reichholf)
- *Building a New World Order: Sustainable Policies for the Future* (Harald Müller)

The public debate

What gives me the courage to carry out this project and the optimism that I will reach civil societies in this way, and possibly provide an impetus for change?

For one thing, I have observed that, because of the number and severity of natural disasters in recent years, people have become more sensitive concerning questions of how we treat the Earth. For another, there are scarcely any books on the market that cover in language comprehensible to civil society the broad spectrum of comprehensive sustainable development in an integrated manner.

When I began to structure my ideas and the prerequisites for a public discourse on sustainability in 2004, I could not foresee that by the time the first books of the series were published, the general public would have come to perceive at least climate change and energy as topics of great concern. I believe this occurred especially as a result of the following events:

First, the United States witnessed the devastation of New Orleans in August 2005 by Hurricane Katrina, and the anarchy following in the wake of this disaster.

Second, in 2006, Al Gore began his information campaign on climate change and wastage of energy, culminating in his film *An Inconvenient Truth*, which has made an impression on a wide audience of all age groups around the world.

Third, the 700-page Stern Report, commissioned by the British government, published in 2007 by the former Chief Economist of the World Bank Nicholas Stern in collaboration with other economists, was a wake-up call for politicians and business leaders alike. This report makes clear how extensive the damage to the global economy will be if we continue with "business as usual" and do not take vigorous steps to halt climate change. At the same time, the report demonstrates that we could finance countermeasures for just one-tenth of the cost of the probable damage, and could limit average global warming to 2° C – if we only took action.

Fourth, the most recent IPCC report, published in early 2007, was met by especially intense media interest, and therefore also received considerable public attention. It laid bare as never before how serious the situation is, and called for drastic action against climate change.

Last, but not least, the exceptional commitment of a number of billionaires such as Bill Gates, Warren Buffett, George Soros, and Richard Branson as well as Bill Clinton's work to "save the world" is impressing people around the globe and deserves mention here.

An important task for the authors of our twelve-volume series was to provide appropriate steps towards sustainable development in their particular subject area. In this context, we must always be aware that successful transition to this type of economic, ecological, and social development on our planet cannot succeed immediately, but will require many decades. Today, there are still no sure formulae for the most successful long-term path. A large number of scientists and even more innovative entrepreneurs and managers will have to use their creativity and dynamism to solve the great challenges. Nonetheless, even today, we can discern the first clear goals we must reach in order to avert a looming catastrophe. And billions of consumers around the world can use their daily purchasing decisions to help both ease and significantly accelerate the economy's transition to sustainable development – provided the political framework is there. In addition, from a global perspective, billions of citizens have the opportunity to mark out the political "guide rails" in a democratic way via their parliaments.

The most important insight currently shared by the scientific, political, and economic communities is that our resource-intensive Western model of prosperity (enjoyed today by one billion people) cannot be extended to another five billion or, by 2050, at least eight billion people. That would go far beyond the biophysical capacity of the planet. This realization is not in dispute. At issue, however, are the consequences we need to draw from it.

If we want to avoid serious conflicts between nations, the industrialized countries must reduce their consumption of resources by more than the developing and threshold countries increase theirs. In the future, all countries must achieve the same level of consumption. Only then will we be able to create the necessary ecological room for maneuver in order to ensure an appropriate level of prosperity for developing and threshold countries.

To avoid a dramatic loss of prosperity in the West during this long-term process of adaptation, the transition from high to low resource use, that is, to an ecological market economy, must be set in motion quickly.

On the other hand, the threshold and developing countries must commit themselves to getting their population growth under control within the foreseeable future. The twenty-year Programme of Action adopted by the United Nations International Conference on Population and Development in Cairo in 1994 must be implemented with stronger support from the industrialized nations.

If humankind does not succeed in drastically improving resource and energy efficiency and reducing population growth in a sustainable manner – we should remind ourselves of the United Nations forecast that population growth will come to a halt only at the end of this century, with a world population of eleven to twelve billion – then we run the real risk of developing eco-dictatorships. In the words of Ernst Ulrich von Weizsäcker: "States will be sorely tempted to ration limited resources, to micromanage economic activity, and in the interest of the environment to specify from above what citizens may or may not do. 'Quality-of-life' experts might define in an authoritarian way what kind of needs people are permitted to satisfy." (*Earth Politics*, 1989, in English translation: 1994).

It is time

It is time for us to take stock in a fundamental and critical way. We, the public, must decide what kind of future we want. Progress and quality of life is not dependent on year-by-year growth in per capita income alone, nor do we need inexorably growing amounts of goods to satisfy our needs. The short-term goals of our economy, such as maximizing profits and accumulating capital, are major obstacles to sustainable development. We should go back to a more decentralized economy and reduce world trade and the waste of energy associated with it in a targeted fashion. If resources and energy were to cost their "true" prices, the global process of rationalization and labor displacement will be reversed, because cost pressure will be shifted to the areas of materials and energy.

The path to sustainability requires enormous technological innovations. But not everything that is technologically possible has to be put into practice. We should not strive to place all areas of our lives under the dictates of the economic system. Making justice and fairness a reality for everyone is not only a moral and ethical imperative, but is also the most important means of securing world peace in the long term. For this reason, it is essential to place the political relationship between states and peoples on a new basis, a basis with which everyone can identify, not only the most powerful. Without common principles of global governance, sustainability cannot become a reality in any of the fields discussed in this series.

And finally, we must ask whether we humans have the right to reproduce to such an extent that we may reach a population of eleven to twelve billion by the end of this century, laying claim to every square centimeter of our Earth and restricting and destroying the habitats and way of life of all other species to an ever greater degree.

Our future is not predetermined. We ourselves shape it by our actions. We can continue as before, but if we do so, we will put ourselves in the biophysical straitjacket of nature, with possibly disastrous political implications, by the middle of this century. But we also have the opportunity to create a fairer and more viable future for ourselves and for future generations. This requires the commitment of everyone on our planet.

Klaus Wiegandt
Summer 2008

An unrelenting flood of publications on the subject of global governance is coming onto the market. I did not actually intend to make a contribution of my own to this debate. However, the challenge of doing just this from the perspective of sustainability – as part of the ambitious project of the Forum for Responsibility – has proven irresistible. At the same time, I could not help but oppose the trend on some issues within the – predominantly 'Western' – debate. This requires an explanation.

One important issue within the debate focuses on making global governance democratic. This issue has a normative orientation, and seeks to apply the values and norms of Western Enlightenment as the guiding principles of global governance, while neglecting to address the friction that such an attempt would cause. My approach starts from a different point of departure: the horrifying risks to humankind and nature which my colleagues have so impressively and chillingly presented in their books in this series, and the unavoidable necessity of initiating measures at the global level to overcome these risks. For me – and thus for this book – that is the primary question: how can a framework of conditions be established within which a solution to these pressing issues will become possible – in the world as it is today and the way it will be in the foreseeable future? The first conclusion which must be drawn in this regard is: there are non-democratic countries in the world, such as China, which have to be part of the solution. If in the course of this process they should become democratic, well and good. If not, it must still be possible.

A further important line of argument regards the state as decreasingly important, and foresees a 'withering away of the state,' a 'denationalization' of world governance. My views are more conservative. I still have considerable faith in the state, both for good and for bad, and believe that without a central role for the separate countries sustainable global governance will not be achieved. I also fear that the potential for individual countries to block measures which address global problems will continue unabated. For this reason, global governance remains primarily governance by nation-states, certainly with appropriate contributions by other players, yet with nation-states and their organizations remaining the focal point.

The hope that humankind will ultimately be able to master the challenges it is facing requires a certain amount of optimistic utopianism. I have mustered the necessary faith, also continuously striving, however, not to lose sight of the hard facts of political reality. I am attempting to construct a framework for global governance by building on the promising models that we already have here and now and which, to some degree, are working. From this basis I am trying to think further, not, however, by starting from preconditions which may exist only in the minds of the very imaginative, and nowhere else. The extent to which this mixture of realism and utopianism is convincing is left up to my readers to decide. I would be pleased if they took the inadequacies of this book as the starting point for further thought and for development of their own models of successful global governance. For in the end, the success of global governance depends on the commitment of many, not on the wisdom of a very few leaders – although this wisdom, a rare quality, is urgently required.

The format of the book series includes dispensing with exhaustive source references, and instead providing a brief Further Reading section. For this reason, I am not in a position to appropriately acknowledge those whose works have supported me in my own lines of thought, as well as those whose standpoints I view critically. I wish to offer a general apology for this.

Many intelligent people have helped me organize my thoughts for this book. Philip Liste and Ulrike Müller provided constructive commentary on Chapter 6; Nicole Deitelhoff, Melanie Zimmer and Thomas Gebauer did the same for parts of Chapters 6 and 7, and Kerstin Martens constructively reviewed all of Chapter 7. Carmen Wunderlich prepared the glossary. I wish to express my great gratitude for this. My friend and colleague Jonas Wolff accepted the task of reviewing the first draft of each chapter and then discussing the completed book manuscript with me as well. Without my conversations with him I would have committed many errors in thought; I cannot thank him enough for the constructive way he immersed himself in my ideas and went beyond them.

I dedicate the book to my friend Piwi, formally known as Heinz-Georg Frey. Ever since the times we shared together as participants in the events of 1968 this indestructible friendship has accompanied me throughout my life. Piwi wrote the most beautiful work on literature that I have ever read – about the women in Goethe's *Wilhelm Meister* – and yet, in choosing to become a teacher he opted for a career far more difficult than mine. He has poured his commitment and energy into his vocation ever since. The poor showing by Germany in the Programme for International Student Assessment (PISA) is truly not of his making. My life would be greatly diminished were it not for his loyalty, brilliant intelligence and incomparable humor. For this reason and because his (and Magdalena's) interest in sustainability may

– due to their three wonderful sons – perhaps be even greater than mine, I dedicate this book to him.

Frankfurt am Main

June 2007

The other books in this series have dealt with individual aspects of treating the Earth in a sustainable manner, one topic at a time. They have critically examined the way we humans deal with the natural resources that our largely benevolent environment lays at our feet. They have made chilling forecasts about what will happen to the air, water, climate and so on, if we continue our current practices without decisive corrective action. Most importantly they have presented ways for changing these practices and leading a life on this planet that does not inexorably lead to catastrophe in one or two generations.

So far, so good. But who is 'we'? All of humankind appears to be implicated. But humankind is not a 'player' – humankind is not a tangible collective in the way your family, your sports team or your company is a group that is able to take action. At the moment, the largest collectives capable of taking action in the world today are nation-states and some very large multinational corporations, well-equipped international organizations (although they generally need nation-states to take effective action!), the churches, non-governmental organizations (NGOs) such as Greenpeace, Human Rights Watch, Amnesty International, or Transparency International, as well as less appealing phenomena such as the Mafia or al-Qaeda. These are by and large the collective 'players' with which 'we' have to begin practicing sustainable global governance.

But what exactly does the concept of 'sustainable global governance' mean? Aren't sustainability and politics inherently contradictory terms? Isn't it true that among politicians in the most powerful and successful countries – which are still the Western democracies (in other words, the NATO world plus Australia, New Zealand and Japan) – the horizon only reaches as far as the next election? And hasn't the anxious illusion that totalitarian countries such as the Soviet Union could be better than we are at pursuing long-term plans vanished into thin air because the Soviets were far less capable of forging a stable future than the apparently so fragmented West? Is it not evident today that despite acknowledging the existence of problems, a non-democratic country such as China has even more difficulties implementing acceptable environmental policy? Hasn't the Chinese population policy, as visionary as it may have seemed at first, in combination with the traditional preference for sons, led to a gender imbalance in the younger generation which in the medium term will create a disproportionately large number of elderly and make our own problems with support for the elderly seem trivial?

Leaving aside the apparently inherent contradiction between politics and sustainability, what does the combination of these two terms mean in the first place? On the one hand, our behavior towards nature should allow the basic natural resources we use – the atmosphere, fish populations, etc. – to be maintained permanently. However, a definition which is so obvious is not what one immediately thinks of for 'sustainable policies.' 'World politics' has strong associations with the eternal heroic struggle of the major powers, with their rise and decline, ongoing rivalries and the perpetual cycle of confrontation in major wars. This is obviously not the answer! However, 'global politics' is not the subject matter here – 'global governance' is. This term, however, raises even more questions and arouses distrust. Citizens have learned to be dissatisfied with political decisions which are far removed from them. We are caught between Scylla and Charybdis: It seems the distant 'rulers' are either inefficient, as with the United Nations, or over-efficient, like the Brussels bureaucracy. Both alternatives arouse neither trust nor sympathy. 'Global governance' sounds suspiciously like 'world government,' and such a structure has already been rejected by Immanuel Kant: He feared that it would be tantamount to tyranny if freedom and resistance no longer had a home anywhere. To deal with this right at the start – to allay misgivings – *Global governance does not mean global government*, although today an increasing number of people see this as the only way out of our problematic situation.

The global problems addressed by the sustainability project affect all people, nations and states, to varying degrees. They can only be addressed successfully when all 'problem producers' and all those who can contribute to a solution work together, and when others who are (as yet) uninvolved pay careful attention to ensuring that they themselves do not become 'problem producers.' First, we need *agreement on the issues*. This is less obvious than one might think, as shown by the attitude of the previous American government towards global warming, or the South African government towards AIDS: Both (democratic!) national leaderships initially refused to accept the majority definition of the problem, and in both cases we are not yet completely out of the woods.

So what is 'global governance'?

'Global governance is a type of governing, and governing means nothing other than identifying promising approaches to solving community problems, defining these in binding rules of conduct, monitoring compliance with these rules and, if necessary, adapting them to changed circumstances. Global governance exists when both the problems and the rules – with the help of which they are to be resolved – do not remain limited to a single political community, but tend to have a global nature' (Volker Rittberger).

For global governance to work the next necessary step is *agreement on the objectives*. This is also not easy to achieve. Even reasonable people can argue about what they want; or what they ought to want. Those who read the books in our series may sometimes have difficulty understanding the sheer possibility of disputes – the facts and the need for action seem so clear. But when one considers that China – at least until recently – regarded maximum increase in their gross national product as a priority even over protection of the air quality in their cities, when one takes into account that the previous American administration under Bush has long fought against cheap AIDS drugs – then one can imagine that even agreement on 'what the issue is' and 'how to proceed' will cost a great deal of high level effort; because this is about ideology and interests, and those are high hurdles.

Defining the objectives is only the first step. If you want to build a house, a rough sketch is not enough. A full set of plans is needed, the structural details must be fully worked out, the division of labor between craftsmen must be agreed upon, a schedule created, orders and purchases carried out, and much more. So too here: what all players – the participants in world politics with states at the center mentioned above – have to do must be determined. That is even more difficult than the objectives: questions of responsibility (for the existing circumstances), inequality of opportunity (between rich and poor), distribution of goods and assets, and equity come into play here. This combination of morality and benefits is highly volatile because it encourages conflict. Most wars in world history have these two elements, in varying combinations, as a starting point.

Second order sustainability

I have now arrived at the 'hard core' of my contribution to the Sustainability Project. It is not a matter of me designing individual systems of rules for successfully regulating and managing, in a sustainable way, the problems my colleagues have analyzed, i.e., it is not about 'first order sustainable global governance.' The main ideas of how this should be done are the subject of the other books. I am more concerned with 'second order sustainable global governance': with the basic consideration of how the conditions can be created for such rules to come into existence. This idea needs to be explained before we can examine it more closely. At first glance it is difficult to grasp that the obvious problems cannot simply be tackled. Is it not just a matter of finding the right experts to create the solutions? The most sensible approach, on which these experts agree or for which there is at least a majority, will be implemented – why can it not simply be done in this way?

The philosophy behind this question is called 'social engineering.' It would be all well and good if it were only a matter of technical questions. But as I have tried to explain, even questions of science – ecology, meteorology – lose their innocence when they come into contact with social and political issues. Then it is about interests and beliefs, about morality and passion, about more and less, about good and evil. Where 'pure science' and its broad, socially and politically powerful applications meet, the scientific community usually splits into polar opposites, groups, parties and sects. The 'experts' are no further help when they argue among themselves. Their disputes are already – often unconsciously – distorted by values, cultural influences and ideologies. Conversely, the public and politicians choose whatever suits their values, cultural convictions and ideologies from an array of disputed scientific positions.

This sounds like resignation, but it is not meant that way. We repeatedly manage to reach decisions despite these hurdles. Often these decisions are very reasonable and open up further possibilities. The important thing is not that one way is always clearly mapped out and all parties concerned automatically agree on this path (the world would be a boring place if this were the case), but to have made preparations that make it possible to deal with conflicts in such a way that decisions are possible and all parties to the conflict accept them. Reliable procedures that seem sufficiently fair to all parties for them to accept their results, even when these differ from their own preferences, are the basic conditions for sustainable governance. Then it can in fact reasonably be expected that the rules will find sufficient supporters, even among those who regard different rules as better and/or voted against them at the time of their adoption. It is the secret of our democratic constitutions that, despite loud dispute, this always happens. Sustained global governance requires creation of similar conditions at the global level.

The qualities of rules that lead to people accepting them as binding can be divided into four categories:

1. When the rules are applied, the situation must be improved; people must feel that the problem being addressed by the rule in the first place is closer to a solution, that their own prosperity is growing, or undesirable circumstances being reduced ('output legitimacy').

2. The rule must have come into existence in an acceptable way. People must be able to identify with it. 'Ownership' is the key word, indicating that an agreed-upon solution does not belong to just a few, but to as many as possible. This sense of 'ownership' usually results from some kind of involvement in the rule-making process ('input legitimacy')

– directly, through the participation of representatives, or through surveys or citizens' forums.

3. The rule must be changeable. It could indeed turn out that it does not provide the best solution to the problem, or that the problem changes. Or it may distribute costs and benefits unequally. In these cases those involved must be able to rely on the rules not being set in stone but being capable of being improved within an acceptable time.

4. Stakeholders must accept the 'rule-making community' as appropriate. They must be ready to cooperate with their partners in it. There can be no antagonisms that break up the rule-making community. This is not a property of the rule itself, but of the group(s) of people who are affected by the problem that needs to be solved. If the antagonism is stronger than the stress associated with the problem, then the best rule in the world will not help reach a sustainable solution.

The arrangements needed to establish these four conditions must cope with three interlinked stumbling blocks that stand in the way of sustainable global governance (apart from ignorance, stupidity, greed and ill-will). It is not about individual shortcomings but about fundamental structural problems with worldwide political behavior. These stumbling blocks are dealing with diversity; the dispute over justice; and war.

Dealing with diversity

The world is fragmented. It consists of 192 states and more than 6,000 ethnic groups. Within these states and ethnic groups, world religions such as Christianity (in its many manifestations, often locked in dispute), Islam (with its schism between Shia and Sunni, each with different schools and sects such as Alavites, Druses or Ismaili, considered heretics by the 'strict believers'), Judaism, Hinduism, Buddhism, Confucianism, Taoism, Shintoism as well as animism compete. Not to mention the millions of people who are not religious. Added to which, there are different political ideologies. Liberalism, with its conservative, social democratic and socialist forms; Marxism, which still has its supporters and through Hugo Chavez is developing an unorthodox 'new' form; diverse forms of state authoritarianism, such as China, Singapore or Malaysia, that see 'good governance' as depending on strong, authoritarian leadership; and various hybrids of religion and politics, such as in the Islamic Republic of Iran or the Wahhabi monarchy in Saudi Arabia.

Sustainable global governance must find ways of uniting this diversity so that acceptable decisions become possible. This is anything but easy. In a later chapter I want to cautiously develop proposals that will permit unity to grow out of diversity, at least regarding the big questions.

In the West there is a fairly unanimous opinion about 'global governance' with which all, from the solidarity-displaying idealists of cosmopolitanism to the neo-conservative promoters of American hegemony, seem to agree: it should be done our way. We possess the patent recipe. The combination of a market economy and democracy is the ideal. All problems can be solved in this way, and there is a lot of freedom and human rights over and above that. In this spirit Francis Fukuyama announced 'the end of history' in 1992 (and so demonstrated his deep ignorance of the historical). This would mean that the formula for reaching and implementing worldwide decisions would already be on the table, and further discussions would be superfluous. Except perhaps for fine-tuning the 'how': it is debatable whether this is to be attained through a cosmopolitan democracy, which is through a democratized UN, or through joint decision-making of the democracies that then decide for the others, whose participation is ruled out by their non-democratic character. But the principle is clear.

Now, as a child of democratic post-war Germany I am as committed a democrat as the advocates of world democracy, and believe in our values no less than they. What distinguishes me from them is a readiness for greater humility and respect for those values we do not like very much. Our values have grown along a specific historical path. The fact that this path is obscured by ideological nonsense, such as stating that liberal human rights are the natural product of the 'Judeo-Christian tradition,' further reinforces the dangerous arrogance of the West. It is clear to anyone with even a rudimentary knowledge of the Christian West that the Christians literally waded through blood, that the separation of Church and State (to the extent that it exists!) derived from the happy circumstance of an approximate balance of power between the two in the Middle Ages and early modern times (and where there was no such balance disastrous alliances emerged, such as the post-*Reconquista* in Spain, the Christian equivalent of the Taliban government).

Those who know Western history also know that the democratic separation of powers without the intervention of religion developed from the balance between monarchs, aristocracy and bourgeoisie in early modern times. And they also know that from the Enlightenment until today, human rights had to be won against the opposition of the Church(es). The fact is this historical background does not provide good reason for a sense of cultural superiority. But for global governance something else is crucial: it makes no sense to want to impose on others one's own ideas of the appropriate form for decision-making, when their cooperation is needed. Nor does it lead anywhere if people believe that the 'good' can impose their decisions on the 'wicked.' Both approaches provoke resistance and rejection. That is exactly what is not needed for sustainable world politics. Resistance and rejection stand in the way of an effective solution. And even worse: both are the starting point for spiraling violence. They open the door to war.

The overriding principle for dealing with diversity is therefore participation. All voices have a right to be heard, whether they belong to democratic or non-democratic governments (or even non-governmental organizations). Incidentally, it is not at all obvious to us that we constantly listen to an arch-undemocratic institution on a number of political questions, often to our considerable profit: namely the Catholic Church, whose medieval principle of hierarchy must really make the heart of any convinced democrat bleed. We do this with good reason: it is out of respect for millions of believers who willingly allow themselves to be represented in certain questions by the un-elected dignitaries of the Church appointed from on high.

The same respect must in a sense carry over to other, non-democratic countries, as long as citizens there do not show through open rebellion in great numbers that they no longer tolerate their rulers. So once again: our culture is just one of many, though in our view the best and most important. Political principles which arise from this historically evolved culture are not universally valid, even if our wise, living philosophers deduce them with seamless logic from the work of equally wise, dead philosophers. For, the dead philosophers and the rules of inference evolved within our own traditions – so we still move in our own, limited circles, and not in the world at large. Only those principles, norms and rules that are actually recognized by representatives of all the cultures of the world can lay claim to universal validity. Thus, universalism is not what we derive from our own experience, but it is also not impossible, as some contemporary philosophical movements such as communitarianism or postmodernism believe. It is more a matter of the broadest possible agreement. Debate not deduction is the motto. That is exactly why the UN is so important and should not, as some truly believe, be replaced by NATO or a 'global NATO' expanded by including all democracies, or disbanded (when it does not make decisions the way we want). Because only in the UN are all countries, regions and cultures really present – even if, unfortunately, not always with elected leaders.

The dispute over justice

Few values enjoy such high regard as justice, and for scarcely any other has so much blood been shed. Dealing with it requires equal measures of respect and caution. In all cultures there is detailed ethical debate about justice that revolves around the good life and the just order in which it is embedded. Much less thought has been given to justice beyond the society and the state, with one disturbing exception, the 'just war.' Only recently has the idea of distributive justice in the global context been considered, for the time being – not unexpectedly – in a decidedly controversial way.

The 'just war' combines two of our three key problems in global governance. I want to subject this concept to fundamental criticism. With the attribute 'just,' war is transformed from something terrible into something good. That just and good are two sides of the same coin has been an essential part of Western thinking since classical times; this overlap is also not unfamiliar to other cultures. This pair of concepts therefore gives the impression that there are wars that have intrinsically good properties. I dispute that. The 'just war' is characterized by being waged for a valid reason, being decided upon by an appropriate authority (national leadership or today the Security Council of the UN), and that *jus in bello*, i.e. compliance with international humanitarian law regarding the separation of civilians and combatants, is observed. Other ways of remedying the injustice over which the war is being fought must be exhausted, and the use of force must be commensurate with goals and necessities. All these are principles against which nothing can be said. But they do not justify the attribute 'just.'

There are few areas of complete agreement between the different cultures of the world, but they all believe in one form or another that justice means 'to each his own' (and incidentally also 'to each her own'). What 'his' or 'hers' is remains a subject of controversy. But there is agreement about what it is not: the violent death of an innocent man or woman is always unjust. However, war is inevitably accompanied by the death of innocents. Collateral damage is not an avoidable accident but an inherent part of war. It happens as an inevitable accompaniment of every war (this applies also to the deaths of soldiers, pressed into service, who have no chance of refusing). However, if war necessarily causes the death of innocents, a serious injustice, it cannot be intrinsically just. The 'just war' is a conceptual contradiction.

This is not to say that there are no wars that are unavoidable. Defense against an attack or help for people facing a real threat of genocide (and not just the assertion that it is occurring) are justified. But justification is not justice. Even such wars are at heart unjust, because innocent lives are lost. They may be the lesser of two evils, but they are still an evil – and a whitewashed term such as 'just war' is a psychological, or worse, propagandistic attempt to disguise this tragic fact. The discussion of war from the view-point of justice has made the motto, examined more deeply in the following section, even more urgent: if at all possible, war is to be avoided.

The second aspect of justice concerns the distribution of goods. We live in a world of horrendous inequality. The tiniest proportion of its inhabitants is personally responsible for this. People are born to their station in life, which puts up high barriers against achieving the good life. The barriers are not insurmountable, but to work yourself out of such a situation requires so much energy to overcome the obstacles and to put the (sometimes malignant) active resistance behind you that not everyone is successful. It is infinitely easier for the child of gradu-ates, who receives an education that enormously improves his career opportunities; the lawyer's daughter, who already knows in school that she can enter a thriving office; or the failed son of a royal house, who even in the face of the grossest personal failure does not go so far as to sink into a physically miserable life. A certain measure of compensation for these profound inequalities of opportunity does not seem unreasonable.

Inequality does not exist only between individuals, but also between social groups and countries. These have to do with each other. The inequality between countries is on the one hand his-torically derived. The early developers in Europe and the United States brought repression and exploitation to the rest of the world and in this way delayed its development. Through arbi-trarily drawn borders, the fomenting of power struggles among opposing ethnic groups, and the continuing dominance of com-panies based in the colonial power, they mainly left the ex-colo-nies in a state that hindered their advancement. Despite formal independence they have retained special relationships to the det-riment of their clients' development (like France in Africa). The

Western nations have shaped the world economic system in such a way that, despite apparent 'preferential treatment,' developing countries are disadvantaged by the fact that the sectors in which they were and are most competitive have been excluded from general liberalization for a long time (textiles) or to this day (agriculture). Developing countries are not only unable to offer their products competitively in Western markets, but subsidized American and European agriculture is able to flood their markets, despite goods actually being produced more cheaply there. This inhumane practice has ruined millions of Third World farmers, and is responsible for famine and death. The EU's agricultural policy, to put it crudely, is an instrument of murder. One thing it is certainly not: just. But wait – our farmers see it differently. There can be many different ideas about justice – including the traditional Hindu belief that the extreme inequalities of the caste system reflect divine justice, because rank in society is just reward for moral achievements in a previous life, an idea that does not fit with ideas from other cultures and religions.

Despite this unfavorable starting point, we cannot avoid having to look for standards of justice that are somehow compatible with the central maxims of all cultures. If we do not achieve this feat, all measures that we put in place for dealing with the many problems and risks of globalization will remain susceptible to frustration-driven attempts to overturn them. Because – in their own eyes and in accordance with their respective beliefs about justice – disadvantaged parties will regard such measures as illegitimate and wish for different ones. The measures would then permanently remain provisional, which would make even well-intentioned parties hesitate to follow them; because even when rules and norms are accepted the will to subject oneself to them suffers under the fear that others, whose participation is needed, would probably constantly transgress against them.

Such a situation is the opposite of sustainability. What is more, the collision of opposing ideas about justice is dangerous. Justice is not simply one value among many. It is a central one because it is on the one hand inextricably tied up with interests, and on the other, highly emotionally charged. People who feel that their interests have been damaged and attribute this unfortunate fact to a stranger behaving unfairly will regard this stranger as an enemy who is also unethical – otherwise the stranger would not behave so unfairly. The machinery of hostility set in motion as a result is capable of unlimited escalation. Violation of the principles of justice opens the way to war.

Outlawing war

War is the arch-enemy of sustainability. (Suggesting that war is the 'father of all things,' as Heraclitus did, reveals a poor opinion of fathers.) War tears apart many finely-meshed networks, lays waste to the countryside, burns crops, disrupts demographic patterns, and destroys and threatens the environment. It has always been that way. In an age of the most up-to-date weaponry its potential for destroying sustainability has multiplied itself. Who does not remember the defoliated forests in Vietnam? Wars in which biological agents created through gene manipulation were released or nuclear weapons used in large numbers could have unforeseeable consequences.

This point deserves closer examination. In 1995 the world had an unprecedented opportunity to achieve mutual agreement on eliminating nuclear weapons – the most fearsome weapons of our time. More than 180 states which had voluntarily abstained from ownership of our epoch's most powerful instrument of destruction declared their willingness to extend this abstention indefinitely. This happened at a conference in New York, where all signatories to the Non-Proliferation Treaty agreed to remove the previously agreed upon restriction of the life of the treaty to 25 years: the treaty was made valid for an unlimited period. The non-nuclear states demanded a price for this unusual step: the nuclear powers had to commit themselves to adopting certain measures without delay, for instance to make a legally binding end to nuclear testing and the production of fissionable materials for weapons purposes as soon as possible, and to undertake systematic steps towards nuclear disarmament. In 2000 these regulations were extended through a series of additional steps. Little of this has happened; on the contrary: in their arrogance the nuclear powers reached the conclusion that because the treaty was unlimited they had the 'have nots' in their pockets. There is no talk of disarmament. China is arming, Russia is re-arming, Great Britain has just decided to take into service a new generation of missile submarines, and the US and France are building extensive laboratories so they can develop new nuclear weapons, despite going without nuclear tests. The consequences are predictable, and are already occurring: others follow in the wake of the 'great powers.' Their bad example encourages others. If the way things are going does not change, within a generation there will be 30 nuclear powers, with greatly increased risk that these weapons will be used or that they will fall into the hands of terrorists.

Biological weapons are prohibited by the biological weapons treaty. It is obvious that observance of the treaty by the member states is not controlled. To change this unfortunate situation the signatories to the treaty have worked out a protocol. In 2001, after seven years, the US rejected the results of the negotiations, in line with the short-sighted practice of the Bush administration of depending on their own military strength in the place of the agreed-upon arms limitations. With nanotechnology, a further militarily applicable technical revolution has appeared on the horizon, one whose effects are unforeseeable if they are not reined in by law. The potential for destruction of life and property inherent in each of these weapons technologies goes beyond anything that has ever existed in history. The Second World War looks like a brawl among badly brought up lads in comparison with the scenarios that the use of these weapons brings to mind.

Prevention of war must thus be a central goal of every global policy oriented towards sustainability. As utopian as this sounds, it is only the minimal maxim, which we must go far beyond. For even the prospect of war is damaging to the principle of sustainability. Players who believe that future armed conflict is possible have good reason to be cautious when it comes to cooperation with those whom they could possibly meet again on the battlefield. For cooperation brings advantages, and when the enemy, who is the (temporary?) cooperation partner, gets too much of an advantage the enemy's strength increases, and with it the risk of one's own defeat in a future armed conflict. For the sake of one's own survival it may thus be rational to refuse to cooperate, although through this refusal one may, under today's conditions, endanger the survival of all – a genuine dilemma!

To accept the possibility of war means having to be prepared for it. Not to arm would mean being helplessly delivered into the hands of a superior opponent. And so the armed forces are built up and equipped with the ever more effective weapons that are developed in the cycles that occur as a result of technological progress. Through this, however, one's own neighbors are motivated to behave in the same way, even if they initially had no aggressive intentions at all – something that one could not know, or misunderstood. This 'security dilemma,' either to be helpless in the event of an attack or to drive oneself and others into an expensive and risky armament spiral, seems to be a logical consequence of the disorganized state of international relations, of the absence of a universally recognized and practiced system of law: every state is dependent upon its own strength, and the competition with each other of many strong states does not make the world safer but, all in all, more dangerous. The arms race consumes enormous resources, which are then unavailable for other purposes. With one-tenth of the American defense budget, which now amounts to an incredible 500 billion Dollars per year, the conversion of the American energy economy to an environmentally neutral mix of renewable resources could be achieved – to give just one example.

That defense budgets almost everywhere belong to the three most important areas of public expenditures shows the global extent of this – from the point of view of the task of achieving sustainability – gigantic waste of financial resources. If war really breaks out, the costs become limitless. With the money that a politico-legal world order, in which the military would carry out only multilaterally agreed upon 'policing actions' for global well-being, it would conceivably be possible to finance the majority of sustainability projects. Sustainability demands nothing less than the re-structuring of a mentality that is trapped in friend-foe thinking structures: no longer to see in the 'other' a current or potential enemy, but rather a partner with whom it is possible to have differences of opinion but with whom many problems are shared, so that there is mutual interest in solving them. It is not in any way a matter of harmony (which after all can be boring), but simply of acknowledging the 'other' as part of an equal partnership, in which common and opposing interests are mixed. It is difficult today to dismiss this option as purely the utopianism of idealists. In the European Union the idea of war against each other has vanished, and that also includes Switzerland, Norway or Iceland; the same is true for North America. South America is on the way. In the South Pacific the smaller countries have internal problems and conflicts, but there are no grounds for war between neighbors. And the states in Southeast Asia, which have united in the regional organization ASEAN, are embroiled it is true in many territorial disagreements, but since the foundation of ASEAN agree on the cast-iron basic principle that they will solve these problems through consultation and negotiation, never with weapons. In other words, a not insignificant portion of the world's regions has banned war between nation-states from their political thinking. This can be overlooked because of the bloody conflicts that are raging in other parts of the world and about which the media mostly report; for we regard peace as something that goes without thinking, without taking any notice of it (except at the moment of a spectacular peace treaty).

The tasks

These three challenges – dealing in a constructive way with diversity, putting into practice more or less compatible ideas of justice, and preventing a major war – provide the basis for all global political sustainability. Meeting them will be all the more difficult because we are living in an age of change. Massive changes that cause unrest in the world are in progress, and these cannot be suppressed or avoided.

In the first place: global power relationships are changing. At present the world is 'unipolar': there is only one superpower and no other comes even close to it: the United States of America. However, if you look at the crucial data it becomes apparent that this will not remain the case. The US accounts for about 5 percent of the world's population in its territory, produces 20 percent of world gross domestic product, and is responsible for just about 50 percent of world military spending. In the last ten years its economy, the foundation of all power, has grown by 3–4 percent a year. The Peoples' Republic of China has about 20 percent of the world's population, produces about 4 percent of the world gross domestic product, and is responsible for less than 6 percent of world military spending, but has grown in the last ten years by about 10 percent a year. In terms of share of population, India lies just behind China (and by 2030 could be the most populous nation on earth), but its military spending is no more than 2 percent, and its gross domestic product no more than 2 percent of world production. India has grown twice as fast as the US in the last decade. This means that we have to prepare ourselves for a 'power shift' in the course of a single generation: China will overtake the US in terms of potential for power, India will almost catch up. Power shifts are turbulent times. They mostly lead to war. This is something we can by no means afford. The whole of humanity must be interested in change in world leadership proceeding via a civil and orderly process of agreement.

Second: Islam and the rest of the world. Muslims everywhere, particularly those in the Arab world, feel that they are the losers in the world history of the last centuries. Enormous frustration has built up. Justified complaints of unfair and unjust treatment can be heard. Why is Israel allowed to occupy Arab territory without being punished, but when Iraq does the same there is an international execution? Why is it permissible to deny Muslims all their human rights in Guantánamo, but when Iran holds 15 British soldiers the big stick is waved? Why are India, North Korea and Israel allowed to possess nuclear weapons, but threats are made against Iraq and Iran and shots fired? The degree of alienation is a cause for anxiety. Al-Qaeda is the criminal perversion of this widespread feeling. The reintegration of the Islamic and Arabic 'center' into running the world is the second great global political task for humanity in the twenty-first century.

Third: we must create at least the prospect of elimination of need. This sounds hyper-moralistic and impractical. And of course we cannot prevent tsunamis, earthquakes or volcanic eruptions. Catastrophic events of this kind will generate need again and again (which we can however reduce, provided that we make appropriate preparation). What is being talked about here is the structurally-conditioned 'systematic' need in which human beings live; above all this involves Black Africa. The phenomenon of the 'failed state' is nowhere as widespread as on the sub-continent south of the Sahara. If you follow the line of thinking in our media you sometimes get the impression of total misery; is there perhaps deep-seated racism ('People with dark skin are not capable of independent development') underlying this? I am sometimes inclined to believe this, because the boom in India is also strikingly ignored. For Africa too has its highlights: Botswana, admirably governed since its independence; Mali, where a civil society led by women persuaded a military regime to give up, and ended a civil war; Ghana, where a military dictator voluntarily retired and a democracy has since begun to blossom; Senegal and Benin, stable democracies; and Mozambique, a successful example of reconciliation after a bloody civil war.

No, Africa is not a hopeless case. But the phenomenon of failed states and depressing poverty needs to be dealt with across the whole region. The neoliberal trend dismisses too lightly the psychological and political distortions which generate (supposed?) hopelessness among the people. On the other hand, the ideology of many opponents of globalization is apparently blind to the fact that in the last 20 years a substantial proportion of humanity has emerged from poverty into a condition of 'making it' (if not well-to-do): 300 million in China, 250–300 million in

India, 250 million in Southeast Asia, and 100 million in South America. This is still not enough. As long as in excess of one billion people vegetate in apparent hopelessness the rest of the world cannot sleep easily; those whose sleep is not troubled by a bad conscience should stay awake out of concern for their safety. Global social policy is also security policy. German security is not being defended at the Hindu Kush, as a German Minister of Defense quipped, but rather through improvements in the slums of Dar es Salaam or Lagos. To remind my readers: my constant concern here is solely to think about the pre-requisites for setting in motion solutions to the problems that my colleagues have identified so convincingly in the other volumes in this series. In doing this I am not concerned with utopian world designs, but with the very basic conditions under which humanity can survive politically and thus work on the big questions of globalization – the economy, population, environment, health, and so on. In the next chapter I would like to examine models that seek to measure up to these requirements. What different dishes are found when the menu of global governance is read, and how easy are they to digest?

The pressing questions humanity faces have led to a large number of attempts to develop a system through which the world could be governed properly. Such attempts go far back into history; Kant's critical analysis of the idea of the world state and his alternative of a 'league of peace' was not the first proposal, but sets a standard according to which other proposals must be judged, even today. In our era such universal political models are developed with high frequency. This is not surprising: it reflects our justified contemporary concern that the many dangers we ourselves have created could overwhelm us if we do not do something about them very quickly. Those who are threatened by rising sea levels, international terrorism, or water shortages are forced, whether they like it or not, to think about how problems can be dealt with at a global level. However, rather different world models emerge when a US president, the leadership of the non-governmental organization ATTAC, or the Islamic Conference, an alliance of Muslims states, think about this question.

In this chapter I would like to look critically at the most important concepts that have been suggested for the tasks involved in global governance. The first type starts with the status quo and extends it further: a *world imperial power* or world *hegemony* of the (relatively 'nice') strongest state seems to the supporters of this approach to be the best way to deal with the growing risks. The second type is not prepared to give so much power wisdom to any single player, but to a union of the leading power with the next strongest ones: a league of peace among the democracies. The third type – as with the imperial power – goes beyond federal coordination among the states. Instead of the imperial rule of a single state over the rest this approach seeks a kind of global rule by the people, a (stronger or weaker) world republic, which regards not the states but individual people as its basic elements. The fourth type is even more many-sided, global governance: here a large number of players exercise power. In addition to states, corporations, international organizations and non-governmental organizations are involved, and effectively functioning and substantially (relatively) workable global governance emerges from their interaction.

Significantly, all these broad ideas emerge from discussions in the West. Non-Western voices are scarcely heard – and that is also the most serious fault inherent in all these ideas. None of these models has been able to convince me. They do not solve our three problems: dealing with diversity, achieving justice and preventing war. On the contrary, they threaten in one way or another to make matters even worse. As a result, the chapter will end with an oversized question mark.

Imperial government and hegemony – built-in failure

In the course of history, imperial powers have emerged. The Persian Empire, the Roman imperial state, the Mongol rule, the Ottoman Empire and the British Empire are the best known examples: a highly developed center that is stronger than its neighbors succeeds in imposing its rule on them. With the passage of time a more or less well-functioning group of subjects develops. At the borders, however, new challenges constantly arise, for instance from far-distant conquerors, and these force the imperial power to extend itself further. The combination of the empire's resources, good administration, military superiority (resulting from organization, technology, discipline and strategy) and reliable subjects makes it possible to control huge areas with astonishingly little exercise of violence. A minimal military presence in the border areas as a deterrent and as a 'fire brigade' for minor crises, backed up by the possibility of reinforcing it decisively through expeditionary armies, inhibits internal rebellion and external aggression. The provinces provide the center with new resources and open up new sources of recruitment for the armed forces (think for instance of the Celtic and Germanic units in the Roman cavalry).

The poison that destroyed the imperial state was its overextension. The further the front lies from the center the more its power diminishes and, as a consequence, the greater is the force that needs to be applied when the imperial power is attacked. The more varied the peoples who are ruled over, the more likely is resistance in several locations, which makes necessary what the imperial power most wishes to avoid: the application of force in several crises at the same time. The greater the distances, the longer communication takes and the more difficult it is; as a result it is correspondingly more difficult for the center to control its agents at the periphery; these people can play their own games, from unlimited profiteering at the expense of the locals (with the almost unavoidable result of rebellions and the expense of putting them down) all the way to direct challenges to the central authority. Both the Roman Republic and the Roman Empire fell not, in the first instance, as a result of external challenges, but through the accumulation of power on the periphery, which was used to acquire positions of power in the center. In the Mongol Empire the lines of communication were so long at the end that the empire collapsed under the sheer extent of its own expansion.

Today the world has shrunk in size. The problem of over-extension, the central problem of imperial powers, thus seems to have disappeared. This state of affairs encourages theoreticians of an American Imperium, such as neoconservatives at the American Enterprise Institute in Washington, but also European writers, to see the best option of all – because it is realistic – in the systematic extension of the power of the US and its application to the goal of achieving functioning global governance. Today, global communication in real time is possible, indeed via several media. Networks of satellite surveillance and television stations spanning the globe allow visual monitoring of one's own operations on the periphery as well as of movements of possible or actual opponents. The speed of military intervention by means of an expeditionary force supported from the air (in hours or days), a heavily armed force supported from the sea (in a matter of weeks) or, when the danger is acute, a completely automated rapid response with ballistic missiles or long-range rockets (in minutes), in the future possibly with laser weapons from space (in minutes or even seconds), makes possible reaction times in a completely different dimension from what was possible for earlier imperial powers. The United States is thus in a position to support its other instruments of power – its economic strength, its cultural influence – through its ability to intervene militarily anywhere in the world at any time. The deterrent effect of this, according to the people recommending a new imperial power, will limit the necessity of applying it to an affordable minimum; the speed of reaction makes it possible to deal with risks early, i.e., preventively, before they develop into tangible threats, defending against which would require great effort.

The people who support American world rule offer normative

arguments for their preference that are worth examining: the US is a democratic country with liberal-universalist values. It is (relatively) well and properly governed, and has enormous economic and technical resources. Its way of dealing with others is comparatively benign; its interest in colonizing foreign territory (as opposed to controlling it) is relatively limited. Compared to other approaches, both historic and contemporary (Russia; China), the US seems to offer the best alternative. From this premise emerges the expectation that the US will achieve security in a way that will be relatively effective and comparatively acceptable to those involved, which will gain it sufficient support to allow it to avoid the problems of historical imperial powers. In addition, in Washington there is a desire to keep world conditions as stable as possible. The American elite have a definite feeling of responsibility as the sole superpower. This self-image is the pre-requisite for accepting the costs and sacrifices that an imperial power must take upon itself in order to create the world-wide benefit 'security,' on the basis of which other benefits such as well-being, ecological balance, and so on can develop. The US has, through historical circumstances, grown into the role of the imperial power. What is needed now is to fulfill this role consciously, with a sufficient level of concern for the common good.

What would such imperial global governance look like? As world policeman the United States would have the task of dousing down all smoldering security hotspots before they could erupt into major fires – this corresponds fairly precisely to the idea of military conflict prevention as described by the Bush administration in their 'national security strategy' of 2002. If a state were opposed to the global rules laid down by the US it would be the business of the US to place constraints on this enemy power. In the case of both tasks Washington would be able to gain support from a world-wide network of alliances, which would take over part of its duties. Such alliances permit a widespread military presence, and by making available airports, logistical centers, supply depots and harbors also make reinforcement with powerful expeditionary forces easier. The partners in the alliance also form a body of voluntary supporters whose agreement gives the rules laid down by the US, through which the problems of globalization are to be dealt with, their worldwide validity; in return America listens to its allies through permanent consultations. With the help of allies, the US can persuade reluctant third parties to step into line without military measures, through a system of incentives and sanctions.

Hegemony is the gentler alternative to imperial power, with which it shares the leadership role of a centralized state that protects the security of the whole system. A hegemony functions with minimal application of military force and global presence, and more through the instruments of subtle persuasion, such as economic relationships, institutional guidance, cultural persuasion, diplomatic skill and the presence of the media. The larger partners in the alliance – in constant interaction with the central hegemony – play a more independent role, the load is borne somewhat more evenly on more shoulders; in exchange, the central hegemony is required to listen more to its partners and to take into account their interests and views. Nonetheless, at the core, similarities with the imperialist model remain: the hegemony lays down the rules most of the time, and its own military might is the guarantee that the rules are followed, even if it is less often and less visibly applied.

Under today's conditions the prospects for a sustainable hegemony seem at first glance to be good. For the instruments of 'subtle pressure' which are available to the US exceed those of all predecessors. America's economic domination has become less, but with about 20 percent of the world's gross domestic product the US still produces more than any other nation-state (it is true that the EU in total has its nose in front, but unlike Washington it lacks the ability to develop a national goal for these resources and apply them in order to fulfill political goals). American popular culture is penetrating the (youth) cultures of even the bitterest ideological opponents of the US, the diplomatic presence of Washington is felt everywhere, international institutions are structured according to American models, and American citizens, minions, or leaders who depend on the tolerance of the US occupy key positions in such societies. The conditions for establishing imperialist leadership or a hegemony thus look as favorable for Washington as could be imagined.

Many imperialism theoreticians have thus already built reservations into their own models: these reservations are based on the historic experience of over-extension, in which they see a historical law of nature. In fact, there are no historical laws of nature, but only intelligent and ignorant ways of dealing with others. Over-extension belongs to the second category; because setting goals which are unattainable with the resources available is one of the most fundamental errors of any strategy – think of the German Reich. When the problem of over-extension is thought through, it soon becomes apparent that the imperialist form of global governance cannot function, even under today's conditions. The imposition of foreign rule in a world of diversity, whether it is to be achieved through imperialism or hegemony, causes resistance at the periphery (failure because of the problem of diversity); internal political support for the costs of imperialism or hegemony can only be achieved when the dominant nation also gains appropriate advantages, which are achieved at the cost of others (failure because of the problem of fairness). Both arouse resistance, which the imperial power has to put down violently (failure because of the problem of avoiding war).

The critical point of world historical development is precisely that the very circumstances that seem to reduce the problem of over-extension for imperial powers make it possible for their opponents to resist them more effectively: modern communications technology, contemporary means of transport, and the weapons technology of today make it possible for even small groups to co-ordinate their resistance across great distances and even to carry it into the territory of the dominant power and, in doing so, in the worst cases to inflict immense damage. Thus, the relationship of strategic capacity arising from technology plays directly into the hands of the 'Davids': for, the dominant power has to maintain order, an enormously demanding task which can scarcely be fulfilled through military measures alone. The rebel, by contrast, only has to do damage in order to rip apart the fine threads of the network of order over and over again and, step by step, to drive the costs of the leadership so high that the far-off source of imperial rule one day declares: 'We have had enough!' What looks like a hopeless asymmetry in the absolute distribution of the instruments of power to the disadvantage of those rebelling against the rulers proves, from the point of view of the economics of the means-end relationship, to be an asymmetry to the disadvantage of the ruling power: the extension dilemma once again thrusts itself into the foreground at a higher level.

There is no requirement of over-extension: allowing yourself to be drawn by challenges into being bled dry is not an immutable law, but the result of foolish decisions. If the dominant power is to avoid being drawn in, it must allow forms of governance other than imperial ones: in the place of global struggle come agreement with the former opponent, participation of the opponent in making the rules and the settling of conflicts, and pressure for compromise far beyond what imperialist domination and harsh, strongly militarily-supported forms of hegemony will permit. Thus, in the twenty-first century imperial power is a self-defeating form of global governance, which, because of the impossible magnitude of its task, is doomed to failure by its own internal dynamics. The result is either the imperial power being bled dry and, following this, in the worst case anarchy, the opposite of sustainability, or a change to more cooperative forms of governance.

In current world political practice – in addition to the impressive confirmation of these general considerations through the failure of the Bush administration – additional concrete weaknesses of the American imperium have become apparent. The US was following a narrow, largely ideologically shaped agenda. All too arbitrarily it divided the world into friend and foe. Its sense of responsibility in connection with some world problems – inequality, the environment, climate, energy consumption, AIDS – was either under-developed or ideologically so channeled (combating AIDS by promoting abstinence until marriage, instead of condoms and affordable medication) that it showed itself to be largely incapable of setting workable and effective rules. Its claim to stand above the law (how can Donald Rumsfeld admit responsibility for the torture chamber Abu Ghraib but not be punished?) undermines the entire validity of global rules. After the fall of the Soviet Union the US had the chance to build up workable global governance, but failed miserably. That is the sad fact. We must hope that President Obama does better.

The democratic alliance: The 'civilizing mission' in new garb

Thus, the US cannot carry out the leadership job on its own. It is failing because of the impossibility of successful imperial rule and, left to its own resources, lacks the wisdom needed to make workable rules. Consequently, the next alternative changes the more subtle form, hegemony, to an institutional solution in which the role of the United States is reduced to that of 'primus inter pares' (first among equals). Instead of going it alone at the top, America limits itself to embedding its power in a 'league of democracies.' The members of this act together to take upon themselves the difficult task of global governance.

A practical expression of this idea is seen in the suggestion that NATO should be 'globalized.' For several years now the American Government has been exerting pressure on the alliance to develop closer ties with democratic countries outside the Atlantic Alliance, such as Israel, Japan, South Korea, Australia or New Zealand – yes, even to consider their membership. Ivo Daalder and Jim Goldgeier, two political scientists in the US, have developed a concise program for this. They go to considerable lengths to allay, for instance, fears that NATO may be seeking to take the place of the United Nations. Their arguments amount, however, to the following: NATO will support the United Nations as long as the UN does what the NATO democracies want. If this does not happen, the latter will behave according to their own inclinations. This shows that the apparent participation of non-democracies in the UN is purely cosmetic. Even more direct are the supporters of former President Bush, who – in the tradition of American neo-conservatism – declare unashamedly that the participation of undemocratic states in the United Nations undermines its legitimacy anyway, and the West therefore has a perfect right to make decisions and behave according to its own standards.

This model is supported by the fact that democracies are relatively better governed than non-democracies. In democracies there has not yet been widespread starvation, they are often associated with powerful free market economies, and the rule of law is significantly stronger than in non-democracies, something that gives their citizens more security in their everyday life. Regular changes of government limit the extent of corruption and misuse of power, of which, however, democracies are not completely free. The freedoms enjoyed by people in a democratic environment make their life more worth living. All this gives democratic governments a higher level of legitimacy than is enjoyed by tyrannies, single-party regimes, military juntas, 'theocracies' and the like. From a statistical point of view, things do not look bad. According to the definition employed, 50–60 percent of the world's states are democracies today. Most of the most highly-populated states are included: India, the US, Indonesia, Brazil, Japan, Germany, along with the entire European Union, involving more than 500 million people. Democracies produce well over 50 percent of global gross domestic product, and – in the light of the occasional necessity of imposing justice through force – rather important: they spend three quarters of the world's military expenditures.

Those in favor of global governance by a 'democratic league' believe that they are basing their arguments on an extremely admirable model: Kant's league of peace (*foedus pacificum*). Kant rejected the idea of a world state as being impractical (because the states would not surrender their sovereignty) and dangerous (because of its potential for tyranny). He proposed instead a 'league of peace made up of free states' which as a voluntary legally-constituted institution would permanently guarantee peace through mutual rejection of force and building of trust between nations. Apart from the provision of a formal framework governing international relations within 'world civil law,' Kant saw no need for any further regulation outside the nation-states, although it must be remembered that he lived in a time of weakly developed worldwide relationships. He limited world civil law to the right of every person to visit other lands without hindrance, to communicate with the people living there, and to trade with them (the counter-obligation to this was to avoid any use of violence against the people being visited). Global governance today requires greater effort in terms of coordination and cooperation, but the 'league of peace' would be a good foundation, on which the members of the alliance could negotiate a set of global rules.

Insistence on a dominant position for the democracies in world politics is supported in an intellectually overreaching way by the distortion that the liberal theory of international politics reads into Kant's 'Perpetual Peace.' According to this reading, the 'league of peace' discussed there – which ignores the domestic constitutions of its members – becomes a 'club of the democracies.' Confusing the concept 'free state' with 'democracy' distorts its historical meaning. To Kant, 'free state' means a state that enjoys external sovereignty: the 'freedom' of a state is seen in its resistance to the attempts of others to interfere in its affairs, not in its domestic constitution. Naturally only such sovereign units could be independent members of a 'league of peace' among states. It can thus be seen that Kant conceptualized the 'league of peace' as a mixed international organization, in which membership was also open to non-democracies. Such a peace-oriented institution would offer the best conditions for using persuasion and good example to coax the non-democracies into gradually matching their internal affairs to the model of their democratic partners. This is still true today.

By distorting Kant's peace theory the liberal movement is going along a detour whose direction is contrary to its own intentions. The decisive argument here is not based on the 'over-expansion' of the democratic powers. Rather, the focus is on the consequences of the arbitrary act of an alliance of the democracies ignoring the political will of all other states, making global political decisions for them and claiming the right to impose these even against resistance. Such a confrontation produces a new kind of security dilemma at a global level. This dilemma no longer involves, as the classical one did, uncertainty about the intentions of neighbors, but uncertainty about the missionary intentions of liberalism, the only uncertainty being the point in time when one will be targeted by the militant liberal camp.

As a result, non-democracies are confronted with a double security problem: they are only involved in the formation of the world order when the democracies invite them, i.e., in a secondary role or even no longer at all, and can thus not participate in making the rules which define the framework for their behavior, especially for their own national security. As non-participants in the application of these rules they are also in danger of becoming the objects of decisions on intervention made by the democracies. The normal answer to the general security dilemma, as well as to more specific threats, is to try to equip oneself with appropriate means of deterrence and defense. As the case of Iran shows, this actually happens; blocked in its ambition to be the leading regional power, threatened on all sides by the military presence of the US, and as a member of what the previous American Government called the 'axis of evil' facing the risk of a violent regime change, Teheran persists, against the will of the international community, in seeking to create for itself an option for a future deterrent through a 'peaceful' nuclear program. The missionary liberal universalism spurs on the arms race. Because its political protagonists are the world's strongest powers, all that remains to those who feel threatened is the attempt to interrupt the work of the missionaries through particularly terrifying deterrents, i.e., weapons of mass destruction. The result is global arms races and the proliferation of weapons of mass destruction.

In addition: those who seek to 'globalize' NATO in the way just described completely miscalculate the willingness of the democracies in the Third World to enter into such an alliance with the 'West.' Israel, Japan, Australia and New Zealand may still be so inclined. For Brazil, South Africa, India or Indonesia this cannot be assumed to be the case. To be sure, these countries are fully conscious of their democratic structures, which differentiate them from their partners in the non-aligned movement. However, at the same time they distrust the alliance of former colonial powers. In many issues – for instance in connection with the Middle-East conflict or dealing with Iran – they see things differently from the leading Western powers and their allies, and are not willing to allow themselves to be taken for granted. They might well give the invitation to join a global NATO a polite rejection. This means that the division of the world into democracies and non-democracies is joined by a second: 'North' versus 'South.' The 'democratic league' too is wrecked by its inability to cope with diversity. The exclusion of the 'South,' and – something that does not seem to have been noticed by those who recommend a world order led by the democracies – the world's most populous nation (China) will awaken resentment: the problem of justice increases exponentially. The sequence of decree and resistance, already known from the imperial power model, repeats itself. The taking of the world into receivership by the democracies could lead to a world war. It cannot go on like this either.

The world republic – the cosmopolitan dream (nightmare)

Under cosmopolitanism, I understand the imposition of a global society on all human beings. This (supposed) community would be suitable in the opinion of contemporary 'cosmopolitans' as the basis for a – at least 'slimmed down,' i.e., equipped with very few, although decisive, responsibilities – world democracy; the responsibilities foreseen are guaranteeing security, protecting human rights, and the authority to take over decision-making in further areas if this should prove to be necessary. This approach is based on the belief that universal principles can be derived from valid, general, basic considerations, without contradictions and independently of the historically developed ethical convictions of different cultures, and can therefore lay claim to being valid for everybody. This is supported by the contemporary diagnosis that the linking up of the world has now reached a point that makes resolving questions of 'global internal affairs' in the way it is done in single states necessary and possible.

The cosmopolitan discourse not only claims that the norms it propagates are worthy of agreement, but even that they inherently require agreement. These norms require as the basis of global governance a world republic, in which elected representatives decide on war and peace and on over-arching issues of distribution. There are differing opinions about whether these representatives will operate as a third chamber alongside the Security Council and the General Assembly of the United Nations, or whether they themselves will directly elect the world government in the manner of a parliamentary democracy. The quintessence of all models of cosmopolitan democracy is that the principle of elected government is accepted in some form or other at the global level too, and that the nation-states that exist today surrender central areas of their national sovereignty to this organ of world democracy.

Globalization really does produce considerable areas of convergence, amalgamations, networks, and communication among previously separated cultures. It makes the hard shell of the nation-state softer. For the realization of societal goals and projects the cooperation (through action or inaction) of players outside the territorial state, whether they are other states or non-governmental players, is always necessary. This development is, however, only one side of the coin. The other side is the strengthening of the identity of those players who for centuries were robbed of any chance of autonomy by the expansion through force of the Western world. The sovereignty of the state is often understood there – and also by people who are suffering tyrannical forms of rule and fighting against them – as protecting their chances of autonomous development. Typical is the fact that many members of the Iranian opposition oppose a violent change of regime, even though they regard the present system as repulsive: their rulers are unpopular anti-democrats, to be sure, but they are 'their' anti-democrats. What even the minimalist cosmopolitans present as universally valid is actually the result of Western liberal history and culture, and they simply assume its value as a model for the rest of the world.

A great deal can be learned by looking critically at our own blind spot: we have created a system that gives, and has recently increased, disproportional influence on political decisions to wealthy and organized interests, concentrates opinion-making into ever fewer hands, and maintains social inequality (and with it massive inequality of opportunity). Our notion of freedom leads to the constant injuring of the feelings of religious people and the degradation of the female body to the status of an object of male voyeurism and an instrument of commercial advertising. Regardless of constitutional regulations and liberal rhetoric, discrimination (all the way to abuse) of strangers is part of our social and political practice. Our system deals in an almost blasphemous way with the Creation, and lacks any rigorous concept for protecting the future of our environment and society. It has broken up the extended family and is in the process of doing the same with the nuclear family. The neglect of children and the degradation of the old seem to be unavoidable consequences. The consumption of drugs is widespread, and is not opposed in any effective way.

I personally feel comfortable in the liberal world whose dark side I have just described. This is because I grew up in it. People from other cultures and regions must be forgiven if they do not enthusiastically adopt values and institutions that have developed within the traditions of our society; this is the legitimate aspect of the admittedly not disinterested construction 'Asian values.' They adapt rights and responsibilities to each other in a way that differs from what we are accustomed to, according to which we give defense of the individual and individual development the clear priority. They see the relationship of collective and individual differently. For them, individual human beings are only part of the human race through their participation in the community, i.e., indirectly, and not as in liberal universalism, directly. Adding to the leadership ranks by co-opting people (as in the Catholic Church or in corporations) may seem to them to make more sense and be more suitable than selecting leaders through general elections. I personally do not side with the anti-liberals in the case of any of these alternatives. I merely draw attention to the fact that such orientations (still?) exist elsewhere, not only as the ideology of a ruling elite but also as 'popular culture.'

Our liberal-democratic principles have grown up in our culture, and would only be appropriate as guidelines for global institutions if they were capable of winning worldwide acceptance. That is not the case. That a world culture has already come into existence is a pious self-deception of the believers in universalism. When these principles are linked, as in the intellectually fashionable idea of a (quasi) democratic form of governance that replaces states, with the undermining of the hard-won sovereignty of the previously downtrodden, they make a doubly aggressive, hypocritical and repulsive impression: to the Chinese, yes even to the Indians who are accustomed to democracy, the thought that, exactly at the moment when through their own skill, hard work and persistence they have crossed the threshold to becoming a world power, they should give up much of their own existence as a separate state must seem like a concealed attack on their identity: after the West has pursued its own interests for centuries, without any consideration for others, and has disempowered and oppressed these peoples, it is once again trying to strip them of the freedom of movement they had regained with so much effort. From this perspective, cosmopolitanism looks like colonialism through other means, a Western ideology of domination which will once again make permanent the subjugation of the Blacks, Reds, Browns, and Yellows under the rule of the White man.

In the best Western tradition, the cosmopolitans understand the individual as the bearer of inalienable rights. As a result, they assign to the citizens of other states rights whose injury justifies external interference. Those who here and now proclaim a 'human right to democracy,' and support humanitarian intervention, hang the sword of Damocles of a militarily imposed regime change over all non-democracies. For, the practical verdict, at what point in time which undemocratic ruler will be decreed to be a member of the 'axis of evil' who must be removed, is completely arbitrary. The Saddam Hussein of 1985 was an authoritarian ruler who could be tolerated, the one of 2003 a tyrant who had to be deposed. The Milosevic of 1995 was the sought after partner of Dayton, the one of 1999 the target of a massive air war.

Increasing unpredictability inescapably leads to relationships between armed political units – Western and other states – being caught up in the security dilemma. The arms race is its grammar; unwanted escalations are its errors of syntax. That those who are uncertain seek to acquire deterrents – Iran and North Korea – is undesirable from the point of view of maintenance of order, for those in power there are not nice people. However, a disinterested analysis in terms of security policy would not see anything surprising in their behavior: those who threaten generate anxiety about survival, and those who experience anxiety about their survival obtain for themselves effective means of defense.

And then the practical problems: how, if you don't mind, will the world parliament be constituted? No somehow convincing concept for the universal parliament exists. The problem of how to distinguish between the elected members from democratic countries and the appointed representatives of non-democratic countries has not been solved (an all the more embarrassing oversight in view of the fact that according to proportional representation the Chinese members would have to make up approximately a fifth to a quarter of the entire world parliament). How proportional representation could be achieved when the difference in population between the smallest and the biggest countries would be not, as in the EU (where it is already causing difficulties) about 1:320, but 1:220,000 is unclear. To exclude the large non-democracies from the world parliament also seems not to be a good idea if the agreement of these countries (at least of China) would be needed to change the U.N. Charter.

A second problem is the question of the voting system, i.e., deciding between the polar opposites of proportional representation and a winner-takes-it-all system. At first glance it seems that it would be possible – as in the EU – to leave this up to the constitutions of the individual countries. A closer examination, however, yields problems with this. Proportional representation gives more emphasis to diversity and gives minorities a stronger position. Presumably this is what is wanted in a world parliament, especially when the building of coalitions is to involve crossing national, regional or cultural boundaries; such a transregional, transcultural political structure is important for the ability of a world parliament to deal with and eliminate conflicts. If a winner-takes-it-all system existed in, let us say, a democratic China or a democratic India, there would have to be concern about whether this would lead to distorted representation of points of view (or cultural nationalism) in the world parliament. In a politically and culturally relatively homogeneous political union like the EU this can be handled; nonetheless, it was difficult for some partners in the EU to concede the strongest parliamentary delegation to the largest partner, i.e., Germany.

At a global level such an over-representation could seem threatening. Through the unconditional claim of validity that the Western cosmopolitans make for their cultural values and institutional solutions the powerful self-defense instincts that exist in other countries, even without this, are reinforced yet further. The recognition that was constantly denied the 'others' during their colonial history continues to be withheld, with the argument that no other principles of global governance can exist apart from those hatched in the West. The absurd consequence then follows that the well-meaning intention of fostering universality instead leads only to greater fragmentation. Asymmetries in power and the nonchalance of cosmopolitan thinkers in dealing with the problem of violence contribute to this.

The idea of cosmopolitan democracy does not demand – in contrast to the project 'global NATO' – that a group of (mainly Western) democracies rule over all others, but affords the right to participate to every human being, without exception. Nonetheless, it embodies a – no matter how well-meant – imperial project: for, it demands from all others that they subordinate themselves to the principles that have been victorious in the history of Western political culture. What is for instance China to make of the appeals being made for the UN or world politics in general to be run along parliamentary lines? It is well known that China is not a parliamentary democracy. The People's Congress plays the role of a moderate forum of debate, but not that of parliamentary control and decision-making. The demand is thus made of China that it subordinate itself to a system that is not its own. Why for all the world should it be expected that those in power in Beijing will bow to such a suggestion – i.e., without violent resistance? Non-liberal states are confronted with the unreasonable demand that they agree to the establishment of, or tolerate, global political institutions that contradict their own principles of governance. At the same time, they experience the self-granted empowerment of liberal states – occasionally supported by the bearers of the philosophical banner of liberal universalism – to make decisions for the entire world in specific cases and in anticipation of the future realization of a liberal world order. All this leads us directly into the ugly world of cultural conflict and the security dilemma, but not to an ordering of things that will make sustainable global governance possible.

Global governance

Over the last decade and a half, the discipline of international relations has devoted its most intensive efforts – with painstaking consideration of world politics – to the problem of 'world government' as part of the 'global governance' debate.' To its credit, this discussion differs from the cosmopolitan approach by taking the diversity of the world into account, and from the imperial power, hegemony or world-state governance concepts by aiming at horizontal rather than hierarchical regulation of world events. Important in 'global governance' is that this approach lays claim to being able to both describe an observable trend in this direction as well as to work out how this trend ought to be continued to the general benefit of all. Research on global governance involves a wide spectrum of topics and suggestions for solutions.

In one thing they (almost) all agree: the state is losing its role as the central mechanism for ruling beyond national borders. Whereas earlier rules for the behavior of states, legal persons, and individual citizens in international and transnational affairs were exclusively the result of negotiations between governments, and these were also responsible for applying and implementing them, nowadays a varied mixture of players is involved in setting rules and implementing them: the nation-states are still involved, but their importance has shrunk dramatically. International organizations, above all powerful secretariats, play their own independent game. Non-governmental organizations are not only active through campaigns in which they try to exert public pressure to get certain governments to support their positions in negotiations, but they also participate in negotiations themselves and play an important role in the implementation and control of the observation of agreements. Multinational corporations are occupied with setting rules without states, for instance in private trade law. And with private security firms a player has appeared that – like the Condottieri in the early modern era – is active as an independent operator in an area that in the age of the national-state was entirely the state's prerogative: internal and external security, an area that the modern world had previously entrusted to the exclusive power of the state.

Global governance as an answer to the challenge of globalization thus occurs, according to its theoreticians, only in exceptional cases as an interaction between states ('government by the state'), and more commonly in networks, in which the state is only involved as one among many ('government with the state'), and increasingly through freely-made agreements and independent rule-making of non-state players ('government without the state'). With all this the hope is connected that this motley hodgepodge represents progress towards democracy; anyone for whom democracy is more than broad but unregulated participation may doubt this. For, who gave the non-governmental organizations the authority to speak for others? Is it democratic for large corporations, whose economic power is not subject to any democratic control anyway, to be placed in a situation where they can now make laws that cross national boundaries? Is that really better in the sense of democracy than democracies and non-democracies negotiating agreements with each other (where in the former at least the governments are democratically legitimized and international agreements require parliamentary assent)?

My own idea of global governance is based on the judgment that conventional opinion underestimates the importance of the state in the setting and carrying out of rules outside its own boundaries, and has lost its sense of what the state can and – in a normative sense – should do in this area. In saying this I am not denying that other players are (should be) involved. I do maintain, however, that the central position of the state continues to be essential for effective and sustainable global governance. I would like to develop this position further by means of a critical look at the actual effects and fields of activity of non-governmental players and their interaction with the state in today's world.

International organizations, especially those with supranational components and/or their own binding arbitration or judicial procedures, constitute the first norm-making bodies that can act independently of the state. On closer examination, however, these organizations reveal themselves to be models of classical – as the name already says – international cooperation, i.e., cooperation between nations. The body of national-states continues to be 'ruler of the proceedings.' The difference from bilateral or multilateral interaction without organization, as it was practiced in the nineteenth and early twentieth centuries, lies in the higher level of institutionalization, which 'stiffens the backbone' of the agreed-upon norms, and in the secretariats, which become players in their own right. (More about that shortly.) Nonetheless, the international organizations can – like international regimes, i.e., sets of principles, norms, rules, and procedures for solving shared problems, whose guardians international organizations often are – only be efficient as producers and guardians of norms if these norms are enshrined in the practice of the states. It is the states which have the decisive 'voice' in norm production; and the states also have the power to withdraw from central agreements and the organizations belonging to them. This possibility is rarely made use of. For this reason it is understandable that international organizations are accepted as they are, and people tend to assume they have greater autonomy in relation to their members than is justified by their constitution. Not until the US withdraws from UNESCO or North Korea leaves the Non-Proliferation Treaty does the temporary nature and fragility of the international organizations and regimes as a governance structures become apparent: they produce governance 'through the state.'

A further indicator of the central position of the states is the difference in the level of influence among international organizations, in which the differences among the states in level of influence in the international system are reflected: it is true that the smaller states have relatively more influence in an organization, and the larger states relatively less, than the gross distribution of power might suggest, but more powerful states still have more influence than less powerful ones. This state of affairs demonstrates that the states are still the decisive factor in the organization. It is known that these differences are even enshrined in the constitution of some organizations, such as the veto power of the five permanent members of the Security Council in the UN Charter, the dependence of voting rights on the level of currency investment in the constitution of the International Monetary Fund (IMF), or the permanent membership of the major users of nuclear power in the Governing Board of the International Atomic Energy Agency. Obviously, through their institutionalization international organizations have an independent effect on the states. In their behavior, states always take into account what it would cost them to replace a functioning organization or create a new one if the existing one were to be destroyed; they take into account the loss of face that would threaten if they constantly broke the rules. They internalize the norms worked out in the organization until they are part of their own flesh and blood. This is the way an international organization works. This also means, however, that the organization only lives in and from its members. The state is thus its core.

That non-governmental organizations are playing an increasing role in international organizations is true. However, they are doing this mainly as 'handmaidens' of the member states and the secretariats that work for them. It is seldom that they achieve the status of players outside this role as assistants. This should not by any means be under-estimated as progress in global governance. They add additional information, legitimacy, and transparency to international norm-setting and implementation processes and, in this way, by and large improve their quality. Nonetheless, decision-making and implementation powers remain with the states. What about the secretariats? More than anything else, they are the essence and the symbol of the independent personality of the organization and its status as a player. In organizations where the Secretary General or Chief Executive Officer has a strong position, such as the United Nations or the International Atomic Energy Agency, the secretariats acquire the status of an independent player. Nonetheless, their freedom of action continues to be limited by the decision-making powers of the member states. Through their control of the budget the member states retain control over every individual action that the secretariat proposes. An unpopular Director General can be voted out of office as in, for instance, the Organization for the Prohibition of Chemical Weapons, whose chief was replaced before the end of his term of office on account of his leadership style and his problems with managing the budget.

The initiating and controlling functions exercised by the secretariat go beyond a 'free-for-all among nations' and change the form of governance. However, they do not change the fact that the secretariat operates within a system of 'governance by the state' or 'by the states.' At the same time, governance 'with the state' gives it more weight in actual reality than the formula reveals. Negotiating systems or networks, in which the state works 'shoulder to shoulder' alongside other non-governmental players in developing and maintaining norms, give due recognition to the fact that the functions of the state cannot be carried out without (cross-border) cooperation with others – whether they are states or other participants in the particular field of action. Simultaneously, this form of governance also means that without the state 'nothing goes,' that the states retain veto power in norm setting (or reserve for themselves the right to withdraw).

In governance 'without the state,' in which non-state players agree on cross-border norms within their own institutional framework without the cooperation of state representatives, it seems to be more difficult to subsequently monitor norm-setting and control processes. (The most frequently cited example is the lex mercatoria, the regulation of reciprocal legal claims among private-sector corporations operating in an international context. Indeed, the state has withdrawn from active participation in this area.) There is also no disagreement about the growing contribution of non-state players to the creation of norms outside the state and, more and more frequently, control of their implementation too. My position, however, is that the state is involved in events in the background, and that this indirect participation continues to be a necessary condition for governance 'without the state.'

The first background condition is that the state continues to be decisive for the existence of non-state players, and consequently for the possibilities of action in the international sphere. These players – to the extent that they are not underground operations like the Mafia or al-Qaeda – need to have their juristic persona anchored in a territorial state which acknowledges their legal existence, gives them legitimacy through this, and makes it possible for non-state players to be accepted as participants by other states (and non-state players). The recognition of legal status is a function in which the state (or the community of states as a whole) is irreplaceable. When this recognition requires an actual legal action on the part of the state the second function consists of toleration or avoidance of obstruction. The independent norm-setting activity of non-state players only exists because the states do not negate them. If these established opposing laws, or actively opposed the attempts of the non-state players to establish norms, relevant activities would be sure to fail. After all, the state sets up the conditions within which private norm setting functions. As is the case for all norms, it is also true for those established by private bodies: their validity depends upon the existence of a perspective stretching beyond the present. Who is it that guarantees the expectation of stability that opens up the prospects for success of privately worked out norms if it is not the state or the cooperation of the state?

Privately set norms are somewhat different from norms that come into existence through state negotiations. This 'different-ness' is always based on the guarantee function of the state. A special case of this state of affairs is seen when the effectiveness of private norm setting depends on the state also assuming respon-sibility for legal enforcement of the norms, i.e., is expected to use its powers of coercion against those who do not observe the norms; when norms have their roots in the civil law of a state, this is the case. Norm setting done in the private sphere can perhaps survive without this special guarantee of validity from the state, but hardly without the more abstract guarantee of continuation of the conditions that – through the original constitution of the players and/or avoidance of obstructing their activities – made laying down of private law possible in the first place.

Even if, in individual cases, legal norms can come into exist-ence without the state, they still need the 'shadow of the hierar-chy' – either because they are still subject to the power of the state to impose sanctions or because state or international constitution of non-state players is indispensable for the future prospects of any rule that is made. Government 'without the state' is – apart from the arcane worlds of al-Qaeda and the Mafia – to a consid-erable degree an optical illusion (and even these dark rulers of extra-state independence can only operate to the extent that, and as long as, the state fails to set any effective boundaries for them and in a certain sense tolerates them). The state also sits invis-ibly at the table during norm setting and maintenance by private organizations. Its work is merely substantially more subtle than in the case of 'government by' and 'government with' the state.

Among the approaches to world government under the conditions of globalization that have been discussed above, 'global governance' seems to be the one least infiltrated by the Western thirst for dominance. And yet it dramatically fails to take into account the perspective of most Third World countries. There – for instance in China and India, in Malaysia and Singapore, in Mali and Brazil – the age of globalization is often seen as a phase in which the power of the state is increasing, and growing demands are being made of it, demands which it can also to some extent meet. In other parts of the Third World they are struggling to reestablish internal sovereignty, to restore the disrupted power of the state in one way or another, in some cases with external help.

It can thus be seen that in a number of states outside Europe the state has retained its importance as an identification and reference system, or even increased it, and that at the same time it has secured resources that have increased its value and status in the eyes of the peoples that belong to it. For Indians and Chinese it is not a loss of state power when their governments are taken seriously as players in the negotiations of the World Trade Organization. It is more a matter of the extraordinarily satisfying experience of taking part in the processes of global rule-making as an acknowledged and respected participant. At precisely this moment the West is discovering the ideology of denationalization; the theoreticians of global governance describe the supposedly current processes of the shrinking state, while at the same time the cosmopolitans base on it their demand to devalue the state in international politics.

On the threshold of the advancement of two developing nations to world powers and of other potent developing nations (for instance Brazil, South Africa, Malaysia) to positions as serious partners in international negotiations, such a debate must look like part of an attempt by the West to stop this process, in order to preserve the 400-year Western hegemony through other means. For developing nations that are establishing themselves, sovereignty is the safe haven within which their autonomous development can complete itself. It makes little sense to oppose this view with the argument that sovereignty ranges from protecting the evil of 'bad governance' all the way to grave violation of human rights and genocide; for this is not at all what it is all about for the countries just mentioned – as well as for those with undemocratic systems of government. To them sovereignty means the right to choose their own legal and political path, without letting others tell them what to do. 'Global governance' too deals inadequately with the problem of diversity – here: different courses of historical development, including completely different experiences with the globalization epoch. It offends the sense of justice of those players with different experiences, and in this way contributes – contrary to its own intention – to increasing conflict. For Chinese, Indians and others, insisting on sovereignty by no means involves rejection of forms of legally-binding cooperation; but they want to maintain control over which form it takes, which property rights and which legal forms and procedures are chosen, in order to participate on the basis of freely made decisions. This is the justification for the wish that representatives of the state participate, i.e., the perfectly normal production of international law.

Conclusions

For our purposes, nothing appropriate for 'sustainable global governance' is on offer. The models have been designed from a Western perspective and reflect, sometimes unashamedly, sometimes unconsciously, the Western claim to dominance. But that is part of the problem rather than of the solution; I reach this conclusion as someone who believes in Western values and is glad to live in a liberal-democratic land. But these convictions and this well-being are one thing, the hope that a new global order can be based on them quite a different one. The partly over-confident, partly naïve way in which the models discussed draw conclusions about others based on us de-emphasizes diversity, establishes our understanding of fairness as the only valid one, and at the same time heats up the 'clash of civilizations' and the great power rivalries by taking no account of the needs and wishes of emerging nations. All the world order models discussed contain aspects with which we can work further. The suggestions for a new imperial power and for hegemony draw our attention to the fact that the unequal distribution of power must be taken into account in some way. The cosmopolitan approach reminds us of the high value placed on human rights and the link between 'good government' and democracy. Global governance delivers the insight that the participation of non-state players in rule-setting is appropriate to current world conditions. However, its one-sidedness devalues this intellectual credit: by falling short of our three basic targets, we run the risk of incurring a net loss in sustainability.

Some branches of social psychology consider diversity among social collectives to be the unavoidable root of violent confrontation: people need an identity and that always means being different from 'others.' Collective identities evolve within 'in-groups' which, based on their (presumed or real) special characteristics, are distinct from 'out-groups.' The processes of integration into the former group are accompanied by increasing alienation from the latter. The alien ultimately appears to be menacing and threatening. Other social psychologists and sociologists disagree with the blanket prediction that differences must always result in (violent) conflict. Diversity can also arouse curiosity, interest, a sense of complementary enrichment, division of labor, etc. People can identify with aspects of a foreign identity and distance themselves from aspects of their own identity. This softens the hard shell of potentially violent collective identity until it is ineffective. Diversity therefore does not damn us to war. It can lead to this if we do many things wrong. However, we are always at liberty to stop the fatal chain of events which leads from 'difference' to 'violence.'

There are about 6,000 different 'peoples' (ethnic groups) in the world. Our 'world cultures' are larger groupings of these. Samuel Huntington, who formulated the 'clash of civilizations' thesis, lists from six to nine cultures which in his view are grouped around religions: the 'Western' or Roman-Christian culture (which he categorizes together with the Protestant and Jewish communities), the Orthodox culture, Islam, Hinduism, Confucianism (which he then mixes together with Buddhism and Japanese Shintoism), the African (about which he is not sure what it is and whether it exists) and Latino culture (which he sometimes treats separately and sometimes as part of the Roman-Christian category). Upon closer investigation, the lines of demarcation between cultures are less clearly defined and much more fluid than portrayed by Huntington. In the 'West,' secular France has little in common with the Protestant fundamentalism of the American Bible Belt or the deep Catholicism found in Poland. The bloody civil war going on in Iraq underscores the schism between Shi'ite Muslims and Sunni Muslims, as does the distrust Iranians and Arabs harbor for one another. When traveling from Riyadh to the Qatar Peninsula you are traveling within the country of the Sunni Muslims; still, there is little common ground between the Saudi's strictly orthodox Wahhabi beliefs and the liberal-minded Islam of the small sheikdom. In India the tolerant and multi-faceted traditional belief of Hinduism is far different from its orthodox counterpart, which maintains the received scriptures and is the animating factor in radical national Hinduism. And so on and so forth. The 6,000 ethnic groups and the few cultural groups are currently spread across 192 countries. We may speak of 'nation-states,' but nation and state are very rarely completely identical. People who consider German to be their native language live in Poland, the Czech Republic, Austria, Italy, France, Belgium, Denmark, Switzerland and Liechtenstein. Hungarian minority groups live in Slovakia, in the Ukraine and Serbia. Estonia, Latvia, Belarus, the Ukraine, Kazakhstan and other 'products of division' of the earlier Soviet Union have many citizens of Russian ancestry. In the course of globalization, 'diasporas' have formed in many countries, immigrant groups with a lasting bond to their country of origin. In Africa boundaries were arbitrarily drawn between countries by the colonial powers, without consideration for tribes and ethnic groups. This is the reason why in some countries there is majority rule and in other countries minority rule, often at the expense of national and social stability. Diversity is found within each country and even more between countries.

Where does the problem lie? The value systems of cultures center on concepts of a good life. 'Good' means two things in this regard: first, a way of leading one's life which people equate with satisfaction, happiness and fulfillment; second, a way of life which is in harmony with dominant customs and norms, and in the context of each culture is deemed 'right.' These norms shape, first, the view of the society and individuals regarding right and wrong in the sense of 'unwritten laws.' On the other hand, they are guiding principles informing legal systems, in other words the laws that have been put into writing and their application in the courts. Problems resulting from globalization now call for a code of conduct which must be recorded both legally (as rules and prohibitions) and in a non-statutory manner (as acquired habits of behavior which are considered 'right'). Caps on CO_2 emissions for every country and a ban on the use of biological weapons fall under the first category; efficient use of energy or giving up the practice of blood revenge fall under the second. These codes of conduct must also be in agreement with a diverse range of cultural values. Otherwise, the representatives of these different cultural groups will not agree to them.

Cultural integration, cultural fragmentation

The difficulty of the task should definitely not be underestimated. There are certainly circumstances which make the task less daunting compared with the fixed intercultural boundaries invoked by Samuel Huntington. According to Huntington, cultures look like the crystalline structures of hard rock: they have an inner order which has calcified through time, over the centuries and through the generations, and are protected by their hard shell from the influence of other 'cultural formations.' A quite different process plays out in real life. There are cohesive and antagonistic forces at work causing harmonization and differentiation, cross-fertilization and separation, cross-cultural learning and isolation, globalization and fragmentation, dialog and war.

The processes of globalization confront all the world's regions with similar problems. Deeply rooted traditions everywhere are faced with challenges, national governments have to come to grips with the 'willfulness' of the global market and its social consequences, environmental issues such as the hole in the ozone layer or climate change require action, and migration is sharpening the debate on social integration. Problems are distributed unevenly; the resources for dealing with them even more. But all world regions and their countries are confronted with these challenges at varying levels. This simultaneity is new in human history. In earlier times the varying levels of development of societies and the relative isolation of their geographic areas favored the formation of different cultural responses to the same but not simultaneously occurring issues. Today, the simultaneity of these problems presents even greater opportunities for cultural convergence than ever before. In addition, this convergence is also being supported by the fact that the most successful responses are being communicated to even the most remote areas by global media, and the necessary resources offered everywhere on the world market. There is an exchange going on across global networks about values, norms and cultural guiding principles. Optimists speak of a 'world culture' that is emerging or possibly already exists. In opposition to this is, in many places, the partly instinctive, partly authoritarian tendency to protect one's own traditions from foreign influence.

At times like this, traditions are normally reinvented 'behind the backs of the players' – who reconstruct a supposed authenticity which has little to do with historical models, but in which their creators fervently believe. Fundamentalists who emphasize the purism of originary Islam and the 'actual' primordial meaning of the Koran ignore the historical connection of customs and rituals which have found their way into the Holy Book and, of more serious ramifications, the fact that large parts of the Koran in its written form, as is also true for the Bible, only came to be a part of an immutable canon over long periods, after the founder of the religion had died. Evangelical fundamentalism deals with the Bible exactly the same way as does Orthodox Judaism. Hinduism as a belief system based on received scripture is really an invention of the nineteenth and twentieth centuries.

Guarding that which belongs to a culture against things alien is a phenomenon seen all over the world. In Munich-Untersendling organized Muslim groups want to build a mosque in order to allow the many inhabitants of the surrounding city neighborhoods who are Muslims to practice their religion in an appropriate setting; non-Muslim residents and the Bavarian state government are mobilizing all available resources to stop the project, which had already been approved by the city of Munich. The same is happening in Cologne at the moment. These attempts to bring the construction of a mosque to a halt breathe the same spirit as the bloody attacks on 'enemy' tourists in Djerba or Bali. The players involved are each resorting to the measures available to them; the Bavarian state government is applying the repressive instrument of administrative law, the radical murderers are using homemade bombs. No matter how different the measures adopted, the similarity of the underlying purposes and attitudes cannot be concealed: fending off the foreign which, with the help of globalization, is unstoppably forcing its way into our own front yard.

This defense mechanism in turn engenders counter-movements among those social and political forces which see enrichment in being open to the unknown, more choices and more freedom in greater diversity, and opportunities for better answers to the challenges we face in variety. In addition to the vertical Counter-Reformation of each specific culture at the point where it originated, a horizontal globalization of cultures across all of the planet's communities is also the result. The business elite in Hong Kong and Mumbai are no different from their counterparts in Frankfurt, London, or New York. Human rights groups who feel bound to the various conventions of the United Nations and believe in Western Enlightenment are found within all cultures, and are causing difficulty for authoritarian rulers the world over. Greenpeace has national organizations everywhere in the world because, in particular since the Special Conference of the UN on Environmental Issues convened in Rio de Janeiro in 1992, an ecological value system has taken root everywhere.

This genuine universalizing of values across cultural boundaries stands in contrast to a distribution of specific particular orientations; this development results from globalization-driven migration. The diaspora also introduces the cultures of the former homelands into the countries people migrate to, and divides these into two forms: first there are 'hybrids' involving the more or less harmonious intermingling of both cultures – as can be seen in our European members of parliament of Muslim or Hindu faith, who have creatively blended values from their home country with Western values; second there are subcultures set apart from the mainstream where the defense mechanisms and fundamentalism practiced by groups in the homeland are perpetuated in the new country. The failure of the countries receiving immigrants to integrate the third generation of immigrant families smoothly plays a decisive role in this respect; the administrative attacks against the mosque in Munich mentioned above are a particularly striking example of this counterproductive failure.

Amartya Sen has emphasized the argument that cultural identity is only one aspect of people's multifaceted individuality. Other aspects – nationality, social class, educational background, political orientation, hobbies, etc. – also play a decisive role in shaping identity. Sen has voiced an appeal to place these many aspects of identity in the foreground in order to prevent overly simplistic attempts to use religious and cultural identity for political purposes, attempts he justifiably considers dangerous because of their potential for violence. It nevertheless makes no sense to ignore the fact that such one-sided building of identity exists in many places and determines people's thinking and actions. That a group of committed 'culture purveyors,' from the evangelical TV preachers in the US all the way to Osama bin Laden, actively engage in this oversimplification makes the situation more difficult.

Because this is the way matters stand, openly fighting against cultural and religious identities cannot be recommended. For this battle is waged on the basis of a previously established universalism that itself is the expression of a particular historical-cultural development (see below). The attempt to stop the 'oversimplification' appears to others to itself pose the danger of cultural 'alienation,' and aggravates the situation more than it resolves it.

There is no getting around acknowledging those players in Third World countries long oppressed by the West who take a firm stand against a liberal secular Western worldview, pointing to their historically evolved culture and religion. These players are just as legitimate as people with universalistic views which we like better. This is especially true for governments of non-democratic countries who rule exclusively over peoples who do not belong to the Western cultural sphere. It makes no sense to formulate rules of global governance which are meant to address globalization problems by meeting only with Chinese, Saudi, or Burmese human rights groups, and seeking to ignore the governments of these countries. For, these governments have noteworthy groups supporting them. To imagine that a military 'junta' consists of only a handful of those in power, while all other people without exception thirst for the day they can enjoy Western values, has been painfully refuted by the bloody experience of Afghanistan and Iraq. Jointly formulated peaceful resolution of problems begins with recognition of players who have the power to take action, even if we do not have to (or are unable to) love them, and even if we have our doubts about whether they represent all of 'their' people. But we must – just as during the time of the Cold War with the autocratic rulers in Moscow – come to terms with them (in the course of which, in the meantime the stable support for the 'unalloyed democrat' Putin by the majority of Russia's people demonstrates that they also do not think in an entirely 'Western' way).

The political significance of the cultural factor

At first glance, it would seem to make little sense to search for the cultural factor in politics. After all, there is empirical data showing that major cultural groups are different in many ways and globalization and accompanying migration have gradually made these differences visible in all countries. Is it really justified to speak of the 'West,' which arouses ill will among 'the Muslims' in the world political arena?

All the justified doubts concerning his historical diagnosis notwithstanding, Samuel Huntington has provided us with the important insight that in today's world political situation 'culture' can only attain a political 'form' if it operates through existing nation-states. A closer look at the global players who are still most important today reveals that most of them are dominated by a single defining culture. This may involve a majority of the people (such as the Hindu majority in India) or be a matter of a minority (such as the combination of Salafiti Sunniism and the Arab ethnic group ruling in Sudan), but a decisive factor is still that the state as the ruling political class's instrument of power is culturally defined in a particular direction. This characteristic feature can be even more pointedly accentuated by a culturally-oriented, above all religious and political entrepreneurism. Iran's President Ahmadinejad, the settler movement in West Jordan, or the national Hindu movement in India are typical examples. The culturally-conditioned national policy formed in this way can have an impact beyond a country's borders: multiple groupings of countries sharing similar or the same cultural influences develop a mutual identity directed against (ostensible) rivals.

Differences between cultures are thus not a law of nature, as Huntington would have readers believe, but instead the result of political actions. The continuing repression by Israel of Palestinians living on the 'West Bank' has a unifying effect on political perceptions within the Islamic world, going beyond all divisions into Arab and non-Arab, Sunni and Shi'ite, or Sunni schools for interpreting Shariah law. The caricatures of Mohammed in the Danish press and their reproduction in the media outside Denmark had the same effect. While societal and cultural fragmentation and intermixing within societies remains a fact of society, national government policies are channeled by these developments in a manner that leaves the impression that there is societal and cultural unity within the two opposing camps.

For this reason, when in the discussion that follows 'we' is used, I mean Western countries among which despite all their differences a shared heritage of the Enlightenment is at work, a shared liberal substrate of constitutions, world views and value systems, which makes the commonalities between France and the US, between Germany and Great Britain, and between Sweden and Italy appear still more substantial than those existing between any one of these countries and Saudi Arabia, Malaysia, or China. This 'we' does not deny the growing trend to contact, to mutual permeation of cultures, and to their internal differentiation, but instead takes into account that despite these developments, being a member of a given cultural 'sphere' must be treated as a significant global political factor.

Western cultural dominance as a historical fact and a problem

Diversity forms a magic triangle with justice and non-violence. Its impact on the chances of mutual resolution of problems cannot be addressed without looking back on the history of the past four centuries. This period in history was dominated by the global expansion of Western power. For the West this unparalleled accumulation of power was seen as proof of its own superiority, as a civilizing mission or – in the racist version of the British Empire – as the 'white man's burden.' In Great Britain and France the deep sense of guilt and the fatal long-term effects of this flawed imperial course have still not been adequately worked through.

The reasons for this superiority were sought in the Christian image of humankind – after the excesses of (German-Austrian) anti-Semitism, in shame it was renamed the Judeo-Christian image of humankind. In reality, the superiority of Western weapons, enterprises and organization is attributable to the unique historical development of Europe, which is due to the relative balance of power between the Kaiser and the Pope, the emerging European nation-states, and the strategic groups within these states – court, nobility, and bourgeoisie. Christianity (in its organized form) was more of a reactionary force during this development, wherever possible seeking to stifle the unfolding of the spirit of enterprise, human rights and democracy. The perversions of the 'Christian image of humankind' that are possible can be seen in the Spanish Counter-Reformation, where the church and secular rulers, in contrast to the rest of Europe, did not stand in a delicate balance but instead entered into a symbiosis which had fateful consequences for the development and freedom of the country (and for Jews, Muslims and 'heretics'). That the Churches, left with no other options after the adoption of democracy by the West, developed theologies more or less at one with the spirit of the Enlightenment is evidence of their flexibility. This has little to do with the 'nature' of the Christian image of humankind. And women are still not allowed to be Catholic priests in the same way they are not allowed to drive cars in Saudi Arabia.

For the rest of the world, the three hundred years of colonialism are an unforgotten trauma: foreign rule, humiliation, forced conversion, violence all the way to genocide, enslavement, exploitation. In the historical experience of subjugated people, the West is associated with the excessive denial of human rights. An orientation toward human rights in values counted for nothing as long as the colonial powers ruled the territories in question themselves. It is selectively supressed, for example in the 'war against terror,' when this appears to be strategically advantageous, such as in Guantánamo, the kidnapping activities of the CIA, and their 'black site' prisons outside the United States. The self-righteous attempt to use this orientation as a big stick against regimes not looked upon favorably by the West appears to many people living under such regimes – including those who stand behind the values of the Enlightenment – to be a cynical attempt to perpetuate or reestablish imperialist rule by new means. (That Western criticism of autocratic regimes can nevertheless be justified unfortunately helps little beneath the weight of history.) In the past, imperial rule often accepted cultural diversity or even used it to its own advantage. The domination of the West against the backdrop of globalization is perceived by many people elsewhere as a more or less violent leveling out of diversity. They feel bowed down beneath a uniform yoke of imperial power or hegemony. There is no participation in the setting of rules. Those who are excluded feel this to be extremely unjust. This feeling incites violent resistance.

How should one deal with the dilemma that we 'Westerners' on the one hand believe in our values and are of the opinion that their universalization would be the best for all others, but on the other are forced in the interest of sustainable global governance to make peace, at least for the moment, with autocratic rulers and non-liberal worldviews? All dealings with diversity start with the knowledge that Western universalism, our belief in human rights, equality, liberty, participation in the democratic process, etc., is at the same time a cultural particularism like Islam (in its diverse manifestations), Hinduism or Confucianism. A Muslim who accepts tradition believes in the validity of the laws handed down in the Koran and the Shariah. Our Western moral philosophy has to pursue a meandering path to justify what we actually 'should do.' For a faithful Muslim, tradition provides many answers of (presumably) eternal validity to these questions. Where these are applied in new circumstances, parliamentary law-making is not needed but instead competent theological exegesis. 'Human rights' exist in that a believer is entitled to the most thorough and scrupulous 'search for the truth,' which God's Word requires in each concrete case, because the individual gets on best if he or she is in complete harmony with God's divine will.

In classical Confucianism the decisive human right is that the individual lives in harmony with the social world, within the nurturing family group and under a good government. All three elements are intertwined. The family consists of a fabric of rights and obligations and is the main point of reference in human life. People do not stand above the collective, but, rather, the happiness of people and harmony within the collective are inseparably linked. The risk that competition among families could disturb harmony in society is compensated for by 'good government.' For, the royal officials – the best of the people – ensure there is justice between competing demands. And because people concerned about the interests of their families can rely on the quality of the judgments made, conflicts of interest do not function as a deadly poison for the desired harmony in society. But how can there be a guarantee that the hierarchy of civil servants (including judges) really does consist of the best people?

It is quite obvious, a classical Confucianist would say: because the best seek out the next best, i.e., through co-option. Once the Emperor had by divine decree gathered society's best at the head of the state, perpetuating themselves from one generation to the next is the best solution; certainly much better than to leave this

most important matter to the whim of people's vacillating opinions and their propensity for being seduced by popular sentiment
(the astounding parallels between traditional Confucianism and
the ideology of the Communist party are apparent; this may
explain some of the phenomena in contemporary China). And if
the improbable should happen and the Emperor and government
indeed fail – a view adopted by some branches of Confucianism
– in unusual circumstances the people still have the exceptional
right to mount a rebellion.

I have discussed classical Islamic and Confucianist precepts
of good political systems at such length in order to demonstrate
that the political ethics underpinning them are coherent, take
people into consideration, and are not simply to be discounted
in disdain. Whoever indignantly refers to 'real' Confucianism
and 'real Sharia' (Saudi Arabia or the Taliban regime) should
remember that reality and ideals also differ sharply in our own
world. During its rise, the 'Christian West' also shamelessly
subjugated and exploited black, brown, red and yellow peoples
after the accomplishments of the Enlightenment. Against the
background of colonial history, speaking of human rights is an
unmitigated mockery. And now? In the United States a person
has to be a millionaire to pursue a successful career in politics;
the everyday reality of racism stands in contradiction to the
principles of the US Constitution, and Native Americans or
those who live in the slums are struggling just as much as the
neglected and powerless elsewhere. Germany's parliament has
a disproportionate number of industry association representatives and civil servants in its ranks – equal opportunity, as it is
proclaimed in our constitutions, does not exist in any democratic
system in existence today. Whoever has money has a dramatically
better chance of influencing the results of politics than somebody who is poor. Those with more money have better prospects

of obtaining justice in our independent courts than somebody with limited means, because the quality of legal representation and the financial capacity to survive the whole appeals process depend on wealth and income.

The separation of church and state, which many cultural warriors willingly carry as their banner into battle against Islam, is rarely fully achieved in Western democracies. Equal rights for women and men exist on paper, but one look at the number of women in leadership positions in the German business sector makes one blush. How immigrants are dealt with is mortifying. If Islam, guided by Sharia and Confucianism, can be criticized for the gap between ideals and reality, then we should not overlook the beam in our own eye! When considering the decision-making process and selection of decision-makers in political systems, an aspect where we Western democrats are convinced of the moral superiority of our constitutions, there are models which can offer 'Western' arguments against the Western one. The system of 'elders' in force in many traditional societies can actually be criticized only because of the gender prejudice favoring men. Otherwise, this system offers greater equality of opportunity of obtaining a leadership position than our complex requirements for large sums of money (the US) or protection within a party (most European democracies). If you consider the fact that among the elite classes in Western democracies it is almost only the retired – whether they be generals, admirals, foreign ministers, defense ministers, prime ministers or senators – who have the common sense to actively support complete nuclear disarmament, then the idea of giving the elderly decision-making power not only appears more egalitarian but otherwise seems not at all so bad.

In Ancient Greece government positions were chosen by lot – that creates the greatest equality of opportunity (if one ignores the fact that women and slaves were excluded from the process). The traditional African palaver system precludes a valid decision until a consensus among all has been reached – that is the most democratic form of decision-making, because nobody is excluded. Those who become anxious that because of such demanding requirements no decisions will ever be made underestimate the pedagogical effect of this system on the attitude of those involved: because people know that things depend to the same degree on everyone, they are more persuasive and more willing to strike a compromise. What is the purpose of this 'exotic' discussion? To demonstrate that it cannot be assumed from the start that we children of the European Enlightenment have somehow been spoon-fed wisdom about decision-making models. In addition, the 'dialectic of the Enlightenment' needs to be called to mind, the ambiguity of Western value patterns: those regions of the world not immersed in the Enlightenment have a marred past of their own variety, but they are not responsible for Verdun or Auschwitz and did not 'achieve' a Hiroshima.

Racial extermination of the Armenians by the Turks, the elimination of 'undesirable' classes by the Khmer Rouge, the massacre of Tutsis by Hutus in Rwanda were certainly also genocidal crimes against humanity. The most horrifying rampages of mass murder in human civilization have, however, been reserved for the possessors of the Christian image of humankind. Given our history, the self-righteousness with which we deal with 'the strange' is therefore unjustified. If our own focus on values is thus as tied to history and our cultural context as are the world-views we criticize, if our own system, too, gives grounds for criticism, and if our own history has the most monstrous deviations thus far from the norms we ourselves proclaim, then there is no longer any good reason to demand from others, without a great deal of self-examination, that our values be recognized as universally valid. On the contrary, the exceptional material strength our Western culture possesses sits well with a sizeable serving of humility, tolerance and willingness to acknowledge 'the strange.' We can afford this tolerance without diminishing our sense of self-worth. It is natural that others who do not possess these material and power-political successes find it far more difficult to muster such generosity. We, the ones who historically caused these inferiority complexes, should in no way be surprised by this.

The cultural 'principle of uncertainty'

In the 1920s Werner Heisenberg, later a Nobel laureate, shook the proud belief of natural sciences in objective knowledge with his discovery of the 'uncertainty principle': in the microscopic world of subatomic experiments the measuring instrument – even if it only consists of one photon, a miniscule particle – influences the condition of what is being measured. As a result, speed and location of the object being measured cannot be reliably determined simultaneously. Heisenberg's insight is fundamental: what we measure, see and judge depends on the tools we use. In physics these are instruments. In politics and daily life it is our cultural repertoires.

What implications can be drawn from Heisenberg's concept for our own problem? Let us assume we were in agreement with partners from other cultures that a certain problem exists and that we have to solve it together. A number of decisions must now be made: what is the decisive principle in a given situation? How should the situation be described? How serious is the situation? What countermeasures are appropriate? The 'burdens of judgment' (John Rawls) bring with them the danger that all these questions may be answered falsely. It can never be ruled out that the error is systematic: it is however more conceivable that judgments are distorted by the cultural location of the speaker, that one will hear different judgments from speakers of different cultural origin.

One needs only to consider for example the difficulties related to arriving at a universally accepted definition of terrorism. It was only the high level panel set up in 2003 by Kofi Annan involving leading figures from all the major regions and cultures of the world that showed that it is possible to overcome differences; as it did in other cases, the panel formulated a recommendation apparently acceptable across cultural and regional borders on how terrorism can be defined (more will be heard about this panel later!). The prerequisite was the good will of all members to make a reflective and self-critical effort to come to an agreement in a spirit of cooperation.

The key difficulty for universalist ethics is rooted in what I would like to refer to as the 'cultural uncertainty principle': at the very best one must be aware of the risk that one's own judgment may be clouded by cultural influences. However, in the individual case, an objective standard for determining whether this is the case or not does not exist. For, even those who self-critically reflect upon their own cultural prejudice still do so from within their own particularistic cultural mold. This problem cannot be resolved by a discourse that takes place within one's own culture. The problem of the cultural uncertainty principle does not forbid adopting a liberal point of view. However, it does argue against categorically claiming that it is absolutely correct, and on this basis demanding that it be implemented in political reality. It is, instead, far more advisable to adopt a position of humility which allows one's own position to be advanced subject to possible errors and compromise: one regards what one proposes as correct for the time being, but is aware of the fact that because of cultural blinkers one could be wrong, and that for reasons of political astuteness, even political fairness, compromises with other points of view will be necessary. Only in this way can supposed universality be prevented from becoming a vehicle for disseminating one's own power interests.

Humility and self-confidence

The point of departure for my formula for dealing with diversity in this world is therefore to voluntarily give up the unconditional claim of validity for our values and norms. We must acknowledge that foreign, archaic and – at first glance – rather unattractive worldviews and value systems are entitled to a seat at the negotiating table when mutual global problems are being addressed; a seat which is justified not only because ultimately we will have to negotiate jointly what needs to be done, but also because they are entitled to say a word or two about the principles underlying the distribution of costs and benefits, i.e., in the last analysis moral questions all the way to the question of using force (see chapter 5). Given our ineradicable Western feeling of superiority (which spontaneously rises up in me as it does in most of my readers from the West), this demand that we ourselves yield our position is strong medicine which is hard to swallow. If we want to live in a world that can be governed in a sustainable manner, there is no alternative. We have to come to terms with having a seat at a round negotiating table (and not demand a seat at the head of a rectangular table), or negotiations will not be successful. The most important principle of intercultural governance is the equal participation of all parties in working out practical compromises and concrete solutions to issues. No one has the right to demand avant-garde privileges that would give one side the right to assume the role of moral warden for others in anticipation of an assumed 'future cosmopolitical state' (Jürgen Habermas).

Does that mean we have to completely give up our cosmopolitical ideas straightaway? In Western philosophy this is the conclusion drawn by communitarians and post-structuralists. The communitarians assign great importance to every local culture: all things particular enjoy the same rights, and that which is particular, local or limited in application cannot be subject to something universally valid. The post-structuralists acknowledge the equality of all value systems: all are equally invalid because a review of how they evolved proves their randomness and arbitrariness. What is valid is the result of a (brutal) historical roll of the dice, behind which no universal rule can be found. The hope of agreeing on rules which can claim to be globally valid is thus diminished. We remain mere pawns of globalization and whatever transpires depends on which – random – power relationships hold sway at any given time.

Both ways of looking at the world are refreshingly critical compared to all fundamentalist views and chronic Western self-righteousness. However, ongoing efforts being made by national and non-governmental players from all cultures to arrive at shared policies regulating interdependent areas of action point to the identification of at least one mutual problem: going beyond all differences of opinion about values, norms and appropriate solutions there is apparently agreement across regions and cultures on the fact that all people on this planet are confronted with the same serious challenges which no particular community can solve on its own. And this is not only the view of those from foreign cultural groups which have been convinced by Western ideals. On the contrary, it includes institutions, governments, regional organizations and NGOs cutting across all cultures. This thus makes clear from the start – on a truly universal basis, i.e., by agreement with state and non-state representatives from all regions of the world (and thus from all world cultures) – the necessity of trying to get closer to solving mutual problems with universally-recognized norms and rules that transcend cultures.

Acknowledging existing diversity as I have proposed in this chapter does not categorically rule out the possibility of norms and rules capable of universal validity. It does repudiate once and for all the right of one of the existing particularisms of its own accord to stipulate for all others what should be universally valid. This one player cannot, in anticipation of the results of a discussion that has not yet been carried out, claim that its own evolved norms are capable of winning acceptance (that is precisely the 'original sin' of Western cosmopolitanism). For, the validity of norms aimed at achieving a world order can only derive from genuine agreement by representatives of all the world's regions/ cultures (even if 'only' state governments, see chapter 6), as well as, ideally, valid humanitarian law. In order to obtain this agreement, others must first be consulted. To assume that agreement is inevitable because it follows of necessity from our fundamental Western principles is not good enough: for this assumption itself has developed from our particularistic worldview. This thus brings us back to the cultural uncertainty principle.

But can we even hope to achieve such universal accord? There are three reasons why this accord does not appear to be ruled out. First of all, agreement may be achieved because there may now already be a basic set of shared characteristics extending beyond the boundaries of specific cultures and their internal nuances, which could provide the foundation for such universal norms – a kind of 'central core of international law.' Second, it may emerge from a future fusing of normative systems which are different today. Or also – third – from drawn out processes of persuasion in negotiations. Although successful universalism is not a historical necessity – it can also go badly wrong – it is nevertheless possible. It does not arise from apodictic demands, but from patient dialog with one another.

One indicator that practical universalism is possible lies in the fact that there are social movements all around the world which are resisting repression by non-democratic governments and calling for more freedom and justice. Obviously, we must take into account that this protest is often also directed against political structures established in the West, and that these movements often place strong emphasis on their own non-Western identity and place part of the blame for their plight on the West (or the 'North') and the economic institutions supported by them. That is the reason why they cannot be made to turn state's evidence in favor of the Western model without reservation. Perhaps the West is in the best position to initiate a dialog about such norms, all the same. The West should try to do so. But instead of claiming from the start that its own value system must be of universal validity, the point would be to offer it as a basis for discussion. It would then be one contribution at the beginning of a long process, and not the irrefutable result; if it went well, this process could lead to a legally established institutionalization of global control and governance. It can be presumed that the 'humble' West sketched out here would have better chances of getting a hearing for its contributions to dialog than the self-righteous and culturally imperialistic one that has presented itself thus far. A liberal political program for carrying out reform of the world order, on which the democracies agreed and which they proposed to their non-democratic counterparts on a step-by-step basis, would be legitimate. The guiding principle underlying this process would be that each reform step be capable of gaining general approval. This strategy of small steps is supported by the liberal insight that good institutions change for the better those (in this case governments) operating within them. International institutions which offer all participants the possibility of cooperating also create as a by-product the best chances for a political and social evolution of non-democratic systems.

With this we turn to the tricky issue of how democracies can give practical expression to their wish to bring about a regime change in non-democracies – such a process can also be viewed as part of a normative global integration. Unlike John Rawls or the communitarians, I consider such a political practice to be legitimate, as long as it is pursued through appropriate, i.e. strictly peaceful, means. What this entails is a limited, discursive conflict which the non-democratic partners must endure. The guiding principle is the political technique that Ernst-Otto Czempiel called 'profit-free advertising': democracies seek converts to their system and values by setting a good example; by standing up for their values in political discourse; by openly criticizing their partners' practices which violate human rights, but in a measured and non-threatening way. It also appears to me to be legitimate to support non-violent civil society players in other countries. The last two activities require good judgment and, looked at the other way around, tolerance toward comparable yet unpopular activities by others in one's own country which are supported from outside the country (as long as they remain non-violent).

Both of these aspects – international cooperation and standing up for your own cause – basically take place in the process of acknowledging sovereignty and, consistent with this, not using force. 'Basically' of course means that rare, narrowly defined exceptional cases are permitted substantively: drastic crimes against humanity, genocide and the toleration of cross-border terrorist acts initiated on the territory of a state which refuses to or is unable to prevent these acts. The strictest procedural rules must apply for these cases (chapter 5). There are therefore two unavoidable prerequisites for dealing with diversity: first, to disavow the use of force for making one's own values the foundation of global rules; second, to recognize the positions of others in principle as equal (even when one is of a different opinion). You may also hold on to your own universalist expectations without a bad conscience if you also take these two principles to heart and understand your own contributions as suggestions, and not as binding edicts. Of course, ruling by decree is far more convenient – that is why so many dictators resist voluntarily giving up this convenient situation. This still does not make it a viable path toward global governance for the West.

Four encounters outside one's own borders

We therefore scale back our universal claim for our principles by viewing them as an offer to engage in discourse which can only gain universal acceptance if it meets with global approval, for example, if a consensus is attained in worldwide negotiations. We are forced to struggle for the agreement of others in order to achieve reasonable solutions to our shared problems. We may encounter four different types of participants in discussions.

First: we encounter partners who share our opinion on principles and the case in point. That is thankfully easy. Here the concern is only about questions of distribution (Who must pay how much, who receives how much?), not the basic questions of what ethical principles and, above all, what principles of justice (see chapter 4) the solution should be oriented towards. That is the type of question which is dealt with in the European Union, in NATO, in the OECD; granted, such questions are not easy to resolve, but in comparison with the ones below, they are pure luxury!

Second: we encounter strangers who share the problem definition with us and also agree that a solution must be found. Unfortunately, their value systems are different from ours. This is no reason for despair. As has been demonstrated for example by Hans Küng in his 'world ethics' project or Dieter Senghaas established in his comparison of diverse cultures' ability to modernize, there is an astonishingly large area of overlap on which the apparently so different cultural value patterns of this world agree. Identifying these areas of agreement and jointly determining what can be drawn from them as principles for mutually resolving problems will be one of the chief tasks of the coming decades. This will be hard work, but it is not a hopeless task, as long as we keep in mind the necessity of solving shared life-threatening problems. It has always been a rule of thumb of world politics that shared dangers such as a climate catastrophe, a collapse of the world economic system, widespread scarcity of energy, or transnational terrorism foster unity among apparently irreconcilable positions.

Parallel to these direct attempts to establish understanding of principles, an approach based on practical projects seems to be appropriate: let us assume that we are dealing with a partner situated in a desert region exposed to high levels of sunlight. We offer investment and technology transfer in exchange for the use of these favorable conditions to generate electricity, and invest in power lines from there to here. This produces a 'win-win-situation,' i.e., everybody is better off afterwards: we both recognize the problem of providing the world with sufficient energy in an environmentally-friendly way, and make a contribution to its solution. Over and above this, we solve special problems faced by both countries, i.e., our lack of primary energy sources and our partner's oversupply of space that is in economic terms useless – the country's desert expanses. Up to this point we have pursued interests that run parallel and supplement each other. The next step is the rather more difficult problem of distributing costs and benefits. What do we get for our investment and our willingness to transfer technology? What does our partner get for the use of the land and workers? These questions will probably be answered through tough negotiations, through 'bargaining,' and finally through a compromise.

As far as the concrete project is concerned, this would be the end: all the steps necessary for its success have been completed. Perhaps a project commission might be set up to deal in detail with unexpected problems or disputes. Nothing more would really be needed. However, it might be sensible to set up a joint 'ethics committee' to look at the principles of quality of life and justice which had actually been implemented in achieving the solution: which ideas about energy supply and environmental sustainability have we put into practice? Which principles of good cooperation are included in the modes of working together? Which conceptualizations of fairness shaped the compromise that was reached on distribution of costs and benefits, i.e., which basic principles of justice did we apply together? Unlike the – as has already been said – equally sensible attempt to define moral agreements at an abstract level, in this way we look for them in a practical setting. The depth of experience our 'ethics committee' gains increases in proportion to the degree that joint projects based on solving problems evolve. If one imagines a number of such committees which constantly exchange experiences, a process of 'world ethics derived from practice' emerges. The 'bonus' yielded by this method is that, as a 'by-product,' the involved partners also benefit from tangible advantages. This in turn increases their motivation to support the use of this method.

Third: we encounter players who are very different from us and very suspicious of us, and who do not want to have anything to do with us but see no reason to resort to violence. This is most unfortunate because no solutions for the (nonetheless present) joint problems can be found: regrettably, they see no chance of reconciling their values with ours to the extent that the necessary minimum of agreement could be reached (or the reverse: we are unable to see that this chance exists). The intensive contact between them and us that the joint project brings with it is regarded as too great a risk to our own integrity for us to take the chance. This is bad for sustainability, but the possibility still remains of establishing a state of peaceful co-existence with such players with as little interaction and contact as possible, and to hope that the unfortunate situation will change. At least peace is preserved, and with it the hope of improvement. Something can still be attempted. If the partner identifies problems which we see in the same way, even though we cannot agree on principles for cooperation, an approach via an offer of help is possible: we are prepared to support the solution sought by the partner without any institutional structures (for instance, food aid to North Korea). With the passage of time two positive developments can result from this: increased trust that makes further dialog possible; or concrete projects which, even in the case of difficult partners, in the long run bring about a 'world ethics from below.' Peaceful coexistence should never be seen as an ultimate state beyond which it is not possible to go. It is also a springboard from which further progress is possible. Granted, this requires great patience and tolerance for what seem like bizarre behaviors of others.

Fourth: we are dealing with genuine enemies who are not

interested in peaceful coexistence with us because they see in us a fundamental evil that, according to their worldview, should be eliminated. This state of affairs will be extremely rare. Here all that remains is the willingness to defend ourselves. If someone refuses to coexist peacefully with us and others, we have to defend ourselves against them. For sustainability cannot be built upon this basis: those who want war oppose even the humblest attempt in this direction. How this rare situation can occur is demonstrated by the historical existence of Adolf Hitler or the merciless orgies of violence instigated by al-Qaeda against innocent bystanders. The best option is still to contain the potential source of violence and limit its possibilities for external action. Political quarantine of this kind would then make it possible to 'sit out' the bad situation and wait for better times. Over and above this, research on the origins of such situations is called for: where did such developments begin? Which behavior of our own fostered or even caused them? What can be done to prevent the enemy players from gaining more supporters? Who apart from us is a target or a victim and therefore a coalition partner for us?

Precisely this was the line of thought with which the Bush administration enjoyed initial success in forming the anti-terror coalition after September 11, 2001, only to dissolve it into its component parts again through the vast stupidity of the Iraq War and a series of additional errors of global policy (for instance the blinkered insistence on complete military superiority over anybody and everybody). The basic idea, however, was correct: keeping the opponents of a sustainable world order in check is in the interest of and a task for everybody. Handled correctly, even this fourth type of player whom we encounter on the world stage is still of value for our shared goal, because this kind of player encourages the rest of the world to unite; such a player is 'a part of that which constantly seeks to do evil and yet brings about good,' in the words of Mephistopheles in Goethe's 'Faust.' The reverse case, however, cannot be allowed: that we, the Western nations, define another country as 'an evil which must be eliminated' and resort to armed force. Armed force must continue to be limited exclusively to self-defense, and where it is to be applied for the prevention of a major evil – for instance genocide – the decision-making power should not lie with the West (alone). More on this in later chapters.

Ways and means

This review of the types of players we encounter in the practice of world politics has revealed more opportunities than risks. In order to seize the opportunities a broad range of activities must be undertaken; institutions must be supported or new ones created that serve the purpose of examining the risky consequences of diversity and making use of the opportunities it offers. Of course, there are several kinds of 'diversity.' A great deal has been said about the difference between democracies and non-democracies; of course, that is primarily a difference between political systems, not cultures. To be sure, the probability is high that cultural differences underlie differences between systems, or at least could underlie them; still, even if that were not the case I would hold fast to the imperative of giving the society of a non-democratic state the opportunity of developing autonomously.

Consciousness of the fact that the variety of values across cultures is as legitimate as our wish to make our own values universal is a decisive perspective for our interactions with other countries. However, from the perspective of global governance, diversity also needs to be shaped by institutions. It has already found such an institutionalized form in the United Nations, in which all regions of the world are represented by their individual states. To the extent that it has taken root in political units the UN General Assembly reflects the diversity of the world fairly accurately; there are certain exceptions that should be noted: neither the Kurds nor the Tibetans, for example, are represented in the UN, and that is undoubtedly a fault. Nonetheless, the General Assembly is exponentially more representative than the Security Council. The Security Council is an exclusive club with a high level of decision-making powers and only a bare modicum of representativity. The General Assembly is a genuinely representative body – in the sense of representing all cultures and states, not in the sense of being democratically elected – but its decision-making powers are extremely limited. It ought to be upgraded. The step of making the Security Council more representative is also overdue (see chapter 7).

Western preparation: getting ready for diversity

In the following sections, I am also sticking to my agenda of thinking about how we in 'the West' can prepare ourselves to deal with diversity. This may seem one-sided: should then the members of all other cultures and regions be able to retain their own special properties unchanged, whereas we have to sacrifice ours on the altar of global governance? That is by no means the idea. My intellectual starting point is completely different: just as fish start to stink at the head, the change towards sustainable global governance has to start with the strongest part of the world. And that means the Western nations. They can invest the most resources in the transformation of international politics; because of their key positions there they are in the best position to fundamentally and permanently change the parameters of behavior for all, and their activities are the most likely to serve as a model for others. Looked at the other way around, stubborn clinging to traditional forms of behavior on their part (for instance US energy consumption or EU agricultural policy) can do the greatest damage. This underlines the fact that successful global governance, to the extent that the behavior in question involves shared problem areas that need to be regulated, cannot practice limitless cultural tolerance. For it is certain that wasting energy is now part of American everyday culture. Changes will have to be made here, or there will be no sustainable world governance and no sustainability at all will be possible. We know that others – China, India – are rapidly catching up in this area. But they are not yet eye-to-eye, not at all if we calculate the energy consumption of the West not nationally but in aggregate. In addition, the 'cultural uncertainty principle' means that it makes the best sense for authors with the necessary competence and prospects of being heard to address the members of their own Western-liberal culture.

So: get fit – but how? It starts with knowledge. We need to understand better what makes the others tick. And do so at an early stage. This means something quite curious: The 'minor disciplines' of the cultural sciences, which have become an endangered species in the tornado of current business management-oriented, blinkered reform of the universities, will have to be given far more emphasis. They need to become core disciplines in the higher education curriculum and be integrated into teacher training and the training of kindergarten personnel (whose education will have to become more academic). No graduate should be allowed to leave school without at least a rudimentary understanding of Arabic, African, Indian, or Chinese issues. The 'foreign' needs better public representation in our society. It makes one almost ill nowadays to think that the word 'Gastarbeiter' [guest worker] was linked to the expectation that the confrontation with the external world in my own country – unpleasant for many people – was only to be a temporary 'affliction.' Recognition that 'Germany is a migrant-receiving land' was suppressed in a pathological way for many years. This idea still resonates in the 'old German' mentality.

Dealing with things foreign requires an institutional presence in the internal discourse. A short televised homily for Muslims on Germany's main station and foreigners' advisory committees at local government level are beginnings. Why not cross-party 'factions' of members of federal and state parliaments with a migrant background? In the US that is normal and it creates welcome links between the migrant-receiving society and the country of origin. Active participation of the 'strangers' in the media is particularly important. This is not a matter of having Turkish, Indian, or Chinese television channels. That would only mean forming 'ghettos' in the communications media. We need integrated programs in which the interests of immigrants have an appropriate place alongside and with the 'traditionally German'; at least as long as integration has not yet fused 'original inhabitants' and migrants to the point of being indistinguishable. After all, partnerships across boundaries are important. A network of such partnerships – cities, sports teams, non-governmental organizations, trade unions, etc., student exchange programs, visits back and forth, exchanges of letters, Internet chat rooms, and similar arrangements – helps to strengthen communication. Within Europe and the Western world this network is already very advanced. Perhaps precisely this network should be employed for 'triangulation': a German-French city partnership, for instance, makes an Arab city the third partner, or the same school carries out simultaneous exchanges with an Indian and an

American sister school. Money is needed to do this. But peace does not come free of charge.

Conclusions

In this chapter I have looked at dealing with diversity from four angles. I started by trying to show why we have no chance of overcoming diversity by 'laying down' what we think is universally valid. Second, I examined various ways through which, despite all obstacles, we can develop universally valid principles – the most significant insight was that this requires humility and patience. Third, I sketched out the best way of dealing with the different types of 'other' players whom we encounter in the world. And in closing I wanted to make clear that the right attitude to diversity is based on a set of social 'micro-prerequisites.' For, despite 'high diplomacy' being successful in a dialog, things will still go awry if it does not receive grass-roots support. In the sixth and seventh chapters institutional provision will be discussed more fully.

Introduction

The intention of the following chapter is by no means to offer simple patent solutions to extremely complex problems. Global decision-making processes are not easy to handle, especially when trying to link them to a controversial concept like 'justice.' What is the 'problem of justice' in politics? First of all the concept requires justification as, according to widespread – including scholarly – opinion, politics is simply a complicated game played according to the rules of rational choice, a view which seems to leave no place for moral considerations, one of which is justice.

To be sure, justice is a substantial motivating force in human relationships. Research on basic needs has identified 'fairness' as a universal value; even in international negotiations – probably the most common example of relationships focused purely on power and vested interests – it has been shown to be without doubt a factor that shapes outcomes. As will surprise nobody after the previous chapter, there is no consistent notion of justice which could be used as the standard for 'correct' results of negotiations. Apparently, however, in every society there are limits to tolerance for inequality and injustice; they vary, historically, between different political camps (left/right), and between cultures. The 'diversity' that has just been discussed and the problem of justice are thus intimately related.

Discovering 'justice' at the seat of power is thus no reason for pleasure or satisfaction. This is because of the ambivalent nature of justice. On the one hand it is a highly regarded good, without which no human society can be imagined. On the other hand, it is a murderous driving force behind conflicts: this state of affairs builds a bridge to the next chapter, which is concerned with avoiding war. The search for justice takes on this fatal role when parties to a conflict set about eliminating real or imagined injustices by violent means. However, the seeds of such violence are sown when the parties to a conflict hold irreconcilable views on justice and each seeks to make them prevail over the opposing concept. Without consensus on justice and established processes for its step-by-step implementation the threat of violence will always hang like a shadow over international relationships. In considering how to achieve and implement such a consensus, findings from the previous chapter about how to deal with 'diversity' will be useful.

Concepts of the substance of justice

The most universal concept of justice that is found in all world cultures is the principle of 'suum cuique' – 'to each his own.' According to this, justice involves each person receiving what he or she is entitled to. Unfortunately, this general formula is not of much help; it simply defers the problem rather than solving it. For, what it is that everyone is entitled to and how it is to be measured remain unexplained. The fact is that immense differences can be seen in the philosophy and history of the concept of justice. The rank-based concept of justice that dominated in the European Middle Ages, for instance, assigned valid claims according to social position. The peasant had different entitlements from the nobleman (who could still lay justified claim to the jus primae noctis, the first night with the virgin bride of his subjects), the priest from the artisan. The resulting differences were not regarded as at all unjust, but as consistent with justice. Traditional social justice, on the other hand, regards the claims of one's own group as ranking above the interests of rival groups; justice calls for greater loyalty to one's own family, clan or tribe, the folk or one's own nation. In such traditional thinking, inequities in distribution in favor of one's own clan, ethnic group or nation are regarded as just. This notion contradicts the universalism principle that is increasingly becoming anchored in our Western-liberal thinking. The dominant situative understanding of justice in Confucianism does without general principles in favor of context-specific judgments: what is just in one situation can be regarded as unjust in another that displays only comparatively small changes in parameters. The most general notions of justice are identical with a good life lived in a state of harmony of all with all. Disturbances of such a harmonious life thus lead to injustice. What such disturbances might be depends, however, on the nature of the particular situation. What is regarded as just in an individual case can only be determined on an ad hoc basis.

The utopian postulate of complete equality that has stirred up revolts against drastically unjust structures throughout history stands in complete contrast to this: only when all goods and opportunities of participation are equally distributed does justice exist. Institutionalized measures for eliminating spontaneously occurring injustices must be available. This idea must come to terms with the existing – starting with bodily – inequalities between people. Creating absolute equality here has proved to require so great an effort that the attempts to do so mostly result in dramatic curtailments of freedom. Natural inequalities are taken account of better in the concept of performance-based justice: each according to his or her abilities, to each according to his or her performance is the modus operandi. The appropriate benefit is directly related to the degree of effort shown. Moderate compensatory measures in order to avoid differences that are too drastic can be integrated into this concept of justice. However, this apparently simple principle is confronted with the problem of defining 'benefit' and 'performance' appropriately. According to the liberal version of this concept of justice the market will take care of it. However, the impartial observer can scarcely comprehend why the market rewards a posturing film diva or a doped-up racing cyclist with a limitless ego so infinitely better than a policewoman or a fireman who place their life at risk for the public good. The idea of equality is more strongly developed in the social democratic model of progressive redistribution. The basic idea pursued is reducing social disparities. But no future point in time is laid down by which complete justice must be reached; rather, the course of history is understood as a perpetual approach to a utopian goal. Justice is not a state and also not a standard against which existing conditions can be assessed, but an infinite process. Eduard Bernstein's classic sentence, 'The movement is everything, the goal nothing,' encapsulates this idea of justice as a historical process.

A formal liberal model of justice is satisfied with equality purely before the law (which makes a huge difference in comparison with the social standing concept of justice, but in comparison with concepts of justice that call for social equality is far too little), and does not go any further into the concretely existing conditions (such as obtaining justice depending on the ability to pay legal fees). By contrast, the idea of equal opportunity regards justice as only guaranteed when people are offered approximately equal opportunities to obtain qualifications in the first phase of their life and in adult life experience no disadvantages on the basis of attributed characteristics (woman/ origin/foreigner/Muslims, etc.). Finally, there is the pareto-optimum concept of justice that is current in economics, according to which an optimal state is reached when improvement in the position of one player is not achieved through a worsening of the position of some other. However, there can be as many pareto-optimal situations in this sense as you like, among which you have to choose. To the extent, however, that different situations divide benefits differently among the players who receive them (i.e., not only those who are not placed at a disadvantage) a new justice problem of the second order that cannot be solved with the pareto optimum is created.

All these approaches have in common that they seek to fill the concept of justice with content. Remarkably, most of them are part of Western history, and even in the present there are highly contradictory opinions in our society about what justice really is. As a result, one can hardly be surprised when conflicts also arise with concepts of justice from outside Europe. That the Koran with its differentiation between appropriate behavior in the faithful and unbelievers, between men and women, experiences rejection in Western cultures is not surprising. The differing contents collide and at first glance have little in common in their substance – hence the potential for conflict already mentioned, which accompanies the struggle for justice. The unavoidability of this collision has led communitarians to the maxim that justice can only be defined for discrete ethical systems and to abandon the attempt to establish a universal model. If the various communities reciprocally accept the rule that particular models of justice are valid in the 'realm' of the others, the conflicts that are otherwise unavoidable can be prevented. Of course, this path cannot be followed in a globalizing world. The various cultures (and smaller ethical communities) are so inextricably intertwined that they are forced to find rules for shared distribution tasks with which all sides can live. This is not possible without a shared concept of justice.

The procedural way out

The attempt to stop trying to define the contents of the concept of justice and to seek to find the way out by means of formal procedures is logical. Justice must then be looked for in the rules for participation in procedures that decide on the distribution of valuables and goods and in the rules for reaching decisions in these procedures. The construction of such a procedure by John Rawls has become well known. According to this, the basic condition for establishing justice is that the participants in the procedure make decisions without knowledge of their actual position in the world. Rawls has few illusions about human nature; rather, he assumes that in making such decisions people will always behave in their own best interests. However, if they have no idea where their real interests lie they will take care to structure decisions in such a way that they will not suffer any disadvantage, regardless of the role they play in the world. Ignorance thus becomes a vehicle through which justice can be achieved.

Rawls's mind experiment is unquestionably creative and interesting, but is scarcely useful for our subject – sustainable governance in international relations – for, there, all players know only too well where they stand in the real world. The unreasonable demand can scarcely be made of them that they simply ignore their own interests. Over and above this, they would have to ignore their own politically and culturally shaped notions of justice, something which is no less unrealistic. Jürgen Habermas sees the possibility of establishing agreed upon moral norms

– and in this way to establish shared criteria of justice among players with differing interests and orientations. A prerequisite for this is that the decision-making process is carried on as a rational dialog, in which all those affected by the decision have an equal right to participate; in addition, all participants must ignore the actual power relationships – in the form of threats, sanctions, and rewards. That too is a demanding, idealized procedure that is at the same time not completely utopian. For, the court procedures of states governed by the rule of law also have to ignore the power position of participants in the procedures (even if this is not always achieved in the reality of legal processes). The requirement of unlimited participation by everybody affected by the decision is certainly also problematic because of the potentially high numbers involved, which in practice would make such a procedure impossible to conduct or bring to a conclusion. Habermas therefore accepted a watered-down version according to which decisions are just if the results are in principle acceptable for those affected by the decision; in the democratic nation-state this condition is guaranteed to some degree through, for instance, the procedures of parliamentary representation. Anyone who has distributive justice in the sense of principles of content in mind cannot ignore procedural justice in the sense of conditions of participation. A just result arises from a just procedure. Bearing this aspect in mind, we can go more deeply into the subject of international relations.

Differences between 'internal' and 'external'

For domestic social justice, the classic Western, social, democratic and market-economy based welfare state has presented a passably useful model for justice. This model has been losing favor lately in the commotion of globalization, without any alternative model in sight. The risks of this backward step should not be underestimated. In this context, it is calamitous that those who make the decisions are themselves not affected by this development. The type of behavior exhibited by men like Mr. Esser or Mr. Ackermann, although legal, come dangerously close to the naïve reaction of the French Queen Marie Antoinette on the eve of the French Revolution; upon hearing that there was no more bread for the poor, she responded guilelessly and with no ill will that they ought to eat cake. The naïve ignorance which the well-to-do manifest about the life circumstances of their less favored fellow citizens is life-threatening and does not contribute to the goal of sustainable governance even in Germany. The resentment which builds up among globalization losers over such behavior is not to be underestimated in its violent potential. We will not eliminate the welfare state without paying a price.

In the international arena such a model, which was at least temporarily valid, has never existed. Countries outside the Western sphere are exposed to shocks, fluctuations, disruptions and transformations to a much higher degree than Western societies. These can throw countries and societies off balance. War is the most obvious of these dire developments. Unlike nation-states, international relations have lacked and are lacking regulatory mechanisms for cushioning the consequences of such shakeups. International relations have not been organized into a community. At best, first signs of this are to be seen in the establishment of a few legal norms and in the gradual evolution of a civil society spanning national borders which stands up for the values of universal solidarity (worldwide willingness to donate money after the tsunami of December 2004 and the global demonstrations against the Iraq War in the spring of 2003 are indicators of community formation). International relations consist more of nation-states which are conscious of their sovereign status and in negotiations wish to realize their own interests in an appropriate manner.

The term 'appropriate' has underlying concepts of what is acceptable as a 'fair' result of negotiations. However, fairness is nothing other than an aspect of justice. Thus, even in the most hard-nosed diplomatic wrangling normative aspects are raised. And such aspects of fairness and justice are rooted in the national and cultural ethics of the state players and their representatives. The striking contrasts which often emerge in international negotiations are thus not merely to be attributed to inherent 'national interests' but, instead, are related to starkly different ethical codes. That is why there is no unified and binding concept of justice. There is unfortunately also no undisputed decision-making process with rules for participation with which all players would agree. After all, there is no ongoing worldwide intercultural dialog designed to establish such a process; the completely parochial interests characterizing discussions about reforming the United Nations, in particular the Security Council, certainly do not deserve to be given the honorable title of 'worldwide intercultural dialog.'

This debate has been going on since the 1990s; it reached its climax in 2005, but without any outcome. On the one hand there was widespread consensus, to be sure, that the world community ought to establish better representativity of its most powerful decision-making body; a minimal consensus had – gratifyingly – formed on the question of procedural justice. At the same time the five permanent members of the Security Council also sought in secret to prevent or delay a change. And many Member States preferred no reform at all to one which would put a disliked partner or competitor in a better position than they were in. As a result, the attempt to reform the UN General Assembly failed in the fall of 2005. This means international relations have been lagging behind to an extreme degree in their ability to address problems of justice.

Over the past few years this state of affairs – driven by the powerful forces of globalization – has provided more and more impetus to reflection on concepts of global justice. When considering these concepts, it is characteristic of the discourse in Western political philosophy that it is for the most part a monolog based on its own premises, while the goals of the – quite attractive – movement for greater justice are not given a hearing. By a process of strict deductive reasoning (usually in the framework of Kantian philosophy) comprehensive obligations about justice and precisely formulated rules are reasoned out which stumble at times for not being in touch with reality. It is nevertheless completely correct to demand energetic steps toward a global redistribution of benefits and burdens. A global social policy which has as its aim strengthening the weak, rewarding development modules which successfully combat poverty, and halting North-South relations which are exploitative in their design – these are all plausible steps on the way to greater global justice which are meeting with approval also outside the West. However, these involve everyday concepts of justice based on common sense, and do not require complicated deductive processes.

Problems of justice driven by globalization

It has already been noted that globalization has brought problems for the welfare state. The ideology of neoliberalism, which is nothing more than a modish cultural fashion, has contributed to these. Those enthusiastic about globalization on business school faculties, on the executive boards of companies, and in the halls of government tend to praise its positive aspects and to fall silent over its downside. They use the argument of the (indisputable) net advantages of economic deregulation, but do not take into account the problems of distribution that arise from it.

However, globalization produces both winners and losers. The winners are not by any means all in the 'North' in rich industrialized countries. This common stereotype is quite untrue. The number of people who have risen out of poverty into the middle-class in South Asia, Southeast Asia and the Far East, as well as in the key business centers of Latin America, amounts to almost a billion people. Globalization has paid off for them. This state of affairs is stubbornly ignored by many who oppose globalization. The striking differences in how individual countries deal with globalization problems indicate that globalization is not an automatism characterized without variation by the same consequences everywhere. Rather, the margin by which winners 'win' and losers 'lose out' as well as the degree of inequality which results has something to do with the policies with which governments in the different countries are responding to the global challenge. How else can it be explained that in Europe, within a relatively unified economic region, the Scandinavian countries have done so much better over the past 20 years than, say, France, Italy, or until recently Germany too? How does it come to pass that China and Vietnam are benefiting far more than Cambodia or Myanmar, India is better off than Pakistan or Bangladesh? What is the reason for Gujarat prospering within India while Uttar Pradesh has not progressed, and even in a state such as Kerala, which is not undergoing such rapid economic growth, measures to combat poverty are making much more progress than in the wealthy Panjab or in desperately poor Bihar, while at the same time inequality – in contrast with the other two states – has lessened rather than increased in Kerala. Globalization does not have a fixed effect, but instead its consequences are moderated by the responses of governments at the various levels – quite apart from the fact that in key areas globalization is a result of action taken by the state.

To be sure, it cannot be disputed that during the past twenty years a large number of people have fallen below the poverty line due to the combined effects of emerging globalization and government policies. For these people, globalization was a catastrophe. What is even more unsettling: it affects to an above average degree those who are already the weakest members of society – children, women, and the elderly. This demonstrates the mercilessness of the development process, from which solidarity as a universal value is excluded and justice of course, too. The phenomenon is concentrated once again because it affects developing countries and the nations which emerged from the break-up of the Soviet Union to a greater degree than countries in the West, and impacts on Africa more than all other regions. It is apparent that the interests of these weakest and most needy members of world society are not represented to the necessary extent in relevant decision-making processes (see below).

The streams of people migrating across national borders triggered by globalization are spawning new conflicts over distribution and participation. These conflicts are between local and immigrant populations as well as between countries of origin and those to which people immigrate. Through the intermixing of differing cultures migration unavoidably leads to confrontations between opposing concepts of justice. Migration also makes conflicts over participation probable, because the locally established population does not wish to share its own civil rights, whereas immigrants demand to share in decision-making in the society where, after all, they now live.

At first glance, the development of communications connects

regions which were once cut off from each other and should thus have a leveling effect on differences that had previously existed. To a certain limited extent this effect actually is seen, but it is false to attribute this simply to CNN, Aljazeera.com or the Internet. This explanation would overlook the 'digital divide' that exists between and within regions. There is a dramatic imbalance in the level of access to computers and the Internet in rich and poor countries. Within countries, the poorest and the least educated remain excluded from such access. This divide undermines all efforts to establish equal opportunity.

Global environmental problems, which represent a further facet of globalization, have also added another problem of justice to the agenda: compensation from those causing international damage to the environment to those affected by it. It is well-established that the industrialization of the West, its colonial seizure of land, and its current level of consumption represent a disproportionately large share of non-sustainable exploitation of nature. On top of that, we have used up the cheapest fossil fuels, our emissions have already substantially filled the 'sinks,' natural storage areas capable of providing storage (such as the oceans), leaving little room there for others. To derive from this the axiom that the developing countries which are catching up, such as India or China, ought to have the right to follow the same course of development (and thus catapult the planet beyond the threshold of survival) is illogical, as it calls into question the existence of these supposedly privileged countries too. It is also an indisputable fact that economies 'closing in on industrialized countries' which will be forced to accept higher costs for an environmentally sustainable future are entitled to compensation.

Due to their consequences and unresolved status, all the problems referred to point out grave issues related to distributive justice. They all hinge on the question: who should bear the cost which we have to pay for – real or imagined – progress? This question is answered in practical terms each day – even if also with the smallest conceivable link to ideas of justice – in a large number of decisions: governments make decisions strategically with their national interests in mind. Due to the huge differences in power and wealth these decisions have substantially different impacts on third parties; the same divide adds yet more, equally large differences in people's ability to protect themselves from such effects. What Washington decides affects every person in the world. Most of the time, what is decided in Tuvalu affects only the people on that island nation.

The second decision-making level refers to the accumulated effect of individual decisions, with imbalances once again occurring through the resources available to these individuals. Decisions in industrialized nations on whether to buy and drive cars determine the price of oil (and thus the costs borne by farming operations in the Third World); in addition, the thirst for energy of India and China is tangibly affecting the development of price levels. Decisions made by large corporations including major stock market traders – such as American pension funds or speculative hedge funds – affect the fate of many people; these corporations operate with little public control.

In the meantime, international organizations have a strong influence over the course of events. The European Union, which is distinguished from all other multinational communities by its unusual degree of integration, is responsible for the foreign trade policy of Member States (with the exception of arms exports). NATO provides a framework for national defense policies and can – as in the case of Kosovo – apply decisive pressure on its members to participate in combat missions; the magical argument of countries having to live up to 'allegiance' commitments is like a whip with which representatives who have reservations about military action can be persuaded to agree; for, of course, the alliance as such is something nobody wants to voice doubts about because it is part of, for instance, Germany's reason for existing. The Group of Eight, the International Monetary Fund, or the World Bank influence the social opportunity of hundreds of millions of people.

The United Nations Security Council decides over war and peace, over the rescue or destruction of human lives, over intervention or taking a hands-off approach and, in recent years, as global lawmaker has even twice assumed the right to obligate all Member States to institute certain legal measures: in Resolution 1373, which contained measures against the financing of terrorism and required suspicious bank accounts to be frozen – with the Security Council specifying through a committee who was under suspicion; as well as Resolution 1540, which demanded a series of legal and administrative measures in order to deny terrorists access to materials and technology for the production of weapons of mass destruction.

In none of these decision-making bodies is it guaranteed that decision-makers and those affected are identical or that those who 'suffer' through such measures are appropriately represented. The fateful decisions of international organizations in which participation is exclusively or for the most part limited to Western democracies (NATO, OECD, G-8) are not subject to any parliamentary control whatsoever; at the most – as is true for NATO – they have a group of parliamentarians whose yearly meetings may be useful for becoming mutually acquainted with and understanding one another, but have not the least influence on the decisions of the alliance's committees. For other institutions all the way to the Security Council of the UN this is even more true.

Unsolved problems of justice in international relations

In the following section justice issues are addressed as they relate to individual fields of world politics. The list does not claim to be exhaustive. It can also not be about wanting to offer 'just' solutions for these problematic areas. The intention is far more that of outlining the problem, which makes it possible to recognize the scope of the tasks awaiting us.

Economic policy

Globalization redistributes economic benefits on a global scale. Given the constantly shifting balance of winners and losers, how can a halfway reasonable balance between participants be achieved? One widely discussed approach could be social minimum standards, which would be respected by all countries that profit from global trading activity. Demands along these lines have often been made by trade unions in Western countries, as well as being presented by industrial countries in the WTO. The counter-argument is that this demand amounts to veiled protectionism: the West – including its organized workforce – wants to deny developing countries the possibility of using in their own favor their biggest competitive advantage, low wages. It is also pointed out that in the decades of the greatest expansion in industrialized countries – in the first phase of industrialization, the decisive 'leap' into the modern age – the level of wages was also distinctly low in the 'North' too, and only with the increase of widely distributed mass-produced goods did the share of wage earners in gross domestic product begin to increase. However, it must also be kept in mind that minimum standards could also protect developing countries themselves against a 'race to the bottom,' a steep downward spiral of ever diminishing wages in order to compete for markets in industrialized countries.

A second controversy centers on the relationship between justice and economic efficiency. The key point is the opportunities for regulating international markets and the players who operate there. The measures being discussed range from a code of behavior for multinational corporations on the question of human rights all the way to a 'Tobin tax' to be levied on speculative profit. The opponents of such steps argue that regulatory constraints gag the beneficial effects of entrepreneurship; justice can only be obtained in this way at a low level of poverty, which contradicts the objective possibilities for fulfillment and is to that degree also unjust. This argument is anything but convincing. Regulations that corrected distribution were no impediment to the German economic miracle. Problems only occur if such rules are introduced in one domestic market and bring competitive disadvantages in comparison with countries which give free rein to 'predatory capitalism.' Global regulations exist to prevent just such inequities. No reasonable objection can therefore be raised against making the global economy a little more just through international agreements.

The third dispute is about the moral status of the motto 'Whoever pays is prostituting himself/herself.' While the brutality of the statement is at first repulsive and appears to be irreconcilable with ideas about justice, upon closer examination the matter is not so clear cut, as can be shown using the example of development aid with strings attached. The means available for aid are raised by taxes in the industrial countries; the government is responsible to taxpayers, and must meet its obligation toward them to act prudently, which is certainly commensurate with justice. For, the intervention in the welfare of the people of one's own country – rich or poor – which the collection of taxes represents would without question be unjust if the expenditure of those taxes were not beneficial in the broader sense to the public interest. This also applies to development aid. It can hardly be termed equitable if because of a lack of strings attached tax proceeds end up in the coffers of a dictator like Robert Mugabe and his hangers-on in Zimbabwe. In this sense, the unequal distribution of votes within an organization such as the International Monetary Fund, where the countries which contribute the most have the largest share of the votes, is not unjust from the very beginning. This line of thought is revealing not only in the relationship between donor and recipient but also in relation to the effects in the country receiving aid. It is hardly something to be accepted gladly by the people when the amount of resources dictators can access is increased even more by development aid. Conditions relating to human rights and 'good governance' or the support of individual projects which help to alleviate poverty or contribute to infrastructure measures used by everybody, instead of handing over funds not earmarked for any given purpose, as governments prefer, generally helps people in countries receiving support more, and is therefore ultimately fairer.

It must be noted here by the way that, in international economic policy in particular, international cooperation which is considered prima facie to be morally valuable because it fosters peace can have its darker sides. If cooperation – namely between stronger partners – produce negative consequences to the disadvantage of third parties or – between strong and weak partners – produces dramatically unjust distribution patterns, its net effect can be negative; its effect is only unconditionally positive when it satisfies minimal, mutually agreed upon criteria for justice; on the one hand this would require that the affected 'third parties' be included in negotiating the intended regulations; on the other hand, this would also require that those placed at a disadvantage are given compensation.

Environmental policy

The basic question has already been posed above: how can compensation between polluters and those affected by it be realized? A classic example is the relationship between countries along the course of a river. Those 'downriver' have to put up with what those 'upriver' do with the water: widespread rechanneling for the purpose of irrigation, the building of dams for hydroelectric plants. Contamination from industry and agriculture can very seriously impair the health, economic and social interests of countries on the lower stretches of rivers. Without a mutually agreed set of rules, these distribution conflicts are very dangerous, and they can explode into violence. If it is a problem involving a region, the issue of polluter/victim has taken on global dimensions. Destruction of the ozone layer was mainly the result of activities by industrialized nations, but the damage was disproportionately located in the South (where two industrial nations, New Zealand and Australia, have been affected the most). Climate change due to greenhouse emissions too has originated mainly in industrial nations, whereas the main areas affected are small island nations as well as countries such as Egypt and Bangladesh in the Third World. Climate change however also raises another difficult question: how are past sins to be balanced with present and future sins? At the moment India and China are developing into the two main contributors to carbon dioxide emissions. However they demand the right to follow the same (environmentally harmful) path followed before them by today's industrialized countries, although present-day knowledge is able to foresee the damage that will result and – with appropriate investment and practices – growth would also be possible in a less harmful manner.

When a balance between industrial and developing countries in questions related to the environment is sought, the arrangement certainly cannot be carried out in a form that ruins the economies of today's rich countries. To slaughter the goose which lays golden eggs has never been a particularly clever strategy for promoting greater well-being. A series of instruments for such compensation is being discussed. Varying entitlement quotas distribute the allowable emissions among the players. In its liberal form, this leads to emissions trading as set out in the Kyoto Protocol; however the quotas agreed under this protocol are based on today's utilization patterns and thus once again favor the major consumers. Compensation payments for damage would conform to the general practices of civil law. Subsidized technology transfer may, under certain circumstances, help prevent environmental damage in the South, but always raises questions regarding patent and ownership rights. All in all, in the field of international environmental law a series of justice-oriented concepts has been established: the polluter-pays principle, limited North-South compensation, the general principle of mutual though differing responsibility, the concept of a 'joint heritage of humanity,' and the cooperation principle which affords all involved parties participatory rights. The principles are noble but vague, and implementation has not gone smoothly – primarily due to the resistance of the industrialized countries.

Two further unsolved issues deserve mention: how are the interests of future generations in surviving in a favorable environment to be balanced against the well-being of people living

today, how should the interests of those not yet born be represented in practical terms so that they can be considered in the
decisions made? How much importance should non-human life
be given in deliberations about justice? Do we regard the environment we live in with others as a resource for human interests
which needs to be sustained and cared for to the extent that an
optimum level of usefulness for humanity is achieved? Is protection of species sufficient as a principle of preservation? Or are
animals (and possibly plants) the bearers of their own rights to
life which should be respected?

Security

Security is probably the commodity which is distributed most
unequally. Compare Iraq with Switzerland, or the Ivory Coast
with Norway. Even September 11, 2001, a day when a pur-
portedly unassailable superpower was attacked within its own
borders, has not basically changed much about this. As for security itself, the distribution of traditional security policy instruments is also grossly asymmetrical. The United States accounts
for nearly 50 percent of the world's military spending, with the
Western alliance partners together accounting for another 25
percent. The aggregation of military power as found in NATO
is unprecedented in human history. Whether security can indeed
be procured through such arsenals is a different question entirely.
The divide in terms of decision-making power is equally wide.
The US is able to formulate decisions at a national level which
affect the security of all players in every corner of the world.
'Coalitions of the willing' led by the United States are in a position to take violent action even when this defies international
laws and takes place against massive, worldwide political and
social resistance.

These rules in themselves grant the five permanent members

of the UN Security Council the privilege of blocking decisions with their veto. The rules ensure that the vital interests of these five powers can never be restricted via valid international rules, while all other countries are hypothetically forced to accept this situation. The more recent practice of the Security Council of acting as a universal lawmaker (see above) indicates the existence of another asymmetry. If this practice continues, the rest of the world community will be confronted with the situation that at any time 'world laws' are possible which undermine a country's own interests, whereas the five permanent members of the Security Council are always spared such treatment; this is not just.

So far, only countries have been discussed as bearers of claims to justice in security policy. Recent developments in international law as well as the idea of 'humane security' are pointing to a trend towards recognizing individual people as the bearer of such claims. Groups too – think of the Albanians in Kosovo – have already been accepted as the bearers of such rights. It is unclear how these various levels of rights can be brought together, and conflicts between them avoided or resolved. This collision is playing a visible role in the treatment of national sovereignty, which for a long period was the pillar of world order but included the possibility of governments behaving with extreme inhumanity towards their own peoples – or sections of them.

On the other hand, as a defense shield against foreign interference sovereignty offers protection against the effects of asymmetrical power distribution, and is thus an element of international justice. During the last decade the concept of sovereignty has partly been subjected to conditions, i.e., measured against the standard of responsibility: only those countries which do not exceed certain limits in the treatment of their inhabitants – such as committing genocide – or which do not tolerate cross-border terrorist activities within their territories (or at least undertake credible efforts to stop such activities) enjoy protection from the prohibition of interference. In the next few years, refraining from the use of weapons of mass destruction could become a third fundamental principle defining 'responsibility.'

This immediately poses another problem of justice: at least for the time being, based on the Non-Proliferation Treaty, five countries are allowed to own nuclear weapons – until complete nuclear disarmament. The obligation to carry out nuclear disarmament is formulated vaguely and without a time frame. Does 'nuclear apartheid' in this form promote peace and thus ultimately justice? Or does it only heighten existing power asymmetries to the point of intolerability, as many non-aligned countries and NGOs argue? The situation is made worse by the existence of four *de facto* nuclear powers – India, Pakistan, Israel, and North Korea – which are not signatories to the Non-Proliferation Treaty and whose nuclear weapon arsenals (at least those of the first three) are tacitly tolerated, whereas it is made clear to Teheran that an Iran with nuclear weapons is intolerable.

Culture

The initial question in the field of 'cultural justice' is whether there is a right to intact culture. In the course of human history cultures have always interacted and reciprocally affected each other, often by conquest but also through constant communication and mutual permeation. It is hardly justifiable to describe every change in one's own cultural patterns brought about by an outside influence as an injustice. Nowadays cultural penetration occurs through a combination of unequal power distribution – the richer and more powerful countries have a better chance of influencing other countries than vice versa – and the individual decisions of billions of people, such as the choice made by Iranian youth to listen to American pop music. It is very hard to predict how these processes could be managed in an 'equitable' manner. It is certainly true that Samuel Huntington's recommended mutual isolation to avoid the 'clash of civilizations' is obsolete; his model does not do justice to the powerful forces of globalization. However, where a strategic attempt is made to impose cultural values through the exercise of power, injustice inevitably arises. The global cultural struggle of the Bush administration to spread the values of Protestant fundamentalism – such as with respect to premarital sex – has also produced serious injustices – preventable AIDS among the young in developing countries – just as does the reactionary missionary zeal of Saudi Arabia which contributes to a worsening of the position of women in Muslim countries. Finally, the question of the guiding criterion for cultural justice presents itself: is it a matter of maintaining cultural boundaries to ensure the survival and development of all cultural identities existing today? Or is it more important to work toward a universal culture consisting of a mixture, in which every cultural group recognizes elements of its own original identity? And are there appropriate decision-making processes at all for cultural development? For who would the authoritative 'cultural representatives' be who would be brought into such a process?

Conclusions

Justice is a concept that is both fundamentally important as well as highly controversial. This is even more the case in international relations than in matters of state and society. Problems of justice of a substantive or procedural nature are found in all areas of politics. There are no clear, universally acceptable solutions to these problems. A 'silver bullet' for achieving justice can thus only be perceived as an imperialist act, and will produce new violence and thus further injustice.

Instead, more modest patching up on all fronts is advisable. These steps include increasing development aid with sensible conditions, implementation of the Kyoto Protocol, and an intercultural dialog which genuinely allows all sides to be heard. An enduring global social policy is called for, which distributes means from the North to the South on an ongoing basis while exercising caution based on experience with bad government, corruption or senseless prestige projects. Above all, the rights of participation of the disadvantaged must be strengthened. Serious security policy decision-making must be returned to the UN Security Council from the 'coalition of the willing' (chapter 5). A modest reform of the Security Council (chapter 7) would help achieve greater procedural justice through more appropriate representation of diversity. The UN General Assembly needs more effective participatory rights in decisions which have serious consequences; NGOs should be consulted before far-reaching resolutions are passed. In order to narrow the power gap between 'northern' and 'southern' NGOs, civil society in developing countries needs systematic help which would enable it to send its own well-organized and effective NGOs into the international arena.

Consigning war as an institution for collective resolution of conflicts to the scrapheap of history, as has been achieved for the most part with slavery and state-condoned piracy, is the third major task in establishing the underlying conditions for sustainable global governance. Naturally, the risk of armed conflict between disputing parties or the escalation of such disputes into war will continue to exist for a long time to come. Even if warfare is effectively banished, and peaceful resolution of conflict has become a generally accepted norm, it will not be spared the fate of all norms: there will always be those who violate norms, even if the vast majority of players fully respect them.

Given the alternative – war continuing to be global political normality – it appears to be sensible, if not necessary, to make an effort to start by preventing *major* wars, then to end the politically smaller ones, and finally to extinguish the brush fires of local conflicts, to the maximum extent possible. For, if these steps do not succeed, the necessary cooperation between states and world regions will be blocked by an insurmountable obstacle: an existential mistrust which hinders all cooperation. In addition, wars and the stockpiling of armaments tie up resources which are needed to solve problems. Wars tear the threads which hold the world together and make global governance possible. Compared to the past, the risks posed by wars have become unimaginably greater because of the potential for escalation and destruction inherent in modern weapons. This means that it is essential to rein in war, not only in the sense of the 'general welfare' of humanity but also in the interest of individual state players.

The most sustainable containment would be its abolition. Is this utopia? The fact is that there are parts of the world which have to all intents and purposes abolished war, although for centuries the countries in question were at each other's throats. In Western Europe and throughout the transatlantic region, war between nations is no longer conceivable, and this peace zone has spread eastwards. In South America war has become a very rare event; the only noteworthy instance of armed hostility in the 1990s – between Ecuador and Peru – lasted only a few days, had few casualties, and took place in an obscure jungle area. Since its inception in 1967 the founding members of ASEAN (Indonesia, Malaysia, Singapore, Thailand, and the Philippines) have had peaceful dealings with one another for more than a generation. The expansion of ASEAN has extended this peace zone across all of Southeast Asia. Even in the conflict between East and West, states which once were enemies have found a way to avoid major war and develop cooperation. In view of these facts, anyone who considers the abolition of war as described above idealistic is not a realist him or herself, but lives in the world of yesterday. This does not mean that war will abolish itself on its own. Concerted and lasting effort is necessary in order to achieve this goal.

War as an instrument of global governance?

With the trauma of the two world wars, in Germany the term 'war' is loaded with highly negative connotations. That is a good thing, but it was once different. During the First World War soldiers marched singing through crowds of joyous people who waved their handkerchiefs and hats, and the same happened in other European countries. In the age of social Darwinism war was considered the highest test of a people's prowess; the Nazi regime later cultivated this heroism ideology with particular fervor. The 'holy warrior' is also an admired figure in the militant versions of Islam.

At least there is more or less a consensus in Europe today that war must be prevented at all costs; as a 'technique for global governance' war is highly regarded by only a few Europeans. With the advent of 'wars for restoring order' and 'humanitarian interventions' by democracies in the 1990s, war appeared to be regaining stature as a regulatory policy instrument. However, the overall outcome of these missions has been sobering. Ambitious goals and reality differed from each other too much, and the uncertainties of armed conflicts were becoming obvious. The trend today is to resort to arms only in the most extreme circumstances such as self-defense or to prevent genocide. However, there was an entire age – and there are still schools of thought – in which this was viewed or is viewed quite differently. The 'European balance of power' was designed to maintain a sustainable structure of power distribution among the continent's nation-states. The objective was to secure the existence of states and maintain their approximate equality. This required preventing any of them from achieving a position of hegemony. Alliances were formed to oppose the strongest and/or most ambitious, in order to offer a counterweight to its power. War was the ultimate measure of balance. Spanish, French and German domination was prevented through wars. Whether the new power balance was attributable to strategic calculation or to a historical dynamic stronger than the will of individual players is irrelevant: de facto war was an intentional and regularly practiced instrument of European security policy. In some parts of the US today there is the idea of a preventive war to create order. Whenever a risk to American or world security (with both conflated to mean largely the same thing) threatens to emerge, it should be nipped in the bud before it can become a real and genuine menace.

Preventive war, according to this view, is an instrument of world order. The attack on Iraq was a trial-run for this strategy. The state of affairs in the country along the Tigris and Euphrates reveals its risks and side effects. It is in the nature of modern warfare that an enemy can be subdued by military means without it being possible, however, for order to be restored. For, the characteristics of today's military weapons – accessible, light-weight, with high destructive force – work in favor of the forces of chaos as against the forces of order. It is exactly for this reason that war generates chaos, despite its intended purpose of being an instrument for achieving order. A destructive blaze spreads instead of sustainable order. If this is true for an apparently 'minor' war against an opponent which hardly seems able to defend itself – and the Iraq war provoked by the US and Great Britain can scarcely be described as more than that – it is even more true for a 'major war' which theoreticians of a 'power balance' have in mind: a war between superpowers would be waged under conditions which raise doubts about whether the world would ever recover from such a conflict. This is because of the fearsome effect of modern weapons, with nuclear weapons at the fore. However, conventional munitions can also cause extreme damage: US-made 'daisy cutter' aerosol explosives destroy an area of several hundred square meters. A war between superpowers would – apart from the damage to humans and nature – brutally tear apart the intricate network of global economic relations. Supplying humanity with urgently needed goods would presumably no longer be assured. In a nutshell: war to compensate imbalance between the superpowers as

regulatory policy is not a good idea, and the middling to catastrophic results of smaller scale 'wars to restore order' in the
last two decades – including the 1991 Gulf War, Bosnia, Kosovo,
Afghanistan – confirm this assumption more than disproving it.

Preventing war through deterrence

Development of nuclear weapons has allowed another idea to
emerge: preventing war by deterrence. Its proponents share the
view that today war no longer makes sense. They see in the most
powerful weapons of our time the best possibility of realizing
humankind's dream of eliminating war. The foreseeable horrors
of nuclear war, so the speculation goes, keep even daring, aggressive and ambitious heads of state from waging wars of aggression. Because 'the one who shoots first dies second,' no war can
serve national interests any more. Everything becomes senseless
in total destruction. Because the costs of war are far greater than
any conceivable profit to be gained from victory, perpetual peace
reigns. If thought through to the end, this concept calls for the
general distribution of nuclear weapons: the more countries that
have them, the more peace would have to spread. It is in fact true
that US academics such as Kenneth Waltz and John Mearsheimer
have propagated this idea, and Mao Zedong also contemplated
it. Interestingly, though, even convinced advocates of nuclear
deterrence in the East-West conflict have been skeptical about
whether peace could be made universal through wider distribution of nuclear arms. What are the reasons for this skepticism?

First of all, we were very fortunate during the East-West conflict. During the Cuban missile crisis in 1962, when the United
States and the Soviet Union were facing each other down on 'red
alert,' a catastrophe was just barely averted. In 1983 the aging

and paranoid leadership of the Soviet Union was so alarmed by the militant rhetoric of the Reagan administration and its arms buildup that Moscow believed the stationing of intermediate-range missiles in Europe while a NATO military exercise was taking place was for the purpose of starting a blitz offensive against the Soviet Union; strategic armed forces were placed on high alert without the West noticing. This crisis also came to an end. After the collapse of the Soviet Union another alert was sounded when a Norwegian research rocket – apparently heading toward Russia – was identified as a ballistic missile. The ominous 'suitcase' containing the release codes for Russian nuclear weapons was activated. The Norwegian government had informed the Russian side about the experiment; but the message simply failed to make it through middle-level bureaucracy, which was in a relative state of disarray at the time. Russia's leadership was, however, insightful enough not to escalate the matter.

If these episodes are already worrying enough, this is much truer for the real war between Pakistan and India in 1999 in the Kargil mountain region on the edge of the Karakoram, a part of Kashmir claimed by both states. Unlike in the East-West concept of deterrence, Pakistan's military leadership did not regard the possession of nuclear weapons on both sides of the 1948 cease-fire line as an instrument for reliably preventing any war. Army chief of staff General Musharraf – who was the President of Pakistan until August 2008 – and his comrades perceived in nuclear weapons the welcome opportunity of conducting limited wars without the far more powerful opponent escalating the conflict to an all-out attack on Pakistan; and only such a full-scale assault would have threatened the existence of Pakistan. In a situation like this, however, India would have been confronted with the risk of a last-ditch nuclear attack by Pakistan. These prospects would have kept the Indian armed forces from launching an all-out attack – so ran Pakistan's line of thought. Instead of believing in complete deterrence *from* a war, the generals in Islamabad counted on deterrence *during* a war. The conclusion to be drawn from this is that we cannot rely on 'our' system of deterrence working elsewhere in the same way it does in the East-West conflict.

If our deterrence itself were not absolutely reliable, and if nuclear weapons in other parts of the world give rise to different ways of thinking from ours, then the conclusion is inescapable: the proliferation of nuclear weapons increases the statistical risk of their being used. Any use of such weapons at one point on the globe can have a 'catalytic' effect, i.e., lead to reactions of others who interpret the situation differently from the instigator of the first bombing. In addition, the proliferation of nuclear weapons and nuclear weapons factories multiplies the possibilities for terrorists: the danger of nuclear terrorism, a real nightmare of humanity, would therefore increase. 'Peace through proliferation' is not a good idea for these reasons: the risks of this concept failing are too high. The costs of failure are unacceptably high: a nuclear war. The continued spread of nuclear weapons brings us closer to this catastrophe. But, at the same time, it is not a sustainable state of affairs when a few countries with nuclear arsenals can threaten the rest of the world while those so threatened have nothing with which they can counter. The Non-Proliferation Treaty, in which the vast majority of countries have committed themselves to doing without nuclear weapons, therefore provides for the disarmament of all existing nuclear weapons based on the principle: either everyone or nobody! This principle is correct, but the atomic powers do not abide by it. They are not even considering forgoing their privilege. If there continues to be no disarmament, it will be the undoing of the NPT. Its usefulness as a 'barrier' against the decision by governments to procure nuclear weapons will disappear. Then one state after another will follow the example of the nuclear powers, who are sending a signal to the whole world that nuclear weapons are useful in the military theater and guarantee political status, and acquire 'its' bomb, the consequences of which are: see above. Sustainable governance only works if the world works toward general and complete nuclear disarmament.

Deterrence of war through imperial hegemony

At this point an objection could be raised which I addressed in chapter 3: nothing is more effective for deterring major and minor wars than a functioning imperial power. An imperial power is present to some extent everywhere, has its troops stationed here and there, distributes rewards for good behavior, and lashes out if an unruly player disturbs the imperial peace. Then reinforcements emerge from the metropolis at lightning speed and nip the resistance in the bud before it can spread to become a consuming wildfire or become established in the region as an enduring system of violence. Seen in this light, then precisely the opposite of what was just said would apply: then it would be desirable for the central hegemony to have absolute superiority, including the awful capability of nuclear pulverization of the whole planet (and thus all possible disturbers of the peace). In such a system it is not nuclear disarmament but a nuclear monopoly which is the most desirable.

The dilemma of this model has been cited in chapter 3: monopolies are an aggravation. They provoke broad resistance; this is especially true for the era of globalization, in which political mobilization is relatively high. This resistance is not an isolated occurrence which results from the rebel's pathological disposition. It is much more a natural, unavoidable and inevitable product of monopolies. In a world full of diversity, imperial rule by even the most merciful ruler is not acceptable to all too many actors. Their honor, dignity, identity, value orientation, ideology and religion forbid submission and demand rebellion. Far from putting an end to all war, a monopoly spawns war in every quarter. The imperial ruler wishing to bring peace to the world presents it in reality with all-encompassing violence. What in earlier centuries was still conceivable – when most of humanity was concerned with eking out their daily existence in a subsistence economy without any great contact with the outside world – is completely impracticable today, in an age of widespread mobility, literacy, communication by cell phone and the Internet, and the ability to organize. All these things are enhanced by technical possibilities, even for the marginalized lower classes. It is difficult to accept that scientists turn to antique or Early Modern Era models when trying to solve our problems of government, without showing the least sensitivity for the irreversible changes that have occurred in the meantime. They have consigned imperial hegemony as a form of rule appropriate for our problems to the garbage heap of history. It is important to note that imperial hegemony as a model of global governance for fostering peace not only fails to work if the superpower acts as foolishly as under the government of George W. Bush, the worst president since I began to consciously observe US foreign policy; in our pluralistic world, with its modern technology enabling any player, regardless of how weak, always to have just enough power to unleash havoc, it will not function as a matter of principle. People, forget about empires – today there is nothing less politically sustainable.

The international organization

What then? After the two previous chapters, the answer comes as no surprise: there is no avoiding the international organization. This type of institution continues to be the only lifeline which offers hope of containing the scourge of war in the sea of diversity and in the swirling problems of justice. It is, after all, a fact that humankind has an impressive network of institutions in place today. However, it is only rarely used properly. The instinctive feeling that you would be able to get all problems under control if you were only stronger than all the others is reappearing again. This instinct was tangible in the expansion policy of Louis XIV and Napoleon, Wilhelm II and Adolf Hitler, and in Stalin's dreams of global domination. It can also be seen with frightening clarity in the political practices of the most powerful country of all time, the democracy at the forefront of the world – the United States of America. At the same time, the US has been learning a bitter lesson. The Bush administration, for a long time blinded by an ideology which affected those obsessed with it no less than Marxism-Leninism once affected the Bolsheviks or Islamism the supporters of Osama bin Laden today, must reluctantly acknowledge that things do not work without cooperation, without listening, without friends and allies, without multilateral coordination. The point of convergence for all multilateral cooperation is the United Nations. Only there is diversity completely present, only there can discourse on justice be carried on in a world forum, and only there is the key for reining in war located. The key is enshrined in the charter of this organization, in the banning of war, and the strict procedural regulations for all exceptions to this ban. All that is needed is for it to be rediscovered.

It was precisely the United States which with great flair

initially wanted to make this idea a political reality: the League of Nations, the first truly worldwide organization, was the invention of an American president, Woodrow Wilson. At that time, though, the two-facedness of America could already be seen: what Wilson had founded was destroyed by the US Senate. For the upper house of the United States Congress refused to allow what was already the most powerful nation on earth to join, and thus from the first day on ruined the chances of the League of Nations succeeding. The League of Nations eked out a modest existence until the withdrawal of Nazi Germany and dictatorial-imperialistic Japan finally damned it to the level of insignificance. The United Nations, in many respects the child of the Second World War, was supposed to do it quite differently and better. The US had learned a lesson. This time the international organization, which was supposed to prevent war as its fundamental task, was propelled forward by Roosevelt and Truman. There was a special incentive for all significant powers to join: the right of veto and a permanent seat on the Security Council. The Security Council was intended to lend the organization a character going beyond a mere debating society, and raise it to the level of a group capable of taking effective action. A small council in which, alongside the representatives of the various regions, the superpowers were always represented and could always ensure that their vital interests were not neglected was supposed to be far more effective than the more egalitarian League of Nations. The principles of sovereignty and non-intervention remained, but the Security Council generally was given the authorization to negate this in the most extreme circumstances – for it was left up to the Security Council to define what in any given case a threat to international peace and security is and what measures ought to be taken to address such a threat. It was (and is) left up to its judgement whether to order the use of force as a last resort.

That the United Nations was completely unable to meet this expectation during the Cold War is not surprising. Two powerful blocs led by ideologically antagonistic superpowers not only cancelled each other out but also blocked the potential of the United Nations to promote peace. The disturber of the peace for the one was the freedom fighter for the other. If the one was willing to appeal for an intervention, the other had to exercise its veto. The world conflict made it impossible for the United Nations to carry out its regulatory function. This was not the fault of the organization, and certainly not a deficiency in the concept, but instead was an expression of the superpowers' inability to responsibly fulfill the role they assumed. The end of the East-West conflict appeared to open the door to a new era. A 'new world order' was announced by President Bush the elder. And indeed it was true that there had never been a more favorable opportunity than after 1990 to bring the powerful nations together, to reinforce rule by international law, and to address the world's problems in a spirit of cooperation. Russia, weakened by domestic strife and 'moving toward Westernization,' tended to align itself with the one remaining superpower. China wanted economic success and a commensurate degree of influence on events in its region. What it needed most was stability, and good relations with the world's superpower were conducive to that. India's experience was no different, as it was just taking its first steps towards enormously successful economic reform. Japan and Europe were also on the side of the US.

In retrospect it becomes clear how ignominiously Washington failed in this task – unlike after 1945, when a new order was fashioned with vision and energy and, very similarly to post-1918, when short-sighted provincialism sabotaged the plans of President Wilson. The partly nationalistic, partly neoconservative shift to the political right was beginning to tighten its grip on America in the 1990s when the neoconservative-led Republicans gained control of Congress and attacked the far more cosmopolitan and multilaterally-oriented President Clinton. Starting in 2001, the presidency of George W. Bush produced an unimaginable combination of arrogance and ignorance. The younger Bush was already on this path prior to 9/11; the brutal attack and the necessity of self-defense finally gave the most hawkish elements in his administration the upper hand. What came out of this was a disaster for the United States and for the rest of the world. To speak this simple truth openly is almost difficult here in Germany – the war club of anti-Americanism is quickly raised. Yet it is nevertheless true: the US has missed a historical opportunity to establish cooperative global governance, with good chances of having a sustainable effect. We have to attempt this once again today, although the broken crockery of President Bush the Younger must first be cleaned up, which means additional work. The Bush administration took power with a strong dislike of the United Nations, international law and multilateralism – in other words standing opposed to those three instruments which are indispensable for sustainable global governance.

Since the Gulf War in 1991 the world had slowly been getting on the right track: making the UN Security Council the referee in those security crises where the use of force represented possibly the only chance of keeping the peace or of restoring it, where, however, those contributing the armed forces were not acting in self-defense. As early as the war in Kosovo in 1999, NATO deviated from this principle and without a direct mandate from the UN launched a bombing campaign on its own authority. In the case of Afghanistan, the Bush administration had the wisdom to have the Security Council confirm that it really was self-defense, because the Taliban had been harboring the instigators of the terror attack and were not willing to guarantee the United States its legitimate right to security from subsequent attacks. Working with the Security Council was advisable because general chaos could result if every state independently and without any international investigation attributed terrorist attacks to other states. During the Iraq war which started in 2003 Bush and Blair defied all the principles of international law – their flimsy arguments sound no more convincing than those used by the German Reich for attacking Poland in 1939.

The first principle which in a sustainable world political order must bring about the banishment of war is a systematic return to the UN Charter: every country may defend itself when attacked. In all other cases, military action is only allowed under a direct mandate of the Security Council and the case of self-defense concludes with review by the Security Council. Those failing to do this are subject to sanctions. But what happens if one of the veto powers violates the law and then blocks all measures directed against it in the Security Council or protects a violator of the law with its veto? In this case an old practice should be adopted which fell into disuse in the 1960s: the self-granted empowerment of the UN General Assembly based on the 'Uniting for Peace' resolution – also known as the 'Acheson Plan.' The General Assembly would respond to a veto deadlock in the Security Council by calling an emergency session and passing a resolution by a two-thirds majority. It would then consider the contentious issue and make a decision about a remedy. Unlike Security Council resolutions, this resolution is not binding for Member States, but gives legitimacy to their actions. This makes it possible to impose sanctions.

Non-governmental organizations have a powerful lever in their hands. Their potential for mobilization and communication is very impressive today. They only apply it occasionally.

One such case where these means found use was the series of nuclear tests conducted by France in 1995.

The boycott imposed by NGOs on French merchandise hit France hard, and was instrumental in President Chirac's reducing the number of tests, making France 'a paragon of virtue' in the negotiations on stopping nuclear testing which took place at the same time. It would be desirable if the major NGOs could agree to impose a boycott – regardless of on whom – when there is a violation of international law against which the vast majority of UN members (at least two-thirds) want to impose sanctions but are unable to. Such a non-governmental embargo would not be without significance to even the most powerful country.

The United Nations must once again become the central body for making decisions on war and peace. If the great powers of this world – more or less voluntarily – submit to this rule, which has actually long been in force, this would mean that a decisive step has been taken toward outlawing war. Unfortunately, this is still not enough, because the violence includes situations where there is no black and white distinction between aggression and defense, guilt and innocence, but instead events occur in a gray area – such as when, for instance, protracted conflicts escalate step by step without it really being clear who bears the fault for the outburst of violence. It also achieves nothing with other forms of violence – terrorism, civil war, and 'war economies.'

Security communities

I will change my tack in the next step: so far in this chapter I have discussed open violent conflicts. Now I will turn my attention to the subject of a manifest and sustainable peace. This phenomenon – and this is the truly good news for our deliberations on sustainable global governance – really exists. It is called a 'security community'; what is meant by this is an association between two or a number of states between which war as a means of resolving conflict has become unthinkable. It is not about there no longer being any conflicts between them. But these conflicts are generally conducted using peaceful means. A mutually shared value orientation, broad cooperation, and shared institutions exist between such countries; at an advanced stage there is also consideration of shared foreign policy and partial or complete military integration; the borders do not have military fortifications. There is lively communication among elites, perhaps even among the general populaces. A prototype of such a security community is the European Union. And the transatlantic region with its North American components is included, as well as the Nordic Council of Scandinavian countries. In the south of South America none of the members of the organization MERCOSUR would even consider armed combat with neighboring states. There is similar transnational peace in Southeast Asia's ASEAN area: there has been no danger of war between the organization's member countries since 1967. There is violence in this region, but it is internal. The peace between nations is all the more astonishing given the fact that each country is embroiled in some kind of territorial dispute with all the others, and the region is culturally fragmented: between Islam (Malaysia, Indonesia, Brunei), Buddhism (Myanmar, Thailand, Cambodia, Vietnam, Singapore, Laos) and Christianity (the Philippines).

How do security communities help us in our task of constructing institutions for global governance? A lot: the more regions where conditions like those just described prevail, the larger the area of the globe where a massive international war can be 'crossed off.' As a result, these states themselves as well as the international community can focus their resources for promoting peace and their energy on the two remaining problems: the regions with stubborn international conflicts and the smoldering, flickering or blazing internal disputes occurring in certain parts of the world. Seen in this light, it makes a lot of sense for the member states in the international community who are able to take action or have ample resources to offer help to potential candidates for the formation of security communities.

One such region is the south of Africa – there is such an aversion against cross-border strife there that not even the stiff-necked tyrant of Zimbabwe, Mugabe, comes under pressure from his neighbors. We do not like that, because Mugabe is a genuinely despicable dictator who is ruining his country. For overall peace throughout Africa this is, however, not a purely negative sign. It would thus be desirable to provide the organization of this region, SADC (South African Development Cooperation), with sufficient resources to continue to advance cooperation within the region. A further candidate of this kind is found in West Africa, as improbable as that may sound given the massive violence in this region over the past fifteen years. The ECOWAS (Economic Cooperation Organisation of West African States) has drawn attention to itself through several joint peace-keeping and peace-making missions and, despite all the differences of interest and tremendous inequality (compared to its neighbors, Nigeria is a giant country), has maintained peace between its member states. Some member states such as Ghana, Mali, and Senegal or – in the immediate past after terrible civil wars – Sierra Leone and Liberia have been or presently are relatively successful in combating internal conflicts. One particularly innovative institution which is based on African traditions is the 'Council of Elders,' a committee of 'wise statespersons' who in several cases have already energetically persuaded politicians and generals intent on overthrowing a government or already doing so not to carry out their plans. With European support, ECOWAS runs one of the most active programs in the fight to curb the spread of the small arms plague. This organization faces a difficult task because France is actively striving to separate out the Francophone members in an attempt to split up the group – an additional damaging effluence of late colonialism. ECOWAS deserves strong substantive support.

Superpower relations: the forthcoming shift in power

Security communities are thus solid regional pillars of effective, sustainable global governance. Another important requirement must be fulfilled for this to become reality at all: the great powers must not be in conflict with each other. If they are in fear of each other, then they build up weapons stockpiles because they do not trust each other, then they carry on geostrategic games of exercising their influence in precarious regions such as the Persian Gulf, and battle each other for world leadership or even for world domination. In such a hotly contested power struggle the real problems of the world cannot be addressed, because the energies of the largest – in the best scenario – cancel each other out. Even worse, the Damoclean sword of an unimaginably catastrophic Third World War would continuously hover over humanity, because – see above – there can be no absolute guarantee that mutual deterrence is reliable.

What makes things even touchier: we live in a time of power transition. These are historical periods where ambitious powers are growing faster than the dominant power and the power gap between the 'Number 1' and those catching up with it becomes smaller and smaller. In the past, periods like this have always had high potential for violence. The choice between the 'reigning

strongman' and a challenger has usually been settled on the battlefield; the struggle over world leadership only occurred without
dire consequences on two occasions – between Great Britain and
the US and the US and the Soviet Union.

How do things look today? Great Britain, France and Russia
too are declining powers which have not yet completely managed
to bow out of their dominant role gracefully; Russia the least.

Until recently, the Russian Federation had been experiencing
an apparent upswing in its power, and was acting with corresponding boorishness. This apparent progress was founded on
a soap bubble, however, for it was driven by high energy prices.
These led to a tendency for reduced demand and a search for new
resources; even now there is an oversupply, which will then lead
to a fall in prices, and the bubble will burst. No world power in
the twenty-first century can be built on the primary sector; to
do this requires an evenly developed economy with an emphasis
on hi-tech and the service sector. Russia cannot offer these, and
it can hardly be anticipated that the recognizable trend towards
strengthening its state economy will produce the innovation
required for the Russian business sector. This is not good news: for
it indicates that Russia could fluctuate in political cycles between
dissatisfaction and the urge to be a great power. This would perpetuate Russia as a disruptive factor in global governance.

Japan and Europe continue to have a marginal role, despite
their importance in the global economy. Japan is visibly being
overshadowed by China. However, without a regional power base
no country can lay claim to being a world power. Japan is left with
its role as second fiddle in East Asia and an important voice in
the global economy. Europe is world champion in exercising its
'soft power,' the player with the most finely tuned repertoire of
foreign and security policies and – regardless of what one may
hear about the 'toothless' qualities of the Old Continent – also

considerable military power when the potential of its Member States is added together. It must be conceded that the whole here is less than the sum of its parts. Although Europeans spend a considerable amount on defense – more than 20% of the world's military spending – this still takes place with breath-taking inefficiency. European countries also allow themselves to be seduced again and again into placing their individual national pride in the foreground when it comes to the key issues of world politics. But you only count at the conference table of the great powers if you speak with a single voice. The Europeans are notorious for having difficulties with this and the expansion of the EU has not helped to close this power gap; on the contrary. Europe remains a significant power, but still only a marginal figure in the geopolitical arena.

If you look around at the situation in the world, only Brazil has the potential to be promoted to the same league as Japan, Europe and Russia in the foreseeable future, assuming that it achieves continuous economic growth for a lengthy period and overcomes its horrendous social conflicts. Brazil has no security problems in its own region but instead is first among equals among its (not always comfortable) partners, and thus does not have to squander much of its resources for immediate national security. Brazil's size makes it the dominant power in South America, thus giving it a regional power base. However, its resources are too limited for it to be a viable force among the preeminent world powers.

This leaves only two countries as future rivals of the US – China and India. Their potential is immense, and growth rates in recent years of between eight to ten percent indicate that within a generation China, and a half a generation later, India will not only be on a par with the US economically but also in terms of political power. For economic resources can be turned into potential for political and military power. In their 'National

Security Strategy' of 2002, Americans declared their intention not to allow any military rival to come close to their stature. The US has not given away how it plans to achieve this if the other countries grow at a continuously faster pace. Looked at in this way, this statement contains a concealed threat against the two major Asian countries.

Are there models for regulating relations among superpowers in such a way that no fatal obstacle to global governance emerges from their interaction? Indeed, there are such models, in fact two: the 'Concert of Europe' in the nineteenth century and American-Soviet arms control in the Cold War.

The concert of powers

The 'concert' was the response by dominant European powers to the Napoleonic wars, which had been traumatic for the entire continent. In order to prevent the recurrence of decades of slaughter, the major powers – Prussia, Austria, Russia, England and France, which had finally been accepted back into favor – formed a close-knit network of constant conference diplomacy in order to prevent any dangerous crisis from occurring among them or, if it did, to deal with it quickly by diplomatic means. War among them was to be ruled out; if any one of them – regardless of the means, through inheritance or the annexation of a smaller neighbor – were to expand its territorial power, the others affected were to receive compensation. Crises in other countries (such as by overthrow) immediately led to détente diplomacy among the great 'Five.' The politics of each of these five countries was geared to keeping the vital interests of the other four in mind with each strategic move, in other words to pursue a policy of judicious consideration.

The principles of the 'concert' can still be usefully applied today. The first principle that must be upheld is that any action taken by one of the superpowers within the direct sphere of another must be agreed upon in consultation with that power. This is by no means intended to mean sole decision-making power is granted to dominant powers within their regions (more on that shortly). Nevertheless, they do have a legitimate interest in actively participating in the formulation of security policy in their own neighborhood. This interest extends to the point that no power from another region should encourage their neighbors to enter into a hostile alliance or seek to win them over (or to present itself as the dominant power of such an alliance which is committed to the revisionist objectives of a smaller regional power). For, such relationships drive the most powerful countries into antagonistic conflicts with each other, and this obstructs beneficial global governance right from the start. What would the United States say if Russia tried to establish an anti-American alliance in the Caribbean and Central America? The harsh 'neighborhood policy' of the US against Cuba and Nicaragua during the Cold War speaks volumes. And yet Washington currently has no qualms about opposing Russian interests in Eastern Europe, in the Caucasus, and in the Central Asian republics, and to do all it can to limit Russia's influence in its own immediate region. If Moscow responds in an abrasive manner, the Americans wash their hands of any responsibility. Until the 1990s the US and China gave de facto support to Pakistan's Kashmir policy which was intent on having the region, a majority of whose inhabitants are Muslim, break away from India. Of course this caused a strain in relations with the irritated Indians. Only after India carried out its nuclear weapons testing did the picture change.

Respect for the security and influence interests of the superpowers is the first principle of the 'concert'. This does not mean that everything that a superpower subjects its smaller neighbors to should be uncritically accepted; yet criticism must be focused on a solution and be advanced after consultation, and it must remain clear that the use of military force is ruled out.

The 'concert' involves all dominant powers in dealing with regional crises which could have a global impact. This is especially true for the Middle East and Persian Gulf – with the world's interest in a dependable supply of oil – East Africa (with its significance to world trade lanes), and perhaps Central Africa and its huge mineral reserves. In dealing with the Iran dilemma, the 'EU-3 plus 3' approach has already produced good progress: the European Union and its member countries Germany, France and Great Britain, plus Russia, the US and China, are involved in the attempt to find a peaceful resolution to the risks involved in the highly questionable Iranian nuclear program. But where are the two large countries which have the best bilateral relations with Iran: India and Brazil? These countries have channels of communication with the Islamic Republic which the other participating countries, including China and Russia, do not have, despite their intensive economic relations with Teheran. The Middle East 'Group of Four' – the United Nations, the EU, the US and Russia – in turn could also be supplemented by China, given its massive interest in the region, as well as by India, the only power which maintains good relations with all direct and indirect participants in this conflict (with Israel, with the Arab camp, and with Iran). For the conflicts in Sudan, in Somalia and between Eritrea and Ethiopia, which form a chain of destabilization processes in East Africa, there is no multilateral consultative group at all outside the largely unfruitful deliberations in the UN Security Council. At the same time, China and India are the countries which have a strong presence in the region; India also has an influential expatriate diaspora (although this is mostly located in South Africa). A holistic, consultative approach to all three conflicts, involving all the superpowers while giving consideration to the interests of all parties involved, certainly offers more hope of success than America's slipshod attempts in the Horn of Africa. Here, the military intervention of the US and its support of the Ethiopian invasion of Somalia, after Iraq, threatened to set off the next blaze in an Arabic-Islamic country. (The US did not cause this conflict, but the manner in which it dealt with it was as clumsy as can be imagined.)

Another level where a balance of power like the concert of Europe makes sense is the global problems which could indirectly turn the superpowers against each other. These problems are first and foremost trade and the energy question. The struggles for markets and unfair trade practices have been grounds for conflict again and again, and this has placed a strain on relations between the major trade partners; at the same time, trade creates shared and complementary interests. Adding India, China, and Brazil to the G-8 and including these countries and Russia in leadership roles in the World Trade Organization opens up institutional channels for handling problems of this kind. These countries should also be made a part of the International Energy Agency (IEA), an organization created by Western industrial countries which has prepared emergency measures in case of energy crises. The IEA is also supposed to coordinate measures which reduce demand for petroleum.

It is to be hoped that these examples make clear how such a 'concert' can work. The main aspect in the examples was to reduce the potential for conflict between superpowers; how to handle the respective conflicts was not the central issue, but is promoted by such consultations. In addition, it has fortunately emerged that such a consultative system does not have to wait for the blockade which impedes reform of the UN to be dissolved.

The other forums suggested could also carry on their work just as the Middle East Quartet, negotiations with Iran, and the 'six-party talks' on Eastern Asia do – the latter will be discussed below – with the Security Council's approval, though separate from it.

Of course it would be a welcome development if the Security Council, which is actually responsible for this, would take all these conflict resolution processes in hand. But it is not sufficiently representative, important powers are missing, and its decision-making rules – primarily the right to veto – tend to work against rather than in favor of examining solution strategies in a calm and reasoned manner. As long as no reform eliminates these two hindrances, a 'consultation concert' outside the formal structures promises to produce better results. There are two areas today where we must go beyond the conventional 'Concert model': first, it is indispensable today that such multilateral confederations show due respect for the concerns of smaller powers instead of, in cases of doubt, mercilessly protecting the interests of the 'big powers,' as in the nineteenth century; this area is promoted by having strong regional organizations and increasing the standing of the UN General Assembly. Second, a modern-day 'concert of superpowers' must be supplemented by arms control.

Arms control and disarmament

The classic balance of power did not pay any heed to what participating states did with their armed forces during times of peace. Not doing so raises the danger that a security dilemma driven by stockpiling weapons produces deeper and deeper mistrust among them. For of course each country will ask itself at whom the military undertakings of its partners could be aimed.

Particularly in current times, we are experiencing the start of an arms race marked by the American missile defense system, Chinese anti-satellite weapons testing, Russia's suspension of the Treaty on Conventional Armed Forces in Europe, and the arms buildup by all atomic powers – the mistrust spoken of above is already bearing its poisonous fruit.

The beginning of a new age of disarmament has to begin with the end of America's superiority mania. Blinded by its unimaginable success in the East-West conflict, the US has single-mindedly pursued the idea of being militarily superior to all its possible rivals (and combinations thereof). Not only does it want to be able to resist potential attacks by these rivals, it also wants to have superior and promising offensive options available, too. These options are supposed to be at the ready quickly, at short notice and all over the world. For this purpose, the US wants to be clearly superior in all modes of battle–at sea, on land, in the air, in space, and in virtual electronic space.

These notions had already been developed in the 1990s and were concretely formulated in a coordinated way in the 'National Security Strategy' of 2002. Every document which is produced by the US Department of Defense breathes this spirit. At the same time these same Americans are shocked when other countries try to keep pace with lesser means. The former defense minister Rumsfeld in all seriousness once issued a sharp reprimand during a visit to Beijing in 2005 because China's defense spending was growing more quickly than its national product – though according to US estimates it was hardly more than 15% of US military spending at the time! Let us assume for a moment that America would be willing to give up its claim to total superiority. What would then be imperative and perhaps also possible? Perhaps the most pressing need is to generally disavow the introduction of weapons in space. Reconnaissance satellites for the armed forces of all states able to afford them have their place there, but no weapons of aggression, no killer satellites, no rocket launchers or laser weapons which in the future may reach the lower atmosphere or even the Earth's surface. A prohibition of this kind would represent a giant step toward stability, for the prospect of having offensive systems of five, six or eight powers in space which mutually spy on each other and are ready to attack the satellite of the other powers in the event of a crisis is a nightmare.

The second and equally important step is moving towards complete nuclear disarmament. We are already aware that further proliferation of nuclear deterrence does not effectively ensure security. The unbending logic of 'all or none' cannot be avoided; nuclear disarmament is the only remaining option. This cannot happen overnight. Complicated technical steps are required, trust must be built up, and countries such as China which have not been forthcoming must come clean about their stockpiles and production facilities for nuclear weapons; the nuclear powers must agree on individual steps, implement and closely monitor them. The process as a whole will take a generation – in other words, about 30 years. The international community must take measures for the final point within this process, in order to rigorously block all those who violate the new rules and seek to obtain nuclear weapons. However, in a world where the superpowers no longer have nuclear weapons, their agreeing on such preventive measures would be far more likely than it is today, for now they can still lean back, seemingly certain of the nuclear deterrence of their weapons. If a new country becomes a nuclear power – at least one which is not generally antagonistic to the superpowers – neither their national security nor their status is subject to immediate danger. However, if somebody were to be so aggressively bold as to become the only nuclear power in a world free of nuclear arms, then this would pose a danger to everybody, and also raise the issue of status as well.

If the nuclear powers were willing to give up their nuclear weapons, then missile defense would no longer be a pressing issue for those which do not have such a system. For the explosive nature of this project is that nuclear weapons of aggression continue to exist. For Moscow and Beijing it is a nightmare vision that in a crisis the US might feel tempted to use its 2,500 remaining strategic warheads (supported by its equally substantial conventional weapons potential) to launch a first strike aimed at destroying the nuclear deterrence forces of Russia and/or China to the greatest extent possible and then use the missile defense system to intercept the pitiful remaining warheads still left over for a counter-blow. If the US itself no longer has such an offensive option, then its defense system can no longer be so terrifying to others. It would then make sense to put a multilateral missile defense system (should it ever be technically feasible, which is anything but certain!) in place for all those to operate which have completely and verifiably renounced nuclear weapons. China, Russia or Iran – if these states were willing to disarm – would also come under the protection of this 'shield' and would participate in the technology.

Doing away with nuclear weapons will make necessary a stricter system of prohibitions for all biological weapons. The Biological Weapons Convention currently lacks any verification measures. Only modest confidence-raising steps are taking place, though not all parties to the Convention are taking part. That is not enough given the potential for mass destruction represented by biological weapons. An organization is thus called for which gathers all relevant information and inspects all national laboratories and industrial facilities. Negotiations for a comprehensive treaty for such a system had already been completed in 2001 but failed due to the objection of the Bush administration, behind which other obstinate negotiating partners such as Russia, India or China may be concealed. In a world with no nuclear weapons, it can be expected that there will be fewer objections to radical verification measures in order to ensure that there is truly no state producing treacherous biological weapons. The Biological Weapons Convention must be gradually reinforced at the same pace nuclear weapons stockpiles are disarmed.

Ballistic missiles hang like the sword of Damocles over the world: appalling long-range projectiles which within the space of minutes can bring death and destruction to any corner of the globe. Alongside the militarization of space, these nuclear missiles symbolize instability, mistrust and danger. President Reagan had once considered completely eliminating this weapon category. The man was right. In a world which should be governed sustainably there should no longer be room for instant long-distance murder. Because missiles are large objects which are produced and stationed, verifying such a ban would be relatively easy. An ideal ultimate scenario would be one where no individual country is capable of carrying out wide-scale offensive operations without the help of other countries, where the armed forces of a given country only have a portion of the capability required and would have to work with other countries like interlocked jigsaw puzzle pieces to mount a military campaign successfully. It would still be possible for the international community to take action against belligerent upstarts, in extreme cases also using force, but no country would be able to carry out such an expedition on the basis of its own resources alone.

Establishment of multilateral structures: East Asia, Central Asia, and Maghreb

At a time when achievement of a balance in power and arms control mean that relationships among the major powers are in the process of establishing mutual peace, the stage is set to form strong bonds of multilateral cooperation in further regions, and to establish corresponding organizations. The most likely candidates for this are East Asia, Central Asia and Maghreb. The imperative to take action is most urgent in the Far East. There is strong rivalry for control over the region (between China, Japan and the US), and with North Korea and its nuclear weapons program a first-order disturber of the peace is based in this region, one of the most despicable and bizarre dictatorships presently in power. At the same time, though, it is just this strange, militarized one-party country and its personality cult which has triggered the first serious effort to work through the security problems in the region on a multilateral basis. For, all the players involved are united in the desire to place restrictions on North Korea's nuclear weapons program without a sudden collapse of the country or – even worse – a regional war. A way out of the crisis has therefore been sought by diplomatic means; since 2003 the 'six-party talks' involving China, Japan, Russia, the US and the two Koreas. This grouping of countries thus provides a forum which can be used for other purposes as well: such as for regular consultations on regional security issues; as a framework to settle the various territorial disputes over uninhabited islands (between China, South Korea and Japan); as the basis for close collaboration regarding economic, energy and environmental policy.

Central Asia (Turkmenistan, Kazakhstan, Tajikistan, Uzbekistan and the Kyrgyz Republic) once played an important part in history, but only since the collapse of the Soviet Union has this region regained in its own independent significance. This area is where Russian, Chinese and Indian interests confront each other, Iran and Turkey are regional players of significance, and the young, predominantly autocratic Central Asian countries must first establish themselves – partly at the expense of their neighbors. There are territorial disputes, ethnic diversity, and a strong Islamic presence as well. Under the premise of fighting terrorism, but in fact with the goal of ensuring overall stability in the region and to avert a Russian-Chinese competition for influence, Moscow and Beijing instituted the Shanghai Cooperation Organization for Regional Security which, in addition to combating terrorist activities, is also dedicated to other security issues (Turkmenistan is not yet a member). Iran, India and Pakistan are participating as observer countries; the US was not granted this status. America has a military presence in the region and considerable interest in the natural gas and oil reserves located there. Giving Washington observer status at the 'Shanghai table' would be sensible in order to avert a confrontation between superpowers caused by one external player one-sidedly making a geopolitical move in a region close to the borders of another superpower. If promoting collaboration among countries that have entered into a pact for a zone free of nuclear weapons in the region as well as collaboration with countries bordering this region succeeds, then a security community could gradually emerge there.

It is also largely true that this opportunity exists in the Maghreb region: the countries along North Africa's Mediterranean coast are relatively homogeneous in terms of their culture, and at approximately the same level of development. So far, lesser conflicts and larger vanities of the political elite, and the resultant jockeying for status, have prevented close regional cooperation. This is an important task of the European Union, which cooperates with these countries and with all countries from the Mediterranean region as part of the Barcelona Process (now the Mediterranean Union), but not specifically with the smaller group of Maghreb states. This type of cooperation with the objective of promoting the regional unity of these countries could be grouped around the issues of migration and energy. The southern shore of the Mediterranean is the main source of illegal immigration to Europe. Two of the Maghreb countries – Algeria and Libya – have extensive oil and natural gas reserves. However, the region as a whole is also blessed with a high degree of useful direct sunlight. This presents the opportunity of building large solar power plants and exporting the power generated (or using it to split water molecules and export the hydrogen obtained by this method as a source of energy). These are major projects which require a solid financial, organizational and political framework. Regional cooperation closely aligned with the EU would be ideal for this; such cooperation would also make an impact in terms of energy, development and security policy.

In the three regions named, the proposed steps would contribute to preventing conflict; the level of violence in each region is relatively low. The situation is different in the two regions which are discussed in the following section: the focus in these parts of the world over the past few years and still now is on limiting the violence and bloodshed, in other words, preventing escalation and the spread of the conflict to other countries and regions, and gradually lessening the level of violence.

Damage containment: Africa, Afghanistan

The belt south of the Sahara has been one of the regions of the world hardest hit by violence. The bloody track stretched from the disintegration of the West Africa countries like Sierra Leone and Liberia, through the Democratic Republic of the Congo and the Great Lakes of Africa up toward the north into Sudan, and all the way to the east to the Horn of Africa. Added to this are the many casualties of the war between Ethiopia and Eritrea, the chaos of civil war in Somalia and the most recent intervention by Ethiopia and the US in Somalia, in order to remove the 'Islamic Courts Union' from power. This union is a grouping of Islamists who had restored a certain order to the country for the first time for years, but were also suspected of having contact with al-Qaeda.

The foremost concern is to prevent individual conflicts from spilling over into other countries and regions. Compared with ending the conflict, this is initially also the easier task to accomplish. Stationing peace-keeping forces in neighboring countries is already of considerable help if they are deployed effectively. A combination of regional armed forces (those of ECOWAS or the African Union) and auxiliary forces from outside the region is probably the most efficient combination. Second, the tasks of such a preventive mission include stopping to the maximum extent possible the inflow of weapons into the conflict-ridden countries or those parts of the country mired in violence. Third, there need to be material incentives for the population in neighboring regions not to become involved in the conflict, not to support the parties in conflict, and to help stop contraband weapons traffic instead of supporting smuggling for its own advantage. This would cost money, meaning that the highly industrialized countries, i.e., the G-8, which professes its wholehearted support of Africa, must make good on promises to help. In many cases only containment is possible, because the ambition to end the conflict itself has poor prospects given the interests and hatred of the embattled parties, not to mention the personal aspirations of their political and military leadership. The chance of mediating or successfully deploying a peace-securing mission often only arises once the parties are exhausted. Knowing when this point has been reached is a key art of promoting peace for which we have still not implemented sufficient institutional measures. It is logical that this task should fall to the United Nations.

In the meantime the near anarchic condition of Afghanistan is close to that found in the heart of Africa. In Afghanistan, the blending of two different concepts – on the one hand the reconstruction help supported by military forces and on the other the hunt for terrorists and the Taliban, led by the US with little heed for the civilian population – has led to growing alienation between local people and the intervention forces. Gains made in rebuilding are countered by increased violence. State authority has remained ineffectual outside the capital of Kabul, where violence is re-emerging. Warlords have control of the provinces, the country is the world's leading drug exporter, and in the south and southeast Taliban militia, supported by western Pakistani provinces, have grown in strength. Perhaps this war is already lost.

If the tide is to be turned, then the interests of the civilian population must be given first priority, even if this comes at the cost of the war on terrorism. Only a civilian population whose experience is that they are being helped and that the central government in Kabul is also organizing effective relief in provincial areas will refuse to help radicals and resist their temptations. If this about-face fails, then withdrawal and limitation of efforts to containment remain the only options. The armed pursuit of a balance of power in the country was a terrible affliction for Afghanistan in the 1990s, which culminated in the coalition between the Taliban and al-Qaeda; the return of the Taliban to power is possible, as is the disintegration of the country into six or seven smaller and ethnically distinct countries.

The UN Security Council will make it unequivocally clear to the Taliban – should they regain power – that threatened states have the right to intervene against al-Qaeda positions, should it once again be allowed to operate there. Given the many ambitious plans for humanitarian intervention in ongoing conflicts, the recommendation to concentrate on containment may seem too modest to many, even appear to border on cynicism – as with the title of an essay by strategy researcher Edward Lutwak, who came to roughly the same conclusions in 'Give War a Chance!' I am (or have become) so reserved because the overall record of peacekeeping and nation-building interventions has not been outstanding. It has often only made matters worse.

Conflict management and resolution: South Asia and the Middle East

Finally, we must take a look at the two most potentially explosive regions of the world: South Asia and the Middle East extending to the Persian Gulf. The volatility of South Asia lies in the fact that two states armed with nuclear weapons stand face to face and have had a territorial dispute with each other for decades over the mountainous Kashmir region. There have already been four armed conflicts between the countries in the region. In 1948, immediately after the two countries were founded, in 1965 when Pakistan believed that India had been weakened after losing a war to China, in 1971 when an Indian military operation in Bangladesh – formerly East Pakistan – split Bangladesh from Pakistan, and in 1999 when Pakistan attacked India in the Karakoram Range at Kargil in northern Kashmir. If there is any place where nuclear war seems possible, then it is in South Asia. This makes resolving the conflict between the two countries a high-priority project for sustainable global governance. It is fortunate that the prospects for success are not all that bad, although the risks remain high.

Ten years ago a confrontation seemed almost unavoidable. In India, militant anti-Islam Hindu nationalism was gaining in strength and in Pakistan a radical Islamist movement was spreading ever more strongly in the secret services and armed forces. The support of the anti-Indian terrorism in Kashmir, yes, even the fomenting of a limited war as in Kargil, were viewed by Pakistan's top leadership as legitimate forms of foreign policy. Today the picture is different. India is dealing with this conflict more calmly. India's position – to make the current cease-fire line its national border – presents the only feasible option, and in the meantime is supported not only by Russia but also by the US and China. Even Pakistan's former president, Pervez Musharraf, tentatively suggested that he would be willing to consider such a solution if the Indian Union granted Kashmiris greater autonomy. Such a change in course by Pakistan would have to be accompanied by massive aid, debt forgiveness, and investment throughout the country. Without measurable advantages for the population, no Pakistani leader who gave up Kashmir for good would have a chance of survival. The residual risks lie within the borders of Pakistan: this country is an unstable, fragmented country with a high proportion of radical Islamists, who continue to have influence within the security forces and dominate in the west of Pakistan. A seizure of power by them would bring the easing of tensions between New Delhi and Islamabad to an end. In addition, such a change in power would hand control of Pakistani nuclear weapons to the radicals. This makes a timely resolution of the conflict all the more important.

With that, the most daunting project of all remains: the Middle East and the Persian Gulf. The two-fold foolishness of the Bush administration in neglecting to pursue a solution to the Middle East conflict and instead to see the answer to the region's problems in the democratization of Iraq through the use of force, accompanied by the greed for land of the Israeli right wing, the short-sighted fear felt by Arab leaders towards their own peoples, and the fanaticism of self-proclaimed religious saviors has plunged this region into indescribable chaos. The simultaneous occurrence of so much political shortsightedness and strategic miscalculation is breathtaking and depressing at one and the same time. But we have to get ourselves out of the mess in one way or another.

We should begin with Iraq: of all the negative alternatives, withdrawing the occupation forces is presumably the option which is the least bad and which is now underway. Iraqis would then be given the weighty responsibility of finding their way out of the maze on their own. The unhappy coalition between radical Saddamists and al-Qaeda will presumably end soon, whether Iraq remains a unified nation-state (which can hardly be anticipated) or breaks up into three parts. The incentive for the 'genuine' Iraqis, including Sunni Muslims, to repulse the self-proclaimed holy warriors who have seeped into the country increases to the same degree that the occupying power disappears as a mutual 'red flag.'

Instead of being a deployment area for pro-Iran militia, a Shi'ite state in the south would certainly be eager to stay separate from the would-be Persian hegemony – after all these are Arabs! The Baath party may regain control in the Sunni midlands or not – it is unlikely that a new Saddam will become established and if this should happen it will be reliant on a power base that has shrunk to harmlessness. The Kurdish state in the north will only become a problem if the Turkish military loses its nerve. The national Kurdish leadership would have to be required to break up any bases of the P.K.K. (Kurdish Workers' Party), the Turkish-Kurdish party seeking to break away from Turkey. Turkish Kurds who would rather live in a Kurdish country than in a Kurdish province in Turkey should be allowed to resettle in a new Kurdistan. Of course there would be a serious civil war during the transition period until the outlines of the national disintegration of Iraq come into focus – but civil war is already going on in Iraq today.

The disintegration of Iraq would not be a political catastrophe. The Iranian disputes call for patience. Today's political leadership in Teheran is not representative of Iranian society. The younger Iranian generation thinks differently and is in the majority. Over time their modern and even liberal orientation will open up the pathway to new forms of rule which are appropriate to Iranian culture. In the meantime, it is imperative to contain any aggressive moves of the government now in power. A well chosen combination of composure and vigilance is called for, because Iran is not strong and – as is also true for Pakistan and North Korea – will not become strong even should it successfully establish a nuclear weapons program (which is itself by no means certain). As always, panic is harmful, in particular to the idea of sustainability.

The solution for the Israeli-Palestinian conflict has been on the table so long and is so obvious that one would almost rather not talk about it. The equation 'land for peace' – Israel's withdrawal to the approximate borders as they were in 1967. Where settlements in West Jordan are to remain Israeli territory there must be an exchange of territory under fair conditions (good land for good land, not desert for farmland), and Jerusalem's Old City becomes Arab again. With Jerusalem becoming the capital city of both countries, the Palestinian refugees of 1948 would receive generous compensation payments and forego (except for a symbolic number) returning to their original settlement areas (lying in Israel). The Palestinian state would receive effective security forces, but not an army with sophisticated weaponry. The international community would provide generous economic aid for building Palestine's infrastructure and forming a Middle East economic community, and the Palestinian state would make every effort to fight terror. It would be important for the Israelis not to overreact after the first attack (especially because the Palestinians will certainly also be targeted by fanatics); both must wait patiently for living conditions to improve and thus help dry out the swamp in which new terrorist recruits thrive.

All of this is not new. The Geneva Accord formulated by NGOs contains all these elements which reject and oppose the fanatics on both sides, the national-religious Israeli movements and parties and the Islamist utopians. Only when the international community led by the US fully backs this accord can the issue be settled.

Peace enforcement and humanitarian intervention: who decides and under what circumstances?

As has become obvious, I am making an appeal for rehabilitation of the institution of the state as a protective wall against war and for a corresponding basic prohibition against intervention, as stipulated in Article 2.7 of the UN Charter. 'Basic' of course means that rare, narrowly defined exceptional cases are permitted: drastic crimes against humanity, genocide and the toleration of cross-border terrorist acts initiated on the territory of a state which refuses to or is unable to prevent these acts. This is not a 'Western' program any longer, but instead is already covered by international law and the practice of the international community: since 'Operation Provide Comfort' to aid the Iraqi Kurds and Shi'ites, mandating humanitarian interventions by the Security Council of the United Nations has made clear that beyond the Western camp, too, the limits of arbitrariness, which national governments may not cross in dealing with their own citizens, have been recognized. Since 1996 there have been several Security Council resolutions against al-Qaeda, which have ruled that a state is responsible for cross-border acts of terror carried out from its territory. After September 11, 2001, Resolution 1368 recognized the violation of this responsibility as justification for defensive measures according to Article 51. Not long after this the Security Council passed Resolution 1373 specifying that the threat of terrorism was cause for universal emergency legislation by the Security Council under Chapter VII of the UN Charter. This development makes clear that in the real-world battle against terrorism, a universally shared set of norms has been achieved.

The justification for the intervention which was recommended by the UN Secretary-General's 'High-level Panel' in its report (2004) also points in the same direction. This panel was inter-regionally and interculturally representative in an exemplary manner, for its sixteen members came from all regions of the world. The five criteria according to which the panel deems military intervention justifiable are:

1. Seriousness of threat (in the case of internal conflicts: genocide or other comparable large-scale killing, ethnic cleansing or serious violations of international humanitarian law);
2. Proper purpose (no hidden motives for those intervening);
3. Last resort (all other instruments have been exhausted);
4. Proportional means;
5. The consequences of action are not worse than the consequences of inaction.

We have a minimal, consensus-based set of norms with which the 'responsibility to protect' can be implemented in practice in truly extreme cases, without initiating procedures which exclude the rest of the world from the decision-making process and thus push them in the direction of risky self-help projects. For the question of when and where these extreme situations are present and what reaction is called for depends on difficult and complex practical judgments. This makes necessary inclusive procedures which block the effects of the 'cultural uncertainty principle' and the influence of the hidden motives already mentioned. The starting point should be the existing decision-making process embodied in the Charter of the United Nations. There are procedures available there which, de facto, transcend cultural boundaries and are inclusive, and can be meaningfully supplemented. For example, the Security Council could introduce procedural rules specifying that a decision on intervention must always be preceded by a neutral analysis of the situation prepared by an interculturally and inter-regionally representative commission of experts appointed and chaired by the Secretary-General.

The manipulation of the Security Council by secret service information filtered in a biased manner cannot occur again using such a procedure. Only if the analysis of the situation – for the preparation of which time limits must apply – comes to the conclusion that a state is committing genocide or that transnational terror attacks are being supported from its territory should the Security Council be authorized to impose military sanctions. Even the Security Council in its present form requires the Western democracies to convince members from at least three other cultural areas – China and Russia as veto powers, as well as at least one, often two of the non-permanent members, of which the 'West' never accounts for more than three.

This weakens the problem of the 'cultural uncertainty

principle' by institutional means. Expanding the Security Council would further increase the pressure to succeed by argumentation even outside one's own cultural region. That these decisions generally cannot be made in defiance of the vote of the permanent members of the Security Council would lead after appropriate reform of the Security Council (i.e. including India as a permanent member) to the states taking part in the voting representing the majority of the world's population. Veto power itself can also be seen as a serious problem within the Security Council. The way out of the dilemma cannot however amount to falling back on an exclusive privilege of the democracies to choose to make decisions that increase the effect of the 'cultural uncertainty principle' and the destabilizing consequences it has for global security. It is more important, by means of a broader decision making practice – a qualified majority in the Security Council and the General Assembly – to further expand the 'multiculturality' of those making decisions. This would lead to a return to an expanded 'Uniting for Peace' process: through clear majorities (two-thirds would be reasonable) the Security Council and General Assembly would legitimize the actions of the international community in cases where individual veto powers prevented a mandate in the Security Council from being obtained.

Although this is not a 'democratization of world politics,' it still ensures that non-Western players see themselves represented in the decisions made in one way or another. The exclusion, which can justify an intervention against the party being excluded, should not be based on the hegemonial decision of a liberal group of states as to whom they regard as well-ordered or have already labeled a 'villain.' It should instead be based on the concrete offence by the accused state which violates jointly agreed rules of the international community of states, with the infringement being determined neutrally, and counter-measures requiring approval by a significant majority of states. That inclusive multilateral decision-making procedures also help to curb potential abuse by intervening states acting in their own national interest under the cover of 'humanitarian intervention' (for example, to gain control of oil reserves) is an additional benefit.

Conclusions

The conflicts which we are currently dealing with are either resolvable or can be contained until the belligerent parties become exhausted and their disputes can be resolved. Solutions are often obvious – land for peace in the Middle East, the cease-fire line as a border in Kashmir – and do not call for exaggerated creativity. However, this does not mean that they would be easy to achieve. In the case of protracted conflicts, players are so deeply dug in that it is difficult to get them out of the trenches. Both friendly and sometimes unfriendly external pressure is thus necessary.

In the age of globalization and the jeopardizing of the Earth by human activities, warfare is not a useful means of policy between states or at the local level: a major war threatens to wreak mass destruction. Smaller-scale wars prevent millions of people from building a better reality for themselves. Both types of war act as roadblocks to solving our problems. War destroys more goals than it can help achieve. To eliminate war as an institution through which state and local interests can be realized 'by other means' is thus reasoned *realpolitik*, not pacifist fantasizing. The organized use of force must become a 'police action' exception in extreme circumstances – according to the guideline criteria of the 'High-level Panel' – and lie in the hands of the international community, not occur at the whim of individual players.

The problem of control

The task is enough to make your head spin: there are more than six billion people on Earth, up to 6,000 ethnic groups, depending on how you count them, 192 states, and seven to nine major cultures, without even mentioning languages and political systems (see chapter 3). Ideas about what is just differ within cultures and even more between them. And there are enough conflicts and weapons in the world to make these differences dangerous. All this has to be brought into a governable form that will make sustainable solutions to shared problems possible without the major catastrophic violence that would bring an end to all sustainability. In the last three chapters I have developed some ideas about how to attack bit by bit the three main problems: diversity, justice, and avoiding war. In this chapter I would like to give the reasons why the measures adopted, as well as the solutions to global problems, have to be based on the control mechanism *law*. I base this assertion on the argument that the rule of law is preferable to other possible global control mechanisms – power, morality, and the market – not only because of its own special characteristics but also because the others have to be anchored in law in order to make use of their positive control potential and limit their harmful side-effects.

Living in a democratic constitutional state sounds trivial to us: how else could we deal with diversity, justice, and conflicts among ourselves; how else could we get a grip on the way we deal with the environment, the issue of migration, water and energy supplies, social policy, equal rights for women and so on, if not through recourse to law? Of course we make use of administrative procedures, out-of-court measures, mediation, sorting things out for ourselves, and other informal and non-legal instruments. We do this, however, in the comforting certainty that we can always fall back on the legal system. Even though we occasionally find laws nonsensical or wrong, and sometimes feel that judicial verdicts are unjust, the security that our environment, steeped in the law, gives us is priceless.

This becomes apparent above all when one unwittingly finds oneself in a situation where the rule of law does not hold sway, for instance in a collapsed state. Trivial though the sentence 'Let's sort the matter out in court!' sounds to us citizens of a democratic constitutional state, its transfer to the conflict-riddled field of international and transnational affairs is far from something that goes without saying. Is it not the case that, despite all apparent legal advances, in the inhospitable sphere of international relations the rule of the jungle holds sway? Is it not the case that powerful states are willing, without regard for existing treaties and legal regulations, to seize any advantage that opportunity offers? Hasn't the Bush administration shown in the last few years that the law does not apply to the most powerful if it does not wish it to do so? Does talking about international law make any sense?

Before I try to offer an answer to this fateful question, I would like to look at a more fundamental issue. This is not popular with those who regard talk of world government and establishment of the rule of law as idealistic hot air. However, it is necessary in order to cast light on the full extent of the problem we are facing. The question is, what is the alternative? If we assume for a start that humanity has common problems but differing opinions about them – what means are available at all for reaching some sort of result that will not lead to the catastrophe that we all want to avoid?

Means of control

In its entire history, humanity has never been particularly productive when it came to answering the question of how to unite the diverging wishes of the many behind the common goal of survival or increased prosperity. How is it possible to find the common denominator of the varied interests without going through a bloodbath of murder and killing, and despite this to achieve our goals in a more or less effective way? If I understand it correctly, humankind has invented exactly four ways of exercising control: power, the market, morality – and law.

Power

It seems attractive to rely on the exercise of power for this purpose, the ability to impose one's own will even against resistance (Max Weber). As a means of control, power forces all other wills to submit to one. It is capable of holding many conflicting interests in check through the permanent threat of sanctions or the application of force. In this sense it is efficient. The temptation to reply on power in regulating world affairs is great. Those who argue in favor of a new imperial power have succumbed to this temptation, including the representatives of American neo-conservatism who want to capitalize on the current 'unipolar moment' in world history, the short period of absolute American superiority, in order to arrange things once and for all.

In the second chapter we saw that the model of the imperium cannot function under today's conditions. To look at this again: we are not talking about the control and exploitation of limited territories but about world order; and not just about political order but about dealing with innumerable individual problems in such a way that every individual mini-order does not constantly collapse, and has to be built up again from the beginning. An imperium cannot achieve this for reasons that have already been given. And more general reasons that make it clear why no purely power-based system would be in a position to guarantee sustainability can be derived from these reasons. The two most important reasons are practical in nature.

In the first place: control of events through the application of power requires the ubiquitous presence of those who hold power and their representatives; the presence of visible, permanently mobilizable means of imposing sanctions in the immediate vicinity of all places where decisions that must reflect the will of the central power are made. This exceeds the resources of even the strongest state, even when, as in the case of the Roman Imperium or the British Empire, it uses those sections of the 'native' population that are willing to collaborate as extensions of its own power. Under conditions of diversity and demands for justice, any system of regulation based on power produces the dialectic of exercise of power and resistance. Resistance increases the pressure to exert force. The resources that are needed to overcome the resistance increase in proportion to the amount of new resistance provoked by this very application of force. Successful resistance in one place encourages new resistance in others. Concentrated application of force in one region reduces the resources that are available for dealing with resistance in other regions.

The potential of those putting up resistance to cause chaos has become too great to achieve the goals for which power is actually intended. In turn, the demands of the populace are too wide-reaching to allow resources for the more intensive application of power to be made available.

Second: systems based on the exercise of power are of necessity highly centralized. For decentralization breaks up power and leads to dangerous power rivalries, to the 'warlord problem.' However, regulating the processes that are decisive for solving problems is too great a task for the center. That was one of the reasons why the Soviet system functioned worse and worse. The Chinese system did not begin its boom until economic decisions were substantially decentralized. Exercising control involves collecting, receiving, processing and transmitting information. Even in the computer age, the information-processing capacity of central agencies remains limited, because decision-making power is concentrated in too few individuals. Consequently, only two possibilities remain: either all information is processed relatively slowly, and the solving of all problems thus lags behind the emergence of new problems. The result is the catastrophe of doing too little. Or the information for the solution of a few supposedly urgent problems is processed rapidly, but that for other areas blocked. In this case good results are achieved in a few sectors, to be sure, but the neglect of the others risks the breakdown of the entire system. (For example: we handle the climate question successfully, but the supply of drinking water runs out and species that are essential in the food chain die out).

Thus, systems based on the exercise of power are not appropriate for world government. They founder on the impossibility of having credible threats of sanctions for every crisis, on the power/resistance dialectic, and on the information dilemma of centralism. This is not to say, however, that effective control would be possible without any exercise of power. But power cannot be the dominant instrument of control. It must work in combination with more effective instruments, and be subservient to them.

The market

One (allegedly) violence-free regulatory system is the market; this is how the idealized models of economics present it. Until recently this model served especially appealing. The predominant way of thinking tended towards leaving everything up to market forces. This way of thinking is blind to the limitations that even the best functioning market has when it is used for purposes for which its systems of incentives are not appropriate. Significant areas of provision for our existence are entrusted to the market, at the price of neglect of essential needs. Supplying the public with basic necessities, science, justice and law enforcement, yes even sports, lose their functional meaning for the society when they are subordinated to the laws of the market. Four weaknesses disqualify the market as the leading regulatory instrument.

In the first place: the market needs a legal framework: it cannot exist without that. There is too little trust between the economic players for them to enter into large-scale, long-term business arrangements. The law lays down who are legitimate players in the market, what their rights and obligations are, and what corridors of legitimacy there are for agreements (the law of contracts). Even the admirable self-regulation within private enterprise is based, in the final analysis, on the 'shadow of authority' offered by laws backed by the state, on which they can fall back in an emergency.

Second: the necessity of producing public goods, as well as

the externalities that the market produces at the expense of public benefit, make an exclusively market-driven system unsuitable for dealing with problems of globalization. The production of environmentally harmful emissions, for instance, is a logical product of unfettered private enterprise. Only the intervention of higher authorities – through imposition of emission norms, environmental taxes, or trading in emission certificates – brings some relief. For even emission certificates are not a product of the market, but a legal product of the political system. The market makes use of these to fulfill environmental goals. Without action 'from above' the participants in the market would not have given any thought at all to bringing an end to the heedless environmental pollution they were producing.

The same is true of, for instance, the fishing industry: if the politicians do not prescribe quotas, the fishing fleets of the major companies will fish the seas empty, without the slightest inclination towards sustainability. Both nationally and worldwide the market is a nature-destroying Moloch, unless its tendency to low-priced exploitation of anything that is not regulated is opposed. Whether this involves the burning off of natural gas from oilfields or the deforestation of the rainforests, without external regulation the market does not of its own accord produce any public goods that benefit everybody, but which individuals cannot acquire on their own. Participants in the market have to be given incentives to do this, or be forced to do so through instruments from outside the market. The market cannot be blamed for this – it is simply not its job. Only the high priests of neoliberalism must be blamed for not being in a position to recognize the natural limits of the extent to which the market can be steered.

An additional public good that the market cannot create on its own is social justice. At best it provides the means for this. This can be seen on a global scale. The opening up of markets has, on average, brought advances in social welfare. The number of people who can now satisfy their basic needs or even enjoy a modest level of prosperity has increased in both absolute and also relative terms. At the same time, however, the number of the extremely poor has also grown, and they are even poorer than they were before. Certain parts of the world such as central Africa have been cut off from development. This is not only the 'fault' of the market but also a consequence of appalling government in these countries. But the market on its own offers no help to solving the problems of this region. It must also be said that the feeling of being 'disempowered' by the anonymous forces of the world market is risky for the maintenance of political stability. People who see their living conditions as threatened and whose expectations are disappointed look for new orientations, and more easily fall victim to demagogic political opportunists than members of a well-established satisfied middle-class.

Third: as we are just now painfully reminded the market produces unintended side effects which in the long term threaten its own stability. Consequently, the short-sightedness of events in the market exceeds even that of politics, and that is saying something. The financial health of companies (and thus the fate of top managers and ordinary colleagues) is determined nowadays by their quarterly reports. The stock market responds like a seismograph to the slightest rise and fall, because the biggest investors, the American pension funds, have to satisfy the short-term demands of their clients. They buy and sell their stocks from the point of view of making maximum profit as quickly as possible. All this is the result of the fateful decision of America to leave making provision for old age to the market. With a relative increase in the aged population the needs of the companies affected become ever more short-term, for the sums that have to be made available in order to satisfy the needs of their customers are climbing steadily from month to month. In view of the significance these institutional investors have for the stock markets, the orientation of the markets is moving ever further away from sustainability.

Events on the market have – something Karl Marx made into a cornerstone of his fundamental criticism – a tendency towards concentration. Monopoly or oligarchical markets do not, however, function for the purpose of efficient control, but simply provide the favored ones with 'surplus profits', which have to be paid for by the rest. In the absence of any effective global economic regulatory procedures, double exploitation of consumers (they have to pay monopoly prices) and working people develop. It gets even worse when governments mouth neo-liberal catchphrases, to be sure, but their realization is blocked by the interests of well-organized special interest groups, of which Western agribusiness is the prototypical example: the agricultural policies of the EU, the US and Japan are scandalous. It can be seen here that not only an unregulated but also a one-sided market has negative consequences. To function in a sustainable way the market must be protected from its own effects through 'external' measures.

Fourth: an unregulated market is revealed to be amoral. Hedge funds can function as useful investors when banks are unwilling to take risks, but they break up healthy companies too and put their employees out on the street if that promises higher profits. Transport firms ship poisonous waste to developing nations which lack control mechanisms or where the administration is corrupt. Weapons dealers escalate bloody civil wars through their deliveries. The lack of morality of the market seems to reach a peak in the 'war economies' and 'violence markets' in parts of Africa south of the Sahara, or in Columbia. There, the market brings together in orgies of violence warlords, organized crime, and completely legal players on the world market: whoever lives well from war – and that is the way of life of the warlords and their pillaging followers – is not willing to give up war, not even when the opportunity of a peace that is not disadvantageous offers itself. The trade in 'blood diamonds' that maintained the war economies in Sierra Leone, Liberia and Angola – because it motivated the people involved to use violence (to obtain the diamonds) and provided them with the necessary means (through the sale of the looted diamonds) – was suppressed via a combination of moral engagement (of NGOs and churches) and the action of politicians (who yielded to public pressure), but not in any way through the independent action of the market and the companies operating there. They carried out changes only after the public and politicians went on the offensive. Thus, the market does not spontaneously create peace, although most companies flourish better in peaceful conditions than in a violent environment, and thus have at the very least a general interest in promoting peace.

Just as with power, when properly applied the market develops useful regulatory effects. No other instrument makes decisions that are so decentralized, efficient and rapid, and distributes goods and services with less red tape, and in this way helps to promote prosperity. However, the right structural conditions and occasional interventions (or the possibility that such interventions could occur) are needed in order to steer its regulatory function in such a way that the harmful side-effects are avoided and the desired effects occur. To achieve this, the other regulatory instruments have to be put in place and combined with market events in a sensible manner. Unfortunately, we are far from such an ideal, complementary system of fine tuning today, least of all in conflict regions and in weak states.

Morality

Market and morality could not be more different. The first is a relentless mechanism for the efficient distribution of material goods without regard to any normative considerations. The other, full of value-saturated scruples. Occasionally morality prevails among market players. 'Rhineland capitalism' stood out because in addition to profits for the firm it focused on the interests of the workforce and the social welfare of the local community. In US capitalism, supporting good causes and establishing charitable foundations is common as an 'intrinsic obligation' of successful firms and rich individuals. Current efforts to establish self-regulation are introducing moral aspects into companies' dealings ('corporate social responsibility'), admittedly mostly not without external pressure, i.e., as a reaction to 'negative advertising' resulting from scandals and highly vocal NGOs, or in order to fend off more extensive politico-legal measures. These examples of the interaction between morality and market show: morality too can be an effective regulatory instrument. It consists of principles and behavioral norms derived from them which together yield a 'logic of appropriateness': in the ideal case, the members of a morally integrated community know how 'one' should behave appropriately in a particular context. Because everybody knows this and follows the common code, coordinated behavior results. On the basis of their moral code such communities can agree on solutions to new problems that then find their place in the catalog of behavioral norms. To this extent, a moral code is also capable of evolving.

Morality can derive from several sources. One major source is religion. Religious teachings usually consist – apart from ideas about a reality beyond the world and the nature of the sacred, and apart from the creation and redemptive-historical narratives – of explicit, often detailed catalogs of norms; strikingly prominent in these are rules for the sexual behavior of the faithful. These give a particular priesthood power over followers of their religion through the pressure of conscience and the power to impose sanctions. For the rules are of such a kind that breaches are certain to occur: morality becomes the handmaiden of power. Religious morality is above all characterized by a claim to absolute validity, because it is not laid down by humans but is of divine origin, and is thus not subject to any discussion but can only be obeyed. Frequently originally derived from religious traditions, but secularized in the course of history, are moral rules based on tradition ('One doesn't do that,' 'What will people say?'). They can no longer claim absolute validity; it is possible to argue against them and rebel, without the community being challenged being able to react with the big stick of the accusation of heresy, excommunication, and the like. The community is forced at the end – after shock, indignation and attempts at sanctions – to engage in a process of debate, and can even be the loser in this.

The German debate about the 'guiding culture' is a demonstration of the difficulties into which a moral code based on tradition can get when it is challenged. Appealing to the 'Christian-Western tradition' must also carry the stigma of pogroms against the Jews, the Inquisition and the burning of 'witches'. It also comes into unpleasant conflict with binding basic principles of the constitution, which forbid giving preferential treatment to any particular religion, ideology or value system – apart from the values anchored in the constitution itself. As an instrument of control, morality can thus find itself on shaky ground when external circumstances change rapidly and new generations are no longer willing to accept the traditional 'logic of appropriateness' and universally agreed-upon new basic principles are not (yet) available.

Once tradition has begun to be fundamentally questioned and religion has also lost its binding effect, such basic principles can only be derived from a rational discourse within a community which shares basic principles and norms. Such a moral code is, however, constantly confronted by the risk that people will not be willing to follow it. It is no longer sufficiently binding to produce harmonious day-to-day interactions among the members of the society, and its principles are not sufficiently binding to function as a foundation for finding new solutions to problems.

When this line of thought is transferred to the problems of world government it immediately becomes obvious that we cannot find an adequate basis for joint control here. Assertions that we are already living in an age of worldwide culture are based on observation of superficial phenomena (music, clothing, etc.), and overlook the differences in people's values. For there is no world morality; what is referred to in this way in liberal philosophy is nothing more than an attempt to universalize the basic principles of their own culture. Just how divided the world is in this respect is demonstrated by the fundamentalization of world religions. Even if you are no supporter of the thesis of a 'clash of civilizations' their contradictions are so readily visible that you would not want to depend upon moral principles for controlling world problems. Moral unity capable without any further effort of leading to the production of solutions to problems based on common basic principles does not exist.

Nonetheless – just as with power and the market – morality is not without its usefulness for the problems which we are facing. Almost all religion-based moral systems include at some point respect for the creation and the duty to live in harmony with nature. This helps as a basis for the promotion of sustainable environmental policies. Many moral and religious systems include the commandment of solidarity with the less fortunate

– this makes the debate about measures for global redistribution easier; the reality is that development policy in the West has been based from the beginning (even if by no means exclusively) on a bad conscience driven by the norm of solidarity or charity. Elements of differing moral systems that overlap or are even identical in content, even though the systems are quite different from each other, can form the starting point for discussions of joint measures. They also help to anchor the measures in the particular ethical systems of the individual societies, because the people recommending the global measures can show that what was jointly agreed upon is compatible with what the ethical system in question calls for, or is even demanded by it.

The 'world conferences' staged by the United Nations on global issues such as environment, population, or the rights of women are global laboratories, in which work on the development of a world moral code can be carried on. The agitated controversies at these conferences show how difficult this task is. The strange coalitions – for instance between Saudi Arabia, the Vatican, Iran and the United States against medical forms of birth control – demonstrate surprising accords. The closing statements of the conferences as well as the documents produced by participating NGOs raise hope that agreement on a 'basic charter of universal values' will not be impossible in the long run. Then moral values which so often intensify conflicts could serve as a foundation for the most useful of all control instruments that are available to us: for the rule of law.

The law

After writing and the wheel, law is perhaps the cleverest invention in the history of humankind. No other instrument is able to coordinate the behavior of so many people continuously and across so large an area with such a minimum of direct compulsion, and yet remain so flexible and adaptable. These characteristics – coordination of great numbers, extension across space and time, and adaptability – mean that the law is uniquely able to serve world governance too. The law – purged of the sprinklings of power, morality and the market – is according to its basic conceptualization a general system of binding rules that applies to all legal partners, whose purpose is to minimize the risky and expensive application of force, and which only certain specialized authorities are authorized to enforce via sanctions. Both the creation of law – and also its application – obey rules based on law. Thus, the law is binding for all. A society based on the rule of law is a constitutional state (but not necessarily a democratic one – the law is not required to prescribe elections and does not have to allow freedom of speech or the formation of coalitions). In absolutist states, in slave-holding societies, or in dictatorships the law is the slave of power, in theocracies of morality, in corrupt states the servant of the market. It is true that in these cases the law functions as a useful appendage of another, dominant instrument of control. In all three cases, however, its goal of minimizing force as the means of domination is restricted; this makes all the difference. For, as a result it sacrifices substantial elements of its capability for comprehensive coordination, namely its capability to motivate the largest possible number of the people it addresses, i.e., those affected by it, to accept it without the constant application of coercive force or open threats.

From the perspective of sustainability, the time dimension of the law deserves special respect. The law is *enduring*. Its stipulations basically have no time limits, unless they are altered by means of prescribed procedures. This continuity gives it permanence, which is consistent with the requirements of sustainability. On the other hand, the fact that changes are possible when changing circumstances require them makes the law malleable in the face of surprises. It does not collapse when it is confronted with new challenges, but is re-shaped in such a way that it has answers for these challenges too. Continuity and flexibility are the interacting complementary prerequisites for making the control instrument law sustainable. It is the law that assigns other instruments of control – power, morality and the market – to their place in a well-structured worldwide system of behavioral coordination.

The law and power

Unbridled power is the greatest enemy of the law, for those holding the power use it ruthlessly in the pursuit of their own interests, free of a legal basis and trampling on the rights of other people (or other states). On the other hand, without the power to impose sanctions the law is toothless. This does not mean that law needs power to impose direct sanctions at any time and place. Exactly the opposite is the case: the law is respected by most legal partners, both individuals and collectives, most of the time, without the threat of direct sanctions dogging every step of everybody. However, the shadow of this power remains unforgotten in the background. The possibility of threatening force in extreme cases, and also of being able to apply it, is a prerequisite for every system of law. Under normal circumstances it functions without force; this is its point in the practical exercise of control. When confronted with dangerous or hardened habitual lawbreakers the responsible agencies have the task of defending the integrity of the law, although under precisely defined circumstances.

Power must be the servant of the law. Only then are the two attuned to each other. Power exists to help the law overcome every challenge. It has no other purpose. Any goal going further than this would compromise the law and elevate the quantum of force that is necessary for social stability. Power must be harnessed for the purposes of the law, and must bow to it willingly and without plotting behind its back. No-one in power can stand above the law or refuse when the law calls for help in gaining the upper hand against lawbreakers. This relationship – power subservient to the law – is the only one that will flourish. That the laws that are in force reflect in a milder form existing power relationships (see below) is not contradicted by this statement. The subordination of power to the law has far-reaching consequences for systems of order based on the law. This principle protects the many different kinds of subjects of such systems from the arbitrary actions of the powerful. Their own autonomy – as is that of players who have access to greater resources – is limited only by the stipulations of the law. When a state of inequality exists in material reality the law reduces this, at least in principle: it makes those who are unequal equal. That below the level of formal equality before the law, access to law-related privileges exists only for the wealthy, for instance access to highly-skilled lawyers who are completely unaffordable for normal consumers or the ability to hold out to the (where the judgment is negative, bitter) end in the appeals process is the reality. It can be seen that the law in our actually-existing democratic constitutional states has bowed to the market in a certain sense, i.e., there has been a departure from the ideal model.

Equality must exist as a principle on the 'output' side of the law. On the 'input' side it is not necessarily so. Different levels of availability of resources give players differing chances of influencing the substance of the law. Logically, the law will always reflect the interests of the stronger somewhat more than those of the weaker. In a confrontation between the strong and the weak outside the legal framework, however, the strong would win out completely. A legally-defined procedure for making laws that leads to rules that apply for all modifies this power discrepancy. To that extent, a system of law in which the weaker have the chance to participate, even if not exactly the same chance as the stronger, represents progress in comparison with a power-based 'natural state of affairs.' When, as in a democracy, all those affected by the law participate indirectly in law-making through the election of representatives, this advantage increases.

In addition, this asymmetry in the way the law operates is the basic reason why the strong accept, without complaining too loudly, the advanced level of equality of treatment of people subjected to the law, on the 'output' side. That their interests are protected makes the bitter pill – of not being able to make use of their superior power resources in representing those interests – sufficiently palatable to avoid rebellion against the system. The law creates a balance between weak and strong by giving the weaker better chances of being successful than in the 'natural state', but without entirely leveling out the asymmetry, so that the stronger 'toe the line.' The rest is taken care of by the power to impose sanctions that backs up the law and exerts pressure to play by the rules of the system, if you please, on both rebellious weaker participants and arrogant stronger ones.

In the relationship of the law and power the most significant advantage of a legally-constituted system is that in solving conflicts the law offers a chance of reducing the application of force to a minimum that could not be achieved with any other approach. This chance results from two characteristics of the law: its strongly normative nature and the special way it structures the incentives to maintain the law or offer violent resistance. The law, as a set of rules that are binding on everybody and accepted by most people and conform in the main to prevailing ethical norms (see next section), generates strong expectations of one's own behavior in the social environment, and thus promotes a substantial internal tendency to conform. This tendency is probabilistic, i.e., it is a probability that does not hold everywhere and always, but for the overwhelming majority most of the time and in most situations, while it does not inhibit small breaches of the law, but does block large-scale violent rebellion.

The violence-inhibiting effect of the law derives secondly from the way it adjusts the incentives for the various players to consider offering violent resistance: the powerful see themselves as better represented in the existing system of law because it reflects their interests more than those of others. The weaker see more of their interests supported than they would ever be able to hope to achieve in a direct confrontation with the powerful. Thus, the incentive for changing existing conditions by force is reduced for both groups. The threat of sanctions against the lawbreaker completes what is needed to load the scales of the pros and cons against the option of using force. And finally, the law offers the chance of settling conflicts at less cost than would be possible through a violent uprising. The rule of law does not completely exclude the use of violence. But it narrows down the situations where force may legitimately be used, by removing them from the whim of private individuals. Its application is strictly limited to stopping lawbreakers from disrupting good order. In the normal course of events the use of force has no place in interactions between private parties.

The law consists of sets of commandments and prohibitions, per-
missions, authorizations, and conditions, i.e., of a wide variety
of very different norms. After some thinking, moral principles
can be recognized underlying many legal norms. There is a connection between the moral code of a society and its legal code. It
is not a one-to-one correspondence. The law can lag behind the
moral code; extramarital sex was commonplace at a time when
'adultery' was still grounds for divorce and imposed a material
burden on the 'guilty' party. The reverse can be true; the law can
be more advanced than the moral code. Abolition of the death
penalty occurred in Germany before a majority of the citizenry
was opposed to it. A society can survive such time lags. If there
were no longer any overlap at all between the moral code and the
law, if the society's moral consciousness and the system of laws
became completely different from each other, the stability of the
society would be endangered.

The law differs from the moral code through its formally
specified sanctions – this is also true for international law, which
contains the rules for reacting to infringements of the law. The
moral code leaves the reaction to a breach of the rules up to
each member of the community. The possible consequences are
chaotic, and nobody has a guarantee against being punished
by segments of the moral community for behaviors that he or
she judged to be appropriate. As the guardian of the law, the
state guarantees to uphold the legal norms and, if necessary, to
compel compliance with them. The legitimate application of
force is available as the most extreme measure for achieving this.
The constitutional state by no means categorically rejects its
application, but bans force as a universally available instrument
for pursuing one's interests. It restricts the authority to use it to

certain office-holders (e.g., the police), under defined conditions and under strict procedural rules.

At the same time, specialization of the agencies that impose sanctions avoids three risks to which a 'free floating' moral code exposes a society. First, the law is binding for the sanctioning agencies too. They have to handle the same things in the same way and different things differently. This limits their freedom of action. Second, the law limits the possibility of imposing moral claims. Third, it prevents moral anarchy: it is not possible for someone who regards him or herself as possessing absolute truths to impose these on fellow human beings by any means available. It is true that the society too imposes sanctions against morally deviant behavior for which there is no commandment of tolerance or the commandment is not universally accepted. Unmarried couples have a hard time even today in many towns and villages. The sanctions are, however, restricted to symbolic acts. In addition, unlawful sanctions (for instance setting fire to an unmarried couple's house) are forbidden in the criminal law, and action is taken against them by the responsible authorities. The chaotic consequences of the blurring of the boundaries between the authority to impose legally-prescribed and symbolic sanctions can be seen in those Islamic societies where self-appointed guardians of morality harass people who follow a liberal moral code, and in this way a destabilizing potential for violence develops. Reining in this potential for violence requires that the law take precedence over morality.

The linking of law and morality in a society has the advantage that the two kinds of argument can relate to each other. The justification for new laws is often based – in addition to its practical task of laying down binding guidelines for conflicts or coordinating decisions – on the moral principles that the society is bound by. This sometimes causes controversies to break out about what these principles really mean: think of the current debate on stem cell research. If you bear in mind how hotly these issues are debated in what is a morally relatively homogenous society, one can appreciate how difficult it is to create widely accepted, valid international law, step by step. The variety of moral systems in the world initially seems to make the chance of problem-free justification for legal norms a hopeless endeavour. But, at the same time, this enterprise is not really hopeless. For the interpretation of cultural ethics, i.e., our own social moral code is also highly controversial in specific questions: see divorce, the death penalty or stem cell research. Despite these disputes, making laws and reaching verdicts based on the laws succeeds. Various methods are responsible for this success: the ranking of one ethical norm above another contradictory one, their ranging alongside each other in an ambivalent legal formulation; their merging, and their situation-specific interpretation in practical legal application. Like all language, the language of laws is not unambiguous but requires interpretation, just as it also makes interpretation possible. Basically, the same methods can also be applied in transnational and international settings.

For world governance there are three ways of working on this problem. The first is *via acquis*, the total body of international law that has been achieved so far. These function as basic reference points for the further development of legal rules for new problems. However, we should not overlook the problem that substantial sections of international law date back to the period of Western hegemony, and younger states often cannot relate to these rules. For example, the principle of 'freedom of the seas' in contrast to the ocean as a 'common heritage of mankind' originally reflected the interests of the great seafaring powers against those who got the worst of the distribution struggles. This example shows how questions of justice – i.e., moral issues

– spill over into the regulation of practical interests – namely the distribution of economic resources. The more inclusively the further development of international law occurs, i.e., the more it reflects the interests of the different states and regions and their cultures, the more it will be based on a gradually developing world moral code instead of a set of values laid down by the West and forced on the rest.

The second way is based on the moral commonalities between cultures. This is not an empty set, as the world ethics project of Hans Küng and other cross-cultural studies have shown. Where islands of common belief exist – for instance in the fundamental agreement that there should be a certain leveling out between the rich and poor of the world, in the shared commitment to saving the environment, in the rejection of nuclear war or terrorism – it is true that this does not guarantee agreement on the concrete form of relevant measures. But it does offer a basic set of values that greatly facilitates joint efforts to develop such measures. I have already discussed the third way in chapter 4: representatives of the various countries work out legal solutions to concrete problems within the existing process of international negotiations, in which all world regions (and thus world cultures) are represented. In a second step, ethics experts filter out of such solutions the moral principles which – possibly unarticulated – have been incorporated into the compromise. For the negotiators will not agree to any solution which totally contradicts their value system.

Once this path from practical formulation to abstract principles has been followed, this principle, in which the various value systems are embedded, can be used in the future as a basic framework for developing new law. A fruitful circular process from the practical legal compromise to the basic moral principle that underlies the law and then back to practical lawmaking develops.

In this way inroads are made into the jungle of cultural diversity and diverging conceptualizations of justice.

The law and the market

Kant already understood that trade cannot flourish without a legal framework. His 'cosmopolitan law,' which is cautiously formulated, was for him the prerequisite for economic relations to be able to develop. To the visitor (interested in trade) it guarantees integrity of person, body and goods, and to the land offering the right to visit safety from, for instance, any hostile intentions. This creates mutual trust, which frees the economic interaction from fear of the application of force.

This way of looking at things is still relevant today. This is shown by doubts about the rule of law in China. There, on the one hand, the interests of workers carry hardly any weight, and on the other, property rights (namely rights in intellectual property such as patents and copyright) are not observed. Once the euphoria about opportunities in the Chinese market fades, greater reticence and even withdrawal from China could be the result – at least once similar opportunities become available in regions with a higher level of legal security, for instance in India or Singapore. The first function of the law in its relationship with the market is thus: the law must lay down a framework within which participants in the market can operate in safety. Sustainable economic relationships going beyond single successful transactions must be able to rely on legal guarantees. The second function derives from the side-effects of events on the market, what economists call 'externalities,' such as for instance environmental pollution. Only legal barriers raised by politics can steer economic activities in a direction that is reconcilable with private and public interest in a natural environment that is capable of surviving.

The market creates chances of advancement but also chronic inequity. A certain percentage of these inequities may be socially useful, because they offer an incentive that motivates the less well-off to increased productivity, which thus – in that they pursue their most basic interests – simultaneously serves the common good. Admittedly, the market has no sensory organs with which to measure the critical point at which this positive incentive becomes injustice, destabilizing frustration, and anger. Anyone who slaves away for a lifetime without ever receiving the hoped-for reward, whoever as a young worker enters the work world in the expectation of a poverty-stricken old age, will have little sympathy for the social and political institutions that pre-destine this fate. Without a legal right to social compensation for extremely unequal initial opportunities, the future of our community would be resting on feet of clay. The law offers the chance to ensure minimal standards of distributive justice among otherwise extremely unequal players.

In the welfare state, this practice went without saying. Even after its reconstruction and tightening up it would be fatal to believe that we can do without it and trust the benevolence of the market. The market is blind to questions of justice. The law has to help it out. Something that is as true within nation-state as worldwide. And it holds for the whole area of 'public good which, without legal rules, do not come into existence. T market is thus a fantastic instrument for reaching the des level of performance as economically as possible. This proj can be made use of for 'governance.' However, it only fun for the general good when it is protected by the law, is s by the law into avoidance of 'externalities' and social in and when the law, through the exercise of its authority, it with services that it cannot provide for itself. The market and the law round each other out splendidly, as long as the law has the upper hand.

The flexibility of the law

The times change and circumstances become different. For this reason, nothing that is intended to help solve practical problems can be written in stone. This is also true for the law. Above all, four aspects of change must be recognized and utilized: a shift in power relationships in favor of previously underprivileged, upwardly motivated groups, which must – appropriately dampened down – be reflected in the system of laws; technological progress that demands new ways of regulating authorization, permission, limitation and prohibition (think of the Internet or biotechnology); the discovery of new problems that demand a solution (and are often linked with new technical conditions); and the emergence of new rights, demands, values, and moral codes which people would like to see cast in the law. In addition to these changes set in motion from outside the law, it has its own internal dynamics, which makes an important contribution to change. This dynamic derives from the internal legal discourse, whether in faculties of law or judges' verdicts, which constantly creatively develop current law anew.

The law is flexible, because in addition to substantive law – which lays down the norms that we all have to observe – there is also procedural law, which determines the way we reach binding decisions, whether in order to apply existing law or to alter its norms and rules. Every system of laws has its procedure for making changes. In absolutism or dictatorships it is simply the will of the ruler, in non-democratic constitutional states the

decisions of ruling coalitions, in democracies a process of deliberation and the making of decisions by the lawmaking authority, the parliament. The stability of the law and the apparently
ineradicable conservatism of the political class (but perhaps of
the electorate too), the sheer difficulty of establishing a balance
between pluralistic or federal social interests, means that updates
often come too late; in dictatorships, in which necessary reforms
might endanger the position of the ruler, they are often neglected
for long periods of time. Some time or other, however, revisions
occur, and the law is once again up-to-date.

In this connection, the law has an advantage over power
(which displays its own self-threatening resistance to change),
but the market is better still – as long as it is not distorted by
monopolistic or oligarchic structures – except that it produces
externalities that bring new situations with them, while in terms
of stability and flexibility morality ranks equal to or just behind
the law. It sometimes moves faster than the law (as in the case
of the sexual mores of the late 1960s), but sometimes remains
behind it (as in the question of the death penalty). In any case,
the law, with its legally stipulated procedures for making laws, is
flexible enough to carry out its control function.

International law

Well and good – but we are talking here about the situation
outside nation-states. Is everything that has been said about the
possibilities and the limitations of the law, about its cooperation
with and separate functions from other instruments of coordination and control, also true for the allegedly toothless paper
tiger of international law? If it is, we would be back at the question at the beginning of the chapter. Is it clever and justified to

entrust international law with the huge task of being the central instrument of effective world governance? Would this not hopelessly overload the supposedly weak normative nature of this shaky institution? As the American specialist in international law, Louis Henkin, pointedly put it many years ago, most legal partners (i.e. states) obey the regulations of international law in most cases and most of the time. Thus, international law does not perform any worse than domestic law. After all, every one of my readers has crossed the street on a red light, and most readers have exceeded the speed limit, cheated a little bit on their tax return, and so on. Admittedly, international law does not have the same powers of enforcement as domestic law does: the police and prosecutors are required to pursue breaches of the law, and if they do not do so they can be held to account, upon which another agency of our legal system springs into action. In the international system no-one, not even the Security Council, is required to do so: the Security Council itself defines the situations in which it regards international peace and security as endangered, and then takes action. There is no possibility of making a complaint about its inactivity – look at Rwanda 1994. But how, under these circumstances, does international law generate such an astonishing degree of conformity among its legal partners?

The effectiveness of international law rests on seven pillars. First, many provisions of international law are in the obvious interest of the states. They might perhaps do this or that somewhat differently – and for this reason legal regulations are important in order to coordinate their behavior – but all in all they feel that their national interests are well represented in the relevant provisions, and consequently willingly conform to them. Second, governments understand that individual provisions may painfully run counter to their wishes and that they perhaps might well prefer the entire way things are regulated to be somewhat different, but that a completely unregulated state of affairs would be even worse than the currently existing, not always pleasing set of rules and norms. They thus accept existing law as the lesser of two evils, not because they stand behind its contents out of complete conviction.

Third, because of the nature of its particular obligations, international law exerts strong normative pressure to conform. Above, I characterized this as a general property of the law, and it is also true for international law as a part of the whole. Because it is prevailing law, the appropriate behavior for a good 'world citizen,' i.e., a sovereign state anchored in the community of nation-states, is to follow its norms – even independently of their particular content. Fourth, those who are less than enamored of current provisions still have a chance to work at changing them. After all, the law is flexible. The treaty partners, as well as the International Court of Justice, can re-interpret treaties; the nation-states can – with some difficulty – also change them. It is even possible to withdraw from a treaty if the level of injury to one's own interests becomes too painful. International law does not condemn to perpetual suffering or even second-class status any state that is – allegedly or in actuality – disadvantaged by various provisions. It offers the chance of change through a 'struggle for justice.' This prospect keeps many in line. This interpretability of international law has, however, the disadvantage that it gives nation-states the possibility of claiming that their own deviant behavior is consistent with international law – even in the Iraq War of 2003 the coalition of the willing claimed that it was acting legally. In order to strengthen international law's ability to regulate global events, therefore, more provision for binding interpretations of laws needs to be made.

Fifth, all nation-states are concerned about their reputation.

They have to live with their legal partners in an enduring community of states. They want their own interests to be taken into account and respected by the others. Once a state has acquired a reputation as a lawbreaking thug the help of friends fails to materialize when it is needed. For example, a chronic lawbreaker can hardly reckon with sufficient support when it is a candidate for a non-permanent seat on the Security Council. Its citizens find it more difficult to obtain leadership positions in international organizations. 'Shaming and blaming,' public denunciation of lawbreakers in international forums, has more than a merely symbolic effect. It lowers a state's prestige, with substantial material consequences.

Sixth, sanctions loom as writing on the wall. Offenses against the law are often not subjected to sanctions, but sometimes they are. The lawbreaker does not know in advance whether they will be or not, apart from the permanent members of the Security Council, who can use their veto to prevent sanctions against themselves. Otherwise, the risk of sanctions hangs constantly over the head of the evildoer as a sword of Damocles – in extreme cases, a military intervention ordered by the Security Council under Chapter VII of the UN Charter, with the explicit purpose or the side-effect of a change of regime. It is not (unlike within a national framework) a certain, but a possible risk, and to this extent has a deterrent effect against committing major breaches of the law. In this process, the rule of thumb holds that the more serious the offence committed (and the further the delinquent stands from the permanent members of the Security Council) the higher the probability of sanctions.

Seventh, in practice the 'transnational process of law' (Harold Koh) results in nation-states mostly obeying international law. They are embedded in an array of legal relationships with other nation-states (and their courts), with international organizations

– including the International Court of Justice – and with non-state players, all of whom respond when the law is broken. The ongoing, lawful activities of the lawbreaking state are thus deeply disturbed, and this disturbance has to be weighed against the supposed interest that led to the breach of the law. In most cases these considerations lead to behavior consistent with the law in the first place.

Power, the world market, the 'clash of civilisations' and international law

International law must somehow come to terms with the other candidates which could function as regulatory instruments for sustainable global governance. What is its relationship with the power hierarchy of the nation-states in the international system, with the world market, which apparently forces even the most powerful to conform, or with morality, which has increased in influence in the last three decades, mainly in the form of a revitalization of religious activity? In looking at this question I would like to indicate in a cautious way the direction in which rules derived from international law and their products should develop in the interest of sustainability.

International law and international power relationships

The most telling objection to international law comes from the school of 'realists': they regard international law as an attractive way of embellishing power relationships. The strong hold to it as long as it serves their interests. Once this is no longer the case, they break it. This skeptical assessment correctly describes a portion of the reality. However, even powerful states submit to rules of international law that demand sacrifices from them. The US government appeals to the World Trade Organization when it believes that America's trade interests are being harmed without authorization. Germany goes to great lengths to fulfill its obligations under the Kyoto Protocol, even though this brings financial strain and perhaps even (temporary) competitive disadvantage for the most energy-intensive industrial sectors. Of the seven reasons for following international law, at least a few hold true for large states too. Admittedly the power problem should not be trivialized. The shameless way the Bush administration broke international law (in the Iraq War), refused to join in important measures (Kyoto Protocol, International Criminal Court) or sabotaged their coming into existence (Biological Weapons Protocol) offers depressing evidence of the vulnerability of international law when the lawbreaker or law resister is the 'toughest kid in town.' In this case, the community of nations has few resources for making the evildoer see reason. State-imposed economic sanctions pose too great a risk for the initiators, because the delinquent can strike back effectively. Military sanctions could even set off a world war. Alliances cause partners right from the start to express criticism extremely mildly, to remain silent, or to take the side of the rule-breaker, like lapdogs. None of these three behaviors is appropriate for giving international law what it needs: the chance of establishing itself even against strong resistance.

Help can only be expected from two sources. The first is recognition by the strong of their long-term interests. When hegemony and imperialism cannot solve the problems that the leader or the imperial power must overcome, when power is an expensive way of imposing compliance, whose use weakens those having the power the more they have to apply it, then it is in their interest also to make compromises that support the law. Gaining insight into the necessity of doing without short-term superficial advantages in the interest of long-term optimization of one's real goals is difficult for all great powers; you can see from this that a collective consisting of a large number of intelligent people has considerable difficulty functioning above the mental level of a four-year-old. Fortunately, however, this handicap occasionally gives way to insight, without which international law would have it even tougher. The second source is the power of the civil society. This is greater than it itself supposes (see below).

International law and the world market

The law must establish a framework for the world market, and by doing so set limits to its actions. Elements of such a system of laws already exist, but not in a fully developed form. A long overdue basic principle that is consistent with the market is fair access to Western markets for products from developing nations. This would bring an end to the privileged status of agriculture, as well as to the reckless preference for non-competitive industries (dockyards, steel, textiles, and coal), which many industrialized countries still permit themselves. The costs are shared in the common misery of unemployed people in the particular industries in the developing countries and the consumers in our latitudes, while the successful lobbyists live it up to celebrate their successful attacks on the global common good. A second principle could be the establishment of minimum social standards that rise in step with growing per capita income.

Until now the demand for such minimum standards has run up against the collective defensive wall of the developing nations. They remind us of the phase of 'Manchester capitalism' in the West, which Marx and Engels described critically and accurately

– without, however, the farsightedness to see how the dynamic nature of this capitalism would ultimately change the fate of the working class for the better, in a way that was unimaginable for these two authors. With this reminder, the developing nations claim the right to pass through the same period of exploitation in order to progress along the path to prosperity. With a certain degree of justification they protest that those in favor of uniform, universally applying, minimum social standards – for instance Western trade unions – are only interested in securing the privileges of their clients, without any consideration of the development prospects of the poorer two-thirds of the world.

Minimum standards for the poorest nations too would have to be set at such a level that the competitive advantage of lower wages would be maintained, but at the same time avoiding a social dumping race among developing nations, in order to attract investors through ever lower wages. A third principle should be an (enforceable) obligation to behave in ecologically-friendly ways, on a sliding scale according to level of prosperity. Obligations would also bind the poor nations (with appropriate compensation that obligated the rich to give aid). The line of argument here runs parallel to the one for the social issue: since the Western nations behaved until recently like environmental vandals, and still have by far the highest level of harmful emissions on their conscience, the developing nations claim the right – especially those that are on the way up such as China or India – to be permitted to make their own contribution to ruining nature, until they have reached the level of affluence of the West. In the meantime, this short-sighted dogma is giving way to the realization that the self-produced environmental damage is hindering development, and their own interests thus suggest they should follow a different developmental path from the West, one that is oriented towards environmental compatibility from the start.

Fourth, for companies operating internationally there should be universal rules regulating their relationships with host countries and their populations; the UN Draft Norms on Business and Human Rights make a start in this direction. These would include ecologically-sound economic behavior, tax morality that conforms to the law, and respect for social standards and labor laws and the norms of technical safety/occupational health and safety. Of great importance is the prohibition of corruption. Corporations should be required to compensate their host countries for harm to public welfare resulting from their bribery activities, but under the condition that the corrupt officials who are recipients of the money paid or the favors granted are punished. In return, the host nations must give legally enforceable guarantees of the security of material and intellectual property, which can only be revoked under the condition (and through an orderly procedure) that the corporations on their part have not fulfilled their obligations or when, let us say, a national health emergency makes exceptional measures necessary.

Fifth, compensation for the social and ecological consequences of global economics would have to be established. The most practicable and sensible suggestions that have been tabled until now are the Tobin tax on short-term currency speculation and a surcharge on air traffic. In both cases the suggestions would be at the expense of comparatively well-off players, and could be used to help less well-off people or to support environmental policy measures in poor countries. Taxes collected on CO_2 emissions, on the 'ecological rucksack' (see *The Earth: Natural Resources and Human Intervention*, by Friedrich Schmidt-Bleek in this series) or the 'ecological footprint' (also in this series, *Our Planet: How Much More Can Earth Take?* by Jill Jäger) of products affect the wallet more widely, but also promise even larger environmentally-friendly effects. The rights and duties which derive from these measures need to be legally codified. Most effective would be to include especially serious offences against such codified rules – e.g., behavior grossly harmful to the environment or corruption at the expense of poor nations – in the crimes that are prosecuted by the International Criminal Court, in the event that the country of origin or residence does not of its own volition institute criminal proceedings. Managers found to be responsible for corrupt practices in their companies would not then be able to travel internationally without risking being arrested and sentenced. A dictator or a general with war crimes to answer for would probably be able to cope with an effective ban on travel. But for business people that would be the end of their careers.

International law and morality

There is no universal moral code, but at most weakly developed forerunners that are not sufficient to form the foundation of a coherent system of law. Even the Universal Declaration of Human Rights, an example of 'soft' law, can only be regarded with great caution as a manifestation of such a moral code. For it came into existence at a time when the Western nations still clearly dominated the United Nations. Anyone who is shocked that numerous countries are not putting the declaration into practice in their own political behavior should remember that the West ignores with equal determination the conventions on economic, social, and cultural rights that conform less well to its own liberal-individualistic convictions. This selectivity in connection with those international conventions that most closely resemble a codified moral system arouses misgivings. Thus, the job must be done in a different way.

International law should be understood as the decisive instrument for dealing with the risks of violence that result from collisions between differing moral codes – yes, differing universalisms. How that can happen has been demonstrated by the United Nations in the case of terrorism. Until today, it has not been possible to agree on a common definition of this concept. Despite this, there are thirteen individual agreements on combating terrorism. How was that possible? Very simple – because states which did not want to define terrorism in general terms because 'one person's terrorist is someone else's freedom fighter' were able to agree that certain specific acts by non-state players are undoubtedly terrorist in nature, and are opposed to the interests (and the moral codes) of everybody, i.e., airplane hijackings, the kidnapping, mistreatment and killing of diplomats, or nuclear attacks.

Two conclusions can be drawn. In the first place: the fact that a universal moral code does not exist makes it difficult in international settings to create new laws step-by-step, in order to provide a framework for finding answers to the challenges of globalization. Difficult; but not hopeless. It is only necessary to understand clearly that – unlike lawmaking within the framework of a functioning nation-state – no common moral code is 'there' which could support the law; but on the contrary, it develops alongside the body of law. It is perhaps consoling to remember that in the great developmental phases in the history of the Western countries morality and law also developed in spurts, and the moral aspects were extremely contentious (for instance in the religious wars), and were not a stable, established foundation for lawmaking. Second: the worst thing to do in this difficult situation is to seek to establish a universal moral code through extralegal means by imposing one's own particular moral code on the opponents by force, in order later to establish a new system of

laws on this basis. With this we have reached the greatest challenge of the present with which the global system of laws was
confronted: the head-on attack of American neo-conservatism
on international law.

The neoconservative attack

Since the offensive of the axis powers against international law,
no attempt has been made to break open the foundation of international law which has been as serious as that of American neo-
conservatism, which the Congress began in 1994 and the Bush
administration adopted as the basis of government. Of course,
the motives were completely different. For the fascist regimes of
Germany, Italy and Japan international law was an unwelcome
barrier to their efforts to win through conquest a dominant position for their own blood in the Darwinian competition between
peoples and races. The aim of the Bush administration was to
use the 'unipolar moment' offered by the irresistible worldwide
superiority of the US to achieve the final victory for democracy
and private enterprise. Looked at in this way, international law
looks like a lazy compromise between the democracies and their
anti-democratic opponents. The American 'Gulliver' was to be
put in chains by the dwarves and prevented from completing its
universal benevolent work. Over and above this, this law impedes
the development of the American economy (Kyoto Protocol) and
– worst of all – prohibits the US from taking effective action
against the 'rogue states,' which are the greatest danger of the
present time.

From the point of view of the neo-conservatives the result
is clear: prevailing international law lacks a moral foundation,
and is a lame middle way between the – justified – demands of

the democracies and the – illegitimate – interests of the non-democracies. To transcend its limitations and in this way to create new law that is also morally valid is not only justified, but even necessary. In this way of looking at things, morality and power form an alliance against valid law, in order to eliminate it and then renew it from the ground up. Whether the hegemonic power that guarantees the rule of law subjects itself to the law afterwards or continues to stand above the law, prepared at any time to create order according to its own moral code if it does not like the way things are going, remains unclear. Based on the degree of arrogance displayed by the neo-conservatives and the nationalist elements in the Bush administration, from Wolfowitz to Cheney, the absolutist version – the monarch stands above the law – would most likely be expected.

The failure of this attack is obvious today. It is true that the protagonists were able to harm international law, but the new order was not able to establish itself; on the contrary: with every move of the Bush Government disorder grew. In this period the US failed miserably as the leading power. This failure has, among other things, cost the world a lot of time which could have been used for urgently needed global measures. Now the damage has to be repaired, the legal relationship between sovereignty and submission to the law realigned, legal progress blocked by the US set in motion again, and the effort to address gaps in the law (such as, for instance social standards) which could not be closed in the Bush era energetically redoubled. The lessons which we can draw for sustainable global governance from this unholy epoch should never again be forgotten: international law only functions when the most powerful force too is willing to submit to it and to support it. We can only develop it further if the most powerful marches in the lead, or at least in the ranks, and is nonetheless willing to make tolerable compromises with the less powerful. The maxim of the self-imposed submission of the powerful to international law is the 'cast-iron rule' under which, with this as its backbone, world governance can work. This self-imposed submission must be supported by insight into long-term interests. If this insight is missing, then one way or the other things look bad for the future of the world.

Who makes international law?

If international law plays this central role for world government, then of course it comes down to the question of who really 'makes' the law, i.e., who has the authority to establish laws. In more recent discussions of 'Global Governance' a confusing variety of players is active in the field: states, international organizations, the UN Security Council, NGOs and private corporations all participate somehow and somewhere in establishing laws. The diminishing importance of the state is unanimously proclaimed (with a greater or lesser degree of satisfaction).

In contrast to this trend, I represent a far more conservative line of argument: if we really want sustainable, effective and legitimate world government to come into effect, it would make sense to retain the central role of the state, to strengthen the stability of the states where this is possible and necessary, and to consign the other players, whose importance and – nonetheless partial – legitimacy I do not want to under-emphasize, to their appropriate place in the process of creating laws, controlling compliance with them, and enforcing them. States jointly determine, not exclusively it is true but mainly, relationships beyond their territorial boundaries. Their ability to make and enforce laws in a certain territory and in regard to the people who live there is better-developed than that of all competing players. And the shadow of the state's legal function is a pre-requisite for the validity of legal rules laid down by other players. For precisely this reason it also makes sense for effective, sustainable global governance to have its basic rules decided among states or their governments.

The effectiveness of governance is, however, only one argument. The second is that only rules freely agreed upon between states protect the political autonomy of their citizens, because only in this way can head-on assaults against central ethical values be defended against, and appropriate portions of their own values flow into the end-result. Basically, this is true even when the governments are undemocratic, even when in an individual case a corrupt dictator agrees to externally imposed rules in the hope of personal gain: sovereignty does not protect genuine autonomy in every single case at every point in time, but it offers a chance of this, as well as the chance of regaining lost or frittered-away autonomy.

This is not a radical communitarian argument that denies any chance of agreement beyond the boundaries of particular communities. For I assume that the shared problems make joint measures urgently necessary. As long as the world is politically and culturally fragmented, the sovereignty of the nations is the only chance of guaranteeing the possibility of autonomous internal development. In those extreme cases where the internal behavior of governments is answered with sanctions, it is necessary to take account of the risk of the 'cultural uncertainty principle' by accepting that the imposition of sanctions urgently requires the agreement of the particular regional environment.

Globalization offers civil society new opportunities for transnational networking, communication and mobility. These growing capabilities put it in a position to set law-creating processes in motion, yes, through its resistance and its campaigns almost to force the states (or occasionally corporations too) to introduce new rules. The list of successes is growing ever longer: the Ottawa Convention against anti-personnel landmines, the small arms and light weapons program of the United Nations, the Convention to ban Cluster Bombs, the Doha Declaration of the World Trade Organization on the TRIPS Agreement and public health (with the goal of increasing the availability of AIDS medication), the Inspection Panel of the World Bank, the World Commission on Dams, the International Criminal Court, and the Extractive Industries Transparency Initiative for revealing payment flows between corporations and states came into existence as a result of initiatives of or pressure from social movements and NGOs.

What Klaus-Dieter Wolf analyzed as 'the new national interest,' i.e., the growth in power of the executive branch through the deliberate accumulation of decision-making authority at international and transnational levels, in which among constitutional organs only the government still plays a role, is by no means a defect in democracy at these levels and therefore cannot be remedied there. In chapter 2, I gave reasons why the attempt to 'democratize' international relations as far into the future as possible only leads in the wrong direction. It is more a matter of a deficit of execution in national democracies, where the parliaments do not do their homework – debate national positions during treaty negotiations, report on the course of negotiations and later implementation of the treaty; carry on basic discussion of the pros and cons of signing a treaty; regularly report on the benefits of membership – but with real sheep-like patience allow themselves to have treaties imposed on them by the executive with apparently compelling appeals. Today, international politics can only be democratized in the following way: by the parliaments regaining their rights of control.

In order to discharge this duty without endangering the

development of tolerable global rules, the parliaments must substantially increase their authority to deal with global issues: they must be so familiar with the necessities, goals, and processes of global governance that they only pull on the 'ripcord' in the most extreme emergencies; for otherwise 'democracy' will be a huge stumbling block on the pathway to sustainable and viable treaties. Occasionally they could even spontaneously commit themselves – as with the American Congress when it hands over to the president 'fast-track' powers for world trade discussions, i.e., does without checking out every single clause. For the principle of democracy it is decisive that parliaments make such decisions after careful consideration and keep their eyes on the general wellbeing for which they are responsible. Anyone who is concerned about the de-democratization of world politics must look above all at ratification procedures and the subsequent implementation steps. In non-democracies government will remain one way or the other undemocratic, until internal reforms or revolutions bring about a change of system.

Wolf's insights question the diagnosis that the (functioning) state has suffered a loss of significance, as a substantial part of scientific literature on world government, the world republic, and so on assumes. It is true that the state has to put up with other players in international relations (which, by the way, was also the case in earlier times, for instance the Catholic Church, the Communist International, and powerful corporations like the multinational oil companies, whose power was greater in the late 1920s than it is today, and so on). As in the past, however, it towers over them. To be more precise: functioning large states continue to be more powerful than functioning large corporations. It can even be said that the state is increasing in effectiveness, because it can utilize resources of other players for its own purposes. Currently, in the war against terror it seems to be recapturing lost territory, because citizens are more willing than previously to give the executive extraordinary powers, even when their own freedoms are infringed upon as a result.

Players affected in special sectors (corporations, unions, directly affected groups of people such as patients in the health-care sector) and sector experts from the non-governmental arena are heard in the process of international law-making, because this helps raise the quality of the decisions made; it is their role to make expert knowledge available, to see to it that interests and considerations that are under-represented in the world of governments are taken into account, i.e., to see to it that the whole breadth of the agenda is discussed by negotiators. In general, however, they have no business at the negotiating table, except as members of national delegations; such participation, as well as the participation of members of parliament from the countries involved, undoubtedly increases the transparency of negotiations, and thus makes sense, within certain limits. As delegates, representatives of NGOs and members of parliament are subject, of course, to the constitutional prerogative of the government, and have to respect its instructions. This is good, for otherwise negotiations would mostly take place in and seldom between national delegations.

In the (increasingly common) cases in which legal rules are worked out between private players outside national bounda-ries, frequently because the states could not come to agreement – for instance in the important area of international private law – tacit approval by the states, sometimes even formal ratification or incorporation into national or international law, is unavoid-able sooner or later. Otherwise it would neither be guaranteed that these rules would be obeyed if breaking them promised advantages, nor could it be expected that the results – negoti-ated from a sector-based, vested-interest perspective – would foster the general good or even be consistent with the law. Corporations are – it is their job and thus this is not an accusation – concerned about making a profit. When corporations adopt measures among themselves it can never be completely excluded that these may occur at the cost of third parties. For this reason a controlling body is needed that is oriented towards the common good. This is more likely to be the states (or an international organization founded and maintained by them) than a different player. In carrying out this task non-governmental organizations can be the allies or the critical supervisors of the states.

From the point of view of global governance I am coming to the rescue of the honor of the sovereign state with only slight modifications. With an eye to the goal of good world governance it makes sense to regard the state as the central player, not because it is morally without stain and free of error but because many reasons support preferring it as the maker and applier of laws for other players. States are still the legitimate authority in a particular territory. In democracies this legitimacy derives from election by the people, in non-democracies from non-removal of the autocratic government and recognition by other states.

Two 'secondary' players who make international law should not be neglected. These are on the one hand the international organizations, which – like the World Health Organization, the International Labor Organization, the World Bank, or the International Monetary Fund – partly set standards which as 'soft law' regulate international dealings, partly lay down significant rules for the economic and political behavior of states through imposition of conditions on credits and other financial support (unfortunately, it must be said, not always in the sense of well-conceived global wellbeing!).

The second player is the Security Council which, under Chapter VII of the UN Charter, has the right to impose particular behavior on all Member States. In recent years it has made use of this instrument in different ways in order to play the role of 'world lawgiver': by taking steps to make the financing of international terrorism more difficult and by imposing on the states procedures to prevent access of non-state players to dangerous materials and substances. In both cases it reacted to acute danger, and yet its actions provoked unease in many Member States of the United Nations, for it did not seem right to them that a relatively small group in which five countries still possess a veto right can make laws for everybody that go beyond dealing with a momentary crisis (this is the purpose for which Chapter VII was originally formulated). Thus, the Security Council is advised to make sparing use of this power. Precisely because of the doubt about the moral character of many states and the 'lop-sided' makeup of the Security Council that still exists, the possibility of testing in court the binding decisions of international organizations, especially the Security Council, would be desirable. That the Security Council can make law and apply it without its decisions being subject to checks on their constitutionality or to appeal is less a lack of democracy than a deficit in the 'rule of law.' Until now there is only the possibility of scrutiny by the International Court of Justice (ICJ) when a decision of the Security Council affects a legal dispute between states in which the state affected by the decision has already taken its case to the ICJ and the Security Council measures stand in a legal-substantive relationship to this case. As yet there is no procedure for disputing decisions of the Council as such.

Who enforces the law?

Existing law dies off when infringements systematically remain unpunished. This question is decisive for the prestige of international law: how can evildoers effectively be deterred from offending against international legal rules in the absence of any reliable, higher-order force – which does not exist in the international system because the Security Council only sporadically plays this role – including verdicts of the ICJ?

The prevailing international system of law gives states which are harmed by the illegal actions of another state the right to defend themselves with a proportionate degree of force. Individual treaties envisage procedures and penalties for taking action against lawbreakers. International organizations can withdraw their services and suspend membership. If the breaches of the rules endanger or disturb international peace and security, the Security Council is called upon to take action under Chapter VII of the Charter. This includes the possibility not only of imposing economic sanctions but also of authorizing military action, or even of imposing a binding requirement on the Member States to participate in such an intervention.

However, the matter becomes difficult when the lawbreakers belong to the world's most powerful states. The United States, Russia and China have distinguished themselves in recent years through their particular shamelessness and self-righteousness when it was a matter of breaking current law, ignoring it, or blocking newly negotiated material. The Russian war in Chech- nya reached a level of crimes against humanity which had caused the Security Council to take action in other cases – Iraq after the First Gulf War or Bosnia; the unscrupulousness with which China, for reasons connected with natural resources, blocked stricter measures against the criminal regime in Sudan, the

shamelessness with which Washington set in motion a war in Iraq
contrary to international law, ignored the Geneva Convention by
setting up the Guantánamo concentration camp, and boycotted
important international agreements such as the nuclear weapons
test ban, the Biological Weapons Convention, the International
Criminal Court, or the Kyoto Protocol for the prevention of a
climate catastrophe, disturbingly demonstrate the inability until
now of these so-called great powers to carry out their mission
in building a sustainable world order; for standards that do not
apply to the most powerful are incompatible with sustainability
because they egregiously violate criteria of justice. For the rest
of the world the question arises: who will actually see to it that
the laws are observed if the muscle-packed Rambos of world
politics oppose them?

As odd as it may sound, the best chances lie with the civil
society, social movements and non-governmental organizations.
For smaller and middle-sized states the degree of risk in taking
on the great powers is normally too high. Whoever casts the 'first
stone' will feel the full might of the great powers' wrath. For this
reason, a 'dwarf' will rarely have the courage to take the initiative
against a 'giant.' Curiously it is also not advisable for the great
powers to act as guardians of virtue and rake each other over
the coals – unless the lawbreaker were a kind of 'new Hitler,'
and conflict were thus unavoidable anyway. Otherwise, it is of
primary importance for world peace – and thus for sustainable
world government – that no dangerous conflict smolders among
the world's great powers. However, if they accused each other of
violations of the law and sought retribution, the world would
be on course for a risky confrontation of the great powers. This
does not make sense.

But can a non-governmental organization really cause serious
problems for countries such as the US or China? Probably not

one acting on its own. But a union of, let us say, the 50 most important NGOs concerned with ecological and economic reform, peace and international security would bring together immense power. Not power in the sense of military strength or economic weight, but power in the sense of Hannah Arendt's 'to unite people behind a project.' Using the Internet and its global communication the 50 largest non-governmental organizations could inflict substantial economic damage on even the mightiest state in the world if they focused their combined organizational resources on a boycott of the products of the country branded as a lawbreaker and on the avoidance of any and all investments there. Elements of this power were seen in the fight against the apartheid regime in South Africa, during the French nuclear tests in 1995/96, and against the mighty Shell Oil Company during the Brent Spar campaign (even though the assertions of Greenpeace about the damage that would be caused by the sinking of the Brent Spar drilling platform were false – the campaign was effective!). The power of the non-governmental organization (NGO) lies in its power to mobilize. This power partly derives from its reputation as a well-functioning representative of a certain aspect of public interest, of global well being (which, by the way, is the reason why every corruption scandal involving an NGO or one of their representatives involves a serious loss of power). It also derives from the enthusiasm for work and the paid and much more frequently unpaid commitment of their officials, workers and supporters. Both are decisive pre-requisites for the mobilizing capability which manifests itself in the backing the campaign enjoys with the public at large. When this global mobilization machinery springs into action, it can cause serious damage to the evildoer at whom it is aimed.

The most serious question, however, is that of the decision-making process that leads to such a momentous decision. There are three reasons why this instrument can only be applied in extreme moderation. Firstly, standards of justice must not be compromised. Second, mobilization cannot be maintained permanently. Failure immediately blunts the weapon. Third, proportionality must be maintained. From this it can be seen that – unlike prosecution of crimes in constitutional states – the NGOs can only make use of the boycott measure in serious cases in which the mobilization offers prospects of success. This requires careful investigation and legitimate reasons for the decision, which are based on more than the judgment of the NGOs involved. Such support could be the usual procedures of the international community of states: a decision of the Security Council that is overthrown by a veto but has a broad majority among the members of the Security Council (after all, the civil society is not bound by the veto!); a resolution of the General Assembly of the UN; and a verdict or legal opinion of the International Court of Justice. The NGOs could also establish a joint independent investigation and inspection agency which would take action in the event that, in the case of suspicion of serious breaches of the law, the United Nations and the Court were not able to act. This should be a kind of 'council of elders' consisting of 'outstanding people' (i.e., no current representatives of nation-states) from all parts of the world. When powerful states or their favorite clients blatantly break international law, provided that it gives itself the necessary power to act, a civil society offers the best chance (although no watertight guarantee) that it will also be possible to call to order powerful transgressors.

Conclusions

A sustainable world order can function if it is based on the rule of law and the law controls the other instruments of coordination and control: power, morality and the market. And it can only function if those with the power submit to the law as a result of the insight that, in our complex and endangered world, lawless conditions in which order was based on nothing but the exercise of power would also threaten their clear interests to the highest degree. This insight can support civil society at certain points with the help of its ability to set campaigns in action. Of all the players, the nation-states are still in the best position to establish the rule of law in a global setting and to see that it functions. They no longer do this alone, but with the assistance of international organizations and their secretariats, of non-governmental organizations, of corporations, and of other interested parties.

NGOs have a highly responsible role in establishing the rule of law. They may well be the only class of players who are able to influence the decisions of even the most powerful players without at the same time exposing the network of international relations to extremely dangerous conflicts. The NGOs must first become aware of this role. If they develop this (self-)awareness, they will advance to being first-division players within a sustainable world order.

The previous chapters sought to systematically present the conditions, means and ways for establishing sustainable global governance. Occasionally, isolated ideas about implementation were inserted, in order to illustrate 'how it could be done.' As a liberal child of the Enlightenment I have tried hard not to set Western values and institutions as the absolute standard. For those who still suspect me of arguing no differently from the cosmopolitans, I would point out the differences with the help of the following table.

	Values/ Objectives	Type of rights	Type of procedure	Decision-maker	Institutions
Cosmopolitans	Western liberal	Human rights based	Based on civil rights	Democracies only	Western design
Author	Interculturally agreed	Based on international law	Based on rule of law	Universal, all regions/states	Interculturally agreed

Table Differences between 'cosmopolitan democracy' and sustainable global governance

The major difference lies in the fact that I wish to develop values, procedures and institutions inclusively, that is by

transcending regional and cultural boundaries through agreement among the largest possible number of members of the
international community of states, instead of presenting the rest
of the world with a Western-oriented design as a fait accompli.
In chapter 7, I will try to go through players and institutions
as thoroughly as possible. Because this is what global governance is ultimately all about: to bring together in institutions
the players through whose actions the desired goals are to be
achieved or whose undesirable acts could frustrate the goals that
have been set, and coordinate the various institutions in such a
way that obstacles to action are eliminated and new options for
action are opened up. At the same time it is necessary to establish a minimum positive attitude among the players, in order to
make successful cooperation in the institutions possible. I make
use of the line of reasoning that Immanuel Kant applied in his
essay 'Perpetual Peace': to design a sensible approach and then
see to what extent current reality – both the players as well as
the institutions – offers possibilities for putting it into practice.
I am looking therefore for 'mooring places' for sensible political
approaches. The necessity to solve the global problems analyzed
by my colleagues in the first eleven volumes in our series is the
starting point. In chapter one I named three 'spoilsports' that
can prevent humanity from finding a solution to this problem:
their cultural diversity, their dispute over justice, and violent conflicts. Institutions and players must be set up so that they keep
these 'spoilsports' in check, and at the same time offer the necessary preconditions for successfully attacking global problems.

The player/institution combination breaks down into two
large sections that together make up the 'prerequisites for sustainable global governance.' The first covers all international,
legally standardized bodies: the United Nations with its sub-
agencies such as the World Health Organization or the UN

Environmental Program, organizations affiliated with the UN but formally independent such as the International Atomic Energy Agency, the International Monetary Fund and the World Bank, treaty regimes with an organizational structure, for example the Chemical Weapons Convention with the Organization for the Prohibition of Chemical Weapons, international regimes without their own organization such as the Kyoto Protocol, regional organizations as well as the International Court of Justice; these institutions can themselves act partly as players, if they embody a uniform political will.

The second area includes everything necessary for global governance that is not included in the first. These are first of all the countries themselves, especially the major powers and their joint bodies, above all the G8. Non-governmental organizations are included, expert committees, commissions and councils not made up of government representatives, as well as corporations and their attempts at self-regulation. These institutional structures too appear – depending on context and point of view – as players again whenever they wish to act in a unified manner.

Finally, habitual behaviors and repeated patterns of behavior are included in the realm of institutions. In this wide variety of players and institutions it is necessary to assign the respective roles sensibly, to settle cases of 'demarcation disputes' with as little conflict as possible, i.e., to coordinate tasks and work, and to establish a structure in such a way that the largest possible number of players feel acknowledged and at home, while at the same time the urgent tasks can really be completed. In my observations I am guided by the 'reality principle,' which consists of four components. In the first place: neither participants nor institutions should be expected to make leaps that are too large. What I recommend may not be immediately possible, but may not lie too far off. Second: too much must not be demanded of participants. What is demanded of them must be in the context of their clearly understood long-term interests. Third – closely connected with the two previous points: in today's reality, 'mooring opportunities' from which bridges to the desired future can be built must be apparent. These are above all models and precedents. Fourth: opportunities must be available to correct mistakes or failures to follow procedure.

The United Nations: The Security Council

As has already been made clear, I am not interested in making the United Nations the nucleus of a world republic. I am satisfied with attempting to make it more representative and more effective in what it is. The Security Council needs new members who belong to different regions of the world, have large populations, and are also (on a regional scale) political and economic leaders. The pathetic failure of similar efforts in 2005 once again demonstrated the inability of the P-5 to rise above provincial nationalism; the same verdict applies to opponents of reform within the ranks of the General Assembly, whose goal, motivated by feelings of competition and envy, is to keep various potential candidates out of the Security Council (Pakistan against India, Italy against Germany, Argentina and Mexico against Brazil), and from among the Africans, who were incapable of seizing the opportunity for better representation by deciding on two of their three possible candidates (Egypt, Nigeria, South Africa). The arithmetic principle should apply, that countries with membership of the Security Council should always represent a clear majority of the world's population, and at the same time all regions, and thus the necessary cultural diversity. Permanent seats for India, Japan and Brazil, as well as one for the EU would be a good idea, instead of for the two nostalgic garden gnomes Great Britain and France, to which Germany would like to be added as the third and biggest. For Africa, the best solution would be the rotation of two permanent seats among the three countries, South Africa, Nigeria and Egypt. Such rotations could also be set up for others, such as Argentina, Mexico and Venezuela as major Latin American countries, and for Indonesia, Pakistan and South Korea in Asia. If Africa absolutely insists on having a permanent member who never rotates out on the Security Council, then it must agree on a candidate. As long as it does not do this, rotation is the best alternative.

Rotation means that a country leaves the Security Council for two years, and then returns for four years. Countries are thus in most of the time. The other UN members know that after a two year 'sabbatical' they will return to the Security Council, and the permanent members also know this. This also boosts their status during the time in which they are 'on the sidelines': the probability of being involved in informal consultations during this time is high, because many important issues occupy the Security Council for longer than 24 months. In this setup the Council would have seven permanent members and three rotating seats; to which could be added twelve non-permanent seats (i.e., two more than currently) in order to achieve a broader regional representation; since the EU would be represented by a shared seat, the minimum of three non-permanent seats that normally go to EU members would be distributed among the others. The Security Council would definitely become more representative. However, this alternative basically assumes that France and Great Britain give priority to the liberal-cosmopolitan heritage ahead of nationalism, and that is a fairly high hurdle; if it is not overcome, a rotating seat for Germany would also be acceptable.

The new permanent and 'almost permanent' members would

not necessarily need the veto; it will not be possible to abolish the veto of the 'originals' because the current veto powers will not be able to bring themselves to give it up willingly. But what is reasonable is the requirement to give reasons when exercising the veto. The fact that the five permanent members do not even want to fulfill this minimum requirement shows the shocking extent of the lack of responsibility of these powers, which at the same time arrogantly take advantage of this responsibility to maintain their own privileges. The remaining members of the United Nations should no longer allow themselves to be fobbed off over this. The 'shaming' of the Five should be doggedly persisted with, together with civil society, until they give in. The glimmer of hope is that, at least in the three Western permanent members, support for this demand may come from the societies and perhaps even the parliaments. For, citizens or parliamentarians would perhaps also like to know why their government made the decision to use the veto in the United Nations.

If worst comes to worst a veto can be overturned through the 'Uniting for Peace' procedure. If the Security Council and the General Assembly approve a measure by a large majority (at least two thirds), this gives legitimacy to countries (and non-governmental organizations, see below) which then implement these measures. Of course, the General Assembly should make sparing use of this possibility. Because the veto also has a purpose: to prevent the vital interests of a major power from being violated. For a dangerous situation can develop through this. Moderation is therefore required of the entire membership, as it is of the permanent members when using their veto. The current quorum of 9 (out of 15) votes might well be raised to 15 with a total membership of 22 countries. A larger number of permanent or almost permanent members would have the opportunity of reducing the annoying practice of the P5 first reaching agreement among themselves then presenting this agreement to the others on the principle of 'like it or lump it.' Because more votes than those of the P-5 will be needed. If they believe they can maintain their old supremacy, the formation of 'opposition caucuses' is recommended, which can come to Council meetings, with proposals backed by a large number of members. After a short period of confrontational meetings a more co-operative mode of operation should emerge.

In recent years the Security Council has increasingly held 'open' meetings and consultations with all interested members of the General Assembly. In addition, since 1999 there are the 'Arria meetings', named after a former Brazilian representative to the UN. These meetings, officially announced at the start of the month by the presidency of the Security Council, are informal consultations with non-members, in which non-governmental organizations also occasionally take part. The Security Council must make this practice permanent, so that 'institutionalization through habit' results. When it comes to measures according to Chapter VII, i.e., for dealing with serious threats to international peace and security, it should be normal practice for all countries in the affected region to have the opportunity to participate in discussions. The Security Council should make it a rule for decision-making that use of force will not be decided upon against the wishes of the wide majority of regional neighbors in a conflict.

In comparison to the Security Council the Economic and Social Council of the United Nations barely ekes out an existence, as far as its authority and political significance are concerned. This is all the more strange when many of the 'global problems' which are the subject of our series of books fall within its area of responsibility. In the light of its existential importance the Economic and Social Council deserves higher status. I will make a proposal for this further on.

Of all world institutions, the General Assembly of the United Nations is the most representative. All states of the world recognized by the vast majority within the international community have a seat and a vote, even if some political entities which have a quasi-state character but are not recognized internationally are not regular members, such as Palestine, Taiwan, North Cyprus and Somaliland. On the other hand, there are members whose status as states can be seriously called into question which nonetheless enjoy international recognition such as Somalia and Afghanistan. Be that as it may: if one searches for a body in which all countries, regions and cultures of the world can have their voice heard, then this is in the UN General Assembly.

Compared to the legitimacy of it basic structure, the responsibilities of the General Assembly are severely limited. It participates in voting for the Secretary-General and plays an important part in the budget and the appointment of key UN civil servants. Resolutions it passes are not binding, but nevertheless set 'soft' norms just as do the world conferences and special sessions called by the General Assembly on specific issues, norms which influence the international agenda as well as how the member states behave. However, it still remains within the power of states simply to ignore these impulses. The General Assembly may also address security issues – but only as long as the Security Council declines to address such an issue itself, and the General Assembly may only comment on such issues in a non-binding manner (however, see the exception of 'Uniting for Peace' above). Perhaps the most important power invested in the General Assembly is its authority to commission expert committees and negotiation forums in order to work out recommendations or detailed international treaties. The General Assembly officially accepts the text of treaties by passing a resolution, and thus authorizes them for signing.

In this chapter I make the basic assumption that only minimal changes need to be made to the UN Charter. But the 'normative power of factual truth' plays a role in international law which should not be underestimated: if the practice of states changes and then remains consistent for a long period of time, such a practice establishes force of habit and thus new norms. In this sense, the General Assembly could attempt to procure broader rights compared to the Security Council, without calling into basic question the central importance of the Security Council for peace and international security. A decisive step towards strengthening the General Assembly is greater accountability of the Security Council. In order to achieve that, the General Assembly must be willing to vigilantly exercise its right to meet outside its regular (fall/winter) sessions whenever a pressing question of international security is on the agenda or the Security Council is working out an important decision on an issue of general interest.

One initial right to demand accountability is directed at the work the Security Council as a whole: this requires the attention of the Council president (the presidency changes on a monthly basis). The General Assembly should assume the right to demand to receive information about current proceedings, including the reasoning behind each action taken, and the Assembly should acquire the opportunity of stating its position. Doing this would mean violating the prohibition against dealing with security matters which are on the agenda of the Security Council at the same time. This prohibition permits the Council to make a decision running counter to the will of the majority of states in conflict situations, without them even having the chance to make a statement on the matter. In contrast to this practice, it would be desirable for the General Assembly to be able to express its views before the Security Council makes decisions of far-reaching consequences.

The second area of accountability sought after involves the five permanent members. The General Assembly should fight for the right to demand a statement of reasons from any Security Council member which has imposed or even only threatened its veto. This obligation to give reasons was one of the suggestions made during the UN reform debate, but failed due to the arrogant self-importance of the five countries in question. If this does not work through a change to the Charter, then the General Assembly should simply exercise its right to question each of the P5 members. Any member who fails to respond to this demand is forced to expressly and deliberately oppose the declared will of the majority of the Members. That is a higher hurdle for the 'deafening silence' after a veto than the present situation – in which a government exercises its veto and the rest of the world submissively moves on to the next item on the agenda.

How the General Assembly should deal with particularly intractable cases of conflict when a Security Council member exercises its veto in an acute conflict against (practically) the entire world community has been discussed in the preceding two chapters. I would just like to call briefly to mind: through the 'Uniting for Peace' procedure the General Assembly can act in the place of a deadlocked Security Council and authorize its Members to take action against an offender. The subtle distinction is this: the General Assembly cannot force Members to take action. But the Security Council has not done this in the case of military operations in the past either. The decisive factor is that the legitimization of sanctions against an offender is broadly based. The General Assembly is able to show it has such broad support. To the extent that it empowers itself to act during such moments of crisis, it nullifies the arguments of those who, by drawing attention to the pattern of vetoes in the Security Council, scoff at the entire United Nations as incapable of reaching a decision on matters of war and peace and wish to replace the will of the international community of nations with their own whims – whether nationally or as part of a 'coalition of the willing.'

Serious consideration should be given to the possibility of the General Assembly also making use of this method when global issues are involved that have only an indirect but nevertheless far-reaching impact on world security. Climate change is one such issue, and the risk of global epidemics or increasing malnutrition could become others. It may sound odd to encourage the General Assembly and also the Security Council to make a decision in this case. But, in particularly acute instances of danger when hunger, the spread of disease, water shortage or similar hardships threaten millions of people and no alternative approach is in view, it is in a position to become active as the world's lawmaker by resolution and to bindingly commit all Member States to take action. If the Security Council does this on its own authority, this leads to irritation among the Member States. However, if the majority of UN members demand that the Security Council does this, then such global law-making by the Security Council obtains an entirely different legitimacy. A special session of the General Assembly leading to such a demand would be a spectacular event which would not pass by without consequences for its way of operating. For, except for the most rugged governments, most are concerned about their reputation. To be specifically castigated by name on a worldwide basis, as the General Assembly could do via a resolution, would be damaging to a country's reputation, and is not something any country likes. In democracies there are also the unpredictable effects this might have among the electorate. The General Assembly has a strong instrument in its hand for affecting the reputation of the most harmful countries on 'global issues.'

Global justice in decisions: universal democracy and the United Nations

The current decision-making structures at the global level are grossly unjust. In response to this, political philosophy has developed models for universal democracy. These approaches are conceptually on target; they attempt to ensure the participation of all parties in decision-making, to the greatest extent possible in a globalized world. At the same time, what is not considered is that in the foreseeable future we will have to live in a world of heterogeneous systems, in which democracies will have to interact with non-democracies (chapter 3). A gradual evolution toward democracies is perhaps conceivable or even probable, because up until now these systems have proven themselves to be generally more effective. However, no prognosis can be made about how long that will take. Impatient attempts to accelerate the process simply cause even greater injustice and new resentments. In particular, dealing with violations of human rights – at what point is violence justified in order to protect victims? – raises difficult questions if the impression is created that through the application of unequal standards the agenda of a given cultural group is being imposed. To derive the right to intervene in a strictly logical way from the premises of a Western liberal worldview therefore does more to create a divide than to contribute to a worldwide consensus on intervening on behalf of threatened and beleaguered people in the most extreme cases.

All proposals for democratization of the United Nations have their drawbacks. For instance, eliminating the veto is an attractive idea, but it also destroys a protective barrier against dangerous conflicts among the superpowers. Relatively speaking, the principle of 'one state/one vote' takes away the rights of people in heavily populated countries. The principle of weighting votes based on population gives the governments of heavily populated dictatorships special privileges. In addition, 'democratization,' to the extent that the relations between states are meant by this, simply twists the meaning of the term 'democracy.' The term means rule by the people, and includes the right of the individual citizen to participate directly or through representatives in the legislative process. States are not citizens, but instead collectives of widely differing sizes represented by officials with executive power.

This has caused some 'friends of democratization' not to pursue greater representativity among the states, but instead to seek to achieve democratization by establishing a parliamentary structure in the United Nations. Making the United Nations more parliamentary – the introduction of a 'third chamber' alongside the Security Council and General Assembly – brings with it, however, the same problems as the attempt to achieve greater representativity among states: how are dramatic differences in population to be taken into account, or the fact that some are democracies and others are not, so that there is no guarantee that in the latter voting will really be done democratically? The inclusion of NGOs as representatives of global civil society in political decision-making processes as a way out also has its problems: NGOs are not elected, some have authoritarian structures, and because the organizations from the 'North' are more numerous and richer such a step could even double the imbalance in participation.

It is perhaps an even more serious matter that the conception of 'democratization' of the world organization involves imposing the organizational and decision-making principle of only a portion of its members, which is not shared by the rest. This is also an attack on their sovereignty just when sovereignty is beginning to become a reality for countries such as India, China, Malaysia, Brazil or Mexico as a result of their economic and political development. It is therefore not surprising that countries from the 'South,' eager for sovereignty, are beginning to detect imperialism under another name behind the democratization projects.

The Secretary-General and Article 99

More than any other office, the Secretary-General – behind whom stands, something that is often overlooked, a 'government apparatus' with civil servants numbering in the five digits – is the epitome of the United Nations. This personification often distracts from the fact that the Secretary-General has only as much scope for action as the Member States allow and personal charisma creates. When people speak of the 'failure of the United Nations,' the public gaze is mainly directed accusingly at the man (or hopefully one day the woman) at the top. But it is mainly the member countries, especially the most powerful, which are to blame when the United Nations does not function the way most people would like it to.

Strong Secretary-Generals such as Dag Hammarskjöld or Kofi Annan give an idea of what people with vision can do with the legally very limited office if they do not let themselves be distracted by the threats and machinations of the 'major powers.' Annan streamlined the secretariat, consolidated the budget, and instituted reforms such as the creation of a peace-building department. He also did not shy away from openly and unequivocally criticizing powerful countries – such as with regard to the war in Iraq. Precisely because of this the neoconservatives wanted to mob him out of office – the campaign which unleashed the chained dogs of the media in 2004 would have broken a weaker person. (The matter was related to misdeeds of Annan's son which were to be used to hobble the father, using the tried and trusted methods of collective guilt.) Kofi Annan was shaken, but did not give in. A decisive and effective executive can stand up to even the most powerful nation. The Secretary-General can act as the mouthpiece of the world's conscience by being the common denominator that summarizes the multitude of voices in a single voice or lends his voice to the weak. People listen to what he says. When he expresses criticism this is also heard in the countries the criticism is directed at. His choice of personnel leaves its mark on the quality of work done by the organization.

The UN Charter places an (until now rarely used) instrument in his hands: according to Article 99, if he considers the matter of sufficient gravity the Secretary-General can on his own initiative investigate situations through which he fears peace and security are being threatened, and can demand a special session of the Security Council and have the matter he is investigating placed on the agenda. Under the gaze of the world he can thus compel the members of the Security Council to address an issue which, left to themselves, they would have chosen to cover up. It is up to the Secretary-General himself to make use of this instrument in specific circumstances.

Just as the General Assembly should, so should the Secretary-General become accustomed to bringing before the Security Council problems related to unregulated 'global issues' that have an impact on security. Of course both proposals would usher in a period full of conflict for the United Nations. The powerful states which set the tone there are generally the ones who created the most serious problems. The General Assembly and Secretary-General are actors whose institutional status allows them to defy the power derived from affluence and military strength of the largest countries – at least in relation to their capability to keep unwanted and unpleasant items off the agenda.

If they increasingly see the risk that the United Nations could become a tribunal for examining their international policy, economic and ecological shortcomings, the chance of change increases. For civil society such an expansion of the United Nations' function would be encouraging, and an occasional 'pillorying' would encourage campaigns of its own. For civil society in the countries whose governments were criticized this could in turn give occasion to pressure for political change at home.

International regimes

The United Nations has responsibility for all aspects of world politics. It is true, of course, that the world's problems, with their controversial and complex details that are often difficult to grasp, cannot really be controlled from such a central head-quarters. That is why the world organization has from the very beginning created separate specialized organizations which can deal with detailed questions with greater expertise and experience. Some organizations such as the International Postal Union are even older than the United Nations. The organizations often form a 'hard core' of institutions referred to in the academic discipline of international relations as an 'international regime.' Such regulatory systems also exist 'free-standing,' without any connection to the UN. The term 'regime' combines legal, political and organizational aspects. A regime is a network of principles, norms, rules and procedures designed to regulate problems of cooperation and coordination in a certain policy field; for example for cooperation among various police forces (Interpol and the corresponding treaty), for the prohibition of chemical weapons (Chemical Weapons Convention, Geneva Protocol, Organization for the Prohibition of Chemical Weapons), or the Montreal Protocol, which outlaws ozone-destroying gases.

Usually a treaty or accord is the cornerstone on which additional regional agreements and 'soft' political obligations are entered into. It is often the case that an organization administers a treaty, monitors its observance, offers a forum for the exchange of experience and opinions, sees to the further development of rules in the light of new developments or knowledge, makes available assistance, relevant information and expert advice, creates channels of communication for NGOs, etc. The regimes form the core of global cooperation, and offer the best hope of tackling the as yet unsolved global problems one step at a time. To an increasing extent regimes include in negotiations and implementation non-governmental players – companies, associations, NGOs – without which it would not be possible for regulation to be effective; the number of regimes instituted in the private sector is also increasing. Global regimes are accessible to all states and to a growing extent to non-governmental players. They are specialized, flexible, and capable of adapting, open for civil society, and emerge as a result of negotiations and consensus. For this reason all the states involved have a feeling of 'ownership,' because they themselves have taken part in the global lawmaking that is reflected in a regime. This is of course only true if negotiations and their result are more or less fair, and are also perceived in this way by the parties involved.

Regime coordination

There are many regimes. Conventions are mostly entered into without consideration of their interactions: as a result inadvertent negative consequences often result, which reduce the hoped for benefit. The World Trade Organization (WTO) and its conventions are more useful for worldwide economic development than an uninhibited race of national protectionist policies as was seen in the worldwide economic crisis of the 1930s. But they produce harmful side-effects for the environment, poorer countries and people, and internationally codified economic and social rights. Sustainable global governance must correct these side-effects of what on the face of it are sensible regulations, as well the intentionally cemented favored standing of the rich countries.

First, it is necessary that institutions active in the international arena themselves monitor what actions of other institutions influence their own goals. Because such analyses are complex, it is recommended that specialized analytical departments be set up for this purpose. At the same time they should have the task of estimating the effects of their own actions on the goals of other institutions; for example, the United Nations Development Program should regularly carry out an assessment of the social consequences of agreements made by the WTO or of World Bank policies. The departments would have to pass on the findings of both analyses to their respective leaderships. The leadership in turn then has the task of entering into negotiations with the executive bodies of other international institutions in order to optimize the positive synergies of their interactions and to reduce reciprocal obstructions and impairments. This task should be a matter of course, given the fact that the actual purpose of international institutions is ensuring the protection of community assets for the community of states and the peoples they represent, which the states can no longer guarantee on their own; it is not the purpose of these institutions to increase their own importance in the competition with others and, if necessary, at their expense.

However, this task is not easy to fulfill, for two reasons. First of all, it would be naive to believe that the self-centered willfulness of bureaucracies, with which we are acquainted from their internal effects, evaporates as soon as a bureaucracy operates on the international stage. Organizational egoism occurs there in just the same way, and hampers coordination. Second, international organizations consist of states, to which their bureaucracies are responsible. Representatives of countries are often focused on the special purpose of the institution they are to control, and often lose sight of the big picture. It is not uncommon for the ambassadors of the same country working in two different organizations to go in two different directions. It is to be hoped that with the transparency of interactions between organizations that is being sought, governments' awareness of inadvertent and also previously unnoticed contradictory actions will increase and regulation become easier.

If this does not work, a third level comes into play. I would place here the Economic and Social Council of the United Nations (ECOSOC) which stands alongside the Security Council in the organizational system, although it is relegated to a sad Sleeping Beauty existence, because nobody really knows what it is actually supposed to do.

If this group were given the authority to make decisions on disputes between international organizations, then in one fell swoop it would become a significant organ and would fill in the void that has opened up within the system of global governance outside the narrower security problem. Only after these 'security issues in a broader sense' have become an acute danger for a large number of people do they fall, as suggested above, within the Security Council's scope of responsibility. In the event of conflicts below this threshold, they remain within the binding, coordinating responsibility of ECOSOC. How important this function could be becomes evident in the tensions between the actions and goals of the Bretton-Woods organizations, the World Bank, and the International Monetary Fund and – to cite one example – the Development Program or the Environmental Program of the United Nations. If, for example, the World Bank wants to grant a major loan for an environmentally harmful project and the Environmental Program feels that its key objectives are thwarted by this, as things stand today the World Bank could go ahead and grant the loan without batting an eyelid. If the environmental program is able to appeal to the Economic and Social Council as the official dispute-settling forum, then things look different. The same is true if the IMF imposes excessive conditions on debt rescheduling and plunges the social structure of a debtor country into chaos. Here, too, the objections of the United Nations Development Program could lead to corrections by the Economic and Social Council.

Regional organizations

We live in one world and at the same time in regional worlds. The principle of subsidiarity, an important principle in today's models for prudent governance, states that as much as possible should be decided at the 'lower' level of the decision-making system, and only what requires synthesis at a higher level may move to that level. This principle helps to satisfy the self-determination desires of players at the local level as well as the claims to sovereignty of governments of states. It implies that the region must be acknowledged as an important level of international and transnational government.

In most world regions there are regional organizations which are committed to cooperation, economic development, ecological well being and promotion of peace and security in the respective region (chapter 5). How precarious the situation is in the Middle East is borne out by the fact that there is no such organization there. The security risks in East Asia are attested to by the fact that regionalism is only in its infancy there and was only created by a crisis – the North Korean nuclear weapons program; in addition, Taiwan, an important player in the region, still remains excluded from the vulnerable seedling of East Asian regionalism, due to China's veto. Not all organizations operate at the same level of efficiency in their member states, their weight as a frame of reference for member countries varies. The following considerations about how the regional organizations could be used are related to the more or less functioning institutions or to those which are gradually gaining importance at the regional level. If such organizations neither exist nor are in sight, then what remains is direct cooperation with the various countries.

It would be desirable if a systematic strategy of support for budding organizations in other regions emanated from the fully-functioning regional organizations and the United Nations. The simplest means for this is regular contact, something the EU already promotes. In addition, a portion of development help and economic relationships should be handled by the best suited regional organization – with the caveat stated above, that this organization in fact works. Projects in which players from various countries are involved should be given priority. The United Nations and its sub-organizations – including the World Bank, the International Monetary Fund and the World Health Organization

– should maintain joint liaison offices at the headquarters of the regional organizations. Regional development banks should play a larger role, in other words the principle of subsidiarity could tie financing of development closer to the particular region. Instead of every sub-organization working on its own in carrying out projects with member countries of the regional organizations, efforts to bundle activities and to plan them with more emphasis on regions than on single countries should be the main focus. Such a priority should not be made into a dogma: where it makes sense to carry out measures in relation to special national conditions (e.g., for a post civil-war society in a peaceful environment) this must of course be done. But the regional situation should always remain on the horizon of planners. Where solid and effective regional organizations exist, they are given a leading role in keeping the peace – this is also stated in Chapter VIII of the UN Charter.

The United Nations should only intervene – and only be made use of – when the regional organization is overwhelmed by this task or the events in a given region have worldwide consequences. In any case, the authorized representatives of regional organizations should be involved if the Security Council makes decisions under Chapter VII, which authorizes the use of force. For it can be assumed that the representatives of regional organizations 'on the ground' often have more precise knowledge than the powerful nations and their representatives in New York. Regional organizations should also be given responsibility for finding solutions to global problems tailored to their region.

Despite all the praise heaped on the regional level, its weakness should not be disregarded. Some regions – Africa is one case – are economically and politically too weak to be able to take effective internal action. They require support from the outside, and this 'interface' should be prepared very thoroughly. For it should lead neither to external dictates nor to unquestioning flows of material aid without regard to the quality of the political system being supported. On the other hand, the regions are also the site of the worst conflicts – the Middle East represents just such a problem. For this reason, regional players are not in a position to set up urgently needed cooperative institutions using their own resources. In both cases turning for help from external players, above all the United Nations, cannot be avoided. The illusion must be resisted that the European model of regional integration can simply be globalized.

Courts of justice and quasi-judicial proceedings

Courts still play a relatively minor role in international politics. Like other supranational organizations they too have the highest levels of authority in Europe. Yet, because of the special nature of the European integration process this model cannot be transferred to other world regions and is also not necessary in every case. Where the political culture of a region leaves, for instance, the resolution of disputes and conflict management to a more informal, bilateral consultative process, as is the case between the ASEAN states of Southeast Asia, a regional court of justice is superfluous and might even encourage conflict. The model of the 'doyens' that has been tried out in recent years in the West African ECOWAS could also be a culture-specific equivalent of what we are seeking in the European Union with the European Court of Justice: it involves an international committee of public personalities who, in the event of conflicts, first of all speak with the players in order through the force of their authority to coax them to act peacefully. As obvious as reinforcement of legal structures at all levels may seem from a Western perspective, it must also be conceded that different institutional safeguards can be equally successful in other regions.

The matter takes on a different complexion when it is a question of statutory provisions and infringements of the law at the global level. As an intercultural model of arbitration, courts of justice are appropriate as an 'intercultural site' for settling disputes, where otherwise cultural agreement is missing. At the regional level, traditional alternatives for conflict management may make more sense. At the global level there are no such traditions. What powers should be given to court proceedings and their institutions is an equally sensitive question, because the precious asset of sovereignty is put to the test with each case heard. Court proceedings have various advantages. They lead to decisions (although they sometimes take a long time to do it); they are removed to some extent from day-to-day politics (yet not completely, for judges are political appointees); they distinguish clearly between justice and injustice and thus provide the international community and civil society with indicators of when a breach of law has occurred.

Just as with resolutions passed by the Security Council and the General Assembly, a judicial decision can take on the function of legitimizing actions. The jurisdictions of the International Court of Justice (ICJ), the International Criminal Court (ICC) and the International Tribunal for the Law of the Sea (ITLOS) are limited. The ICJ can make rulings on disputes between states if the parties contesting the case recognize its competence. It can issue an advisory opinion. It would be desirable for the ICJ to have the opportunity of acting on its own authority at least by issuing expert opinions on the constitutionality of Security Council resolutions. The potential for unlimited authority, which the UN Charter places in the hands of the Security Council by allowing it to decide on its own what should be deemed a 'threat to international peace and security' and thus possibly incur violent sanctions, would at least be provisionally limited in this way, and the imbalances in power among members and non-members or those with the right to veto or only to vote in the Security Council would be reduced, if not completely eliminated.

The International Criminal Court (ICC) is distinct from the International Court of Justice because it does not make rulings on disputes between states, but instead can apprehend individuals who have violated international criminal law in an especially serious way, such as war criminals or people who must answer for serious crimes against humanity. Cautiously widening the elements constituting an offense over which the ICC has jurisdiction would be worth considering once its membership approaches being universal and, above all, American resistance to the court has faded away. Illegal arms trafficking would be an example, while dealing in substances which can be used for constructing weapons of mass destruction, drug and human trafficking, active corruption inflicting harm on the poorest countries, and embezzlement of international relief funds are potential offenses as well. The principle of subsidiarity applies, meaning the ICC only takes action if the country on whose territory the crime was committed or the suspect's country of origin itself does not (cannot) act or expressly hands the case over to the court. In order to prevent overburdening the ICC – in criminal cases the burden of proof and thus the volume of data is very high – regional branches would be a sensible extension.

Some international regimes have procedures for dealing with rule violations which are very similar to those used in legal proceedings. The World Trade Organization is the most prominent example, where the settlement of disputes is dealt with in independent committees. The state which is lodging the complaint can be given authority by the committees to take punitive action against trade barriers which are in breach of a trade agreement. These committees are quasi-courts which hand down verdicts on violations of the norms of a particular treaty. The finding is binding, although the case remains within the bilateral relationship of the two states in dispute. This distinguishes the WTO's procedures from legal proceedings in a state which, if necessary, enforces the right of the successful party in a legal dispute, even if the unsuccessful party resists. An additional step would be necessary in order to give conflict management measures at the level of a regime such as the WTO the same weight: the dispute mediation committees would need to be able to impose sanctions which were binding for all WTO members against a state found to be in violation of an agreement.

I am exploring the question of how disputes between states or between a state and a powerful private player can be dealt with because the sustainability of international rules depends in large measure on these issues. A ruling can cast a long 'time shadow' on the behavior of states if these can reliably assume that the ruling will be enforced.

Enforcement means that, if necessary, rules can also be enforced despite attempts to break them. If a state violates rules to which it originally voluntarily submitted, this can have three causes. The state may lack the capabilities or resources to observe the rules. In this case sanctions are senseless, as this only makes matters worse. Relief programs must be available in order to put a state with otherwise good intentions in a position to act in accordance with the rules. The second possibility is the laxness of bureaucracy: the people responsible are unaware of the rule in question. They would apply it if they were aware of their own obligations. This problem can be rectified by issuing regular reprimands or even better by requiring reporting of adherence to the rule. The third case is the most serious: the state in question breaks the rule because at the moment it seems to run counter to its interests. A procedure similar to court proceedings for determining breaches of rules and if necessary punishing them instantly increases confidence that the rules are enforceable and in the sustainability of the regime in question.

The 'neutral' forum removes the disputed issue from the immediate conflict ping-pong of the states involved in the dispute, and thus prevents falling back into the classic anarchy of international relations. The prospect of sanctions symbolically strengthens the rule, and simultaneously creates a system of incentives which contributes to its enforcement. It would therefore be desirable if as many international regimes as possible which have been set up to regulate global problems had comparable multi-stage procedures in place: relief measures for ensuring the ability to observe rules; a systematic reporting system which maintains the alertness of politics and administration to their own obligations; and quasi-judicial procedure for resolving disputes at the end of which binding sanctions can also be enforced against an offender. This is particularly true for international environmental regimes, in whose case observance of rules is vital for survival while at the same time the incentive for opportunistically violating them is considerable for states and companies alike. The difficulties of formulating standards for the Kyoto Protocol that apply to all parties give an idea of how difficult the path will be until ways are found for effectively dealing with violations. The idea of an international environmental court which is circulating among international law specialists is not to be rejected out of hand as one possible path.

Does the proposal to give all international regimes devoted to regulating global problems quasi-judicial procedures for settling disputes require too great a sacrifice of sovereignty? There are three arguments which can be raised to counter this objection.

Firstly: in world conferences, in UN General Assembly resolutions, and in existing treaty regimes, the overwhelming majority of states have acknowledged the existence of global problems, as well as accepted that solving them is necessary. If the survival of humanity depends on resolving these problems, then humanity must enter into a compromise between preserving autonomy (sovereignty) and effective control. Second, my suggestion attempts to arrive at such a compromise by resorting to models which already exist. Many regimes already have the possibility of imposing sanctions, so this does not amount to a revolution. Third: states basically retain their sovereignty: in extreme cases they can turn their back on their obligations by withdrawing from the regime; however, doing so comes at the high price that all those who suffer as a result of the withdrawal because the joint problem is now harder to solve seek to recover their losses from the 'defector.' Sovereignty would be defended at the price of material losses. To take this into account or to give higher priority to joint solution of the problem is the sovereign decision of the state considering what to do. To this extent, submitting to the procedures described is compatible with an understanding of sovereignty appropriate to today's conditions of close interdependence.

The superpowers

If one speaks of sovereignty, then one immediately thinks of the superpowers. They are not particularly concerned about the sovereignty of small states and from time to time nonchalantly disregard it, but tend to defend their own sovereignty with a zealous vigilance that borders on the grotesque. Yet even these powers have regularly acquiesced in the last 50 years to controls which contradict an absolute concept of sovereignty unaffected by interdependence. The WTO is proof of this willingness.

This brings us to consideration of one of the most important factors affecting the functioning of a sustainable arrangement for solving the world's problems: the attitude of the superpowers to international cooperation. It is not an exaggeration to say that it would be an absolute 'showstopper' for global governance if one or more of the political heavyweights – the US, China, India, Russia, Japan or the EU – were to play the spoilsport. The excesses of unilateral arrogance shown by the Bush administration have demonstrated for all to see what can go wrong when the most powerful state believes it can rule the world like a lord and master.

Perhaps there is a bright side to this disaster: the catastrophic failure of Bush's policies on all counts could create the point of view in the US and elsewhere that the uncompromising forcing through of national interests and objectives in the globalized world no longer has a future. If this lesson has been learned, the chances of global governance becoming sustainable are not so bad. For it is not about the superpowers no longer pursuing their national interests at all; rather, what is required are two insights. First of all, these interests can only be realized through cooperation. Second, solving world problems – upon which the survival of the people in the powerful countries as well as the continued existence of their power resources also ultimately depends – is in the best interests of the superpowers themselves.

Only when these insights take root can the superpowers play their part(s) in global governance. We do not need an attitude of idealistic surrender of power and unlimited willingness to sacrifice for global well being – that is not to be expected. An attitude of prudent limitation of power and selective exercise of power, measured pursuit of interests, willingness to cooperate, and observance of the law as the 'middle way' is enough to create the prerequisites for effective cooperation.

For, global governance demands several things of the super-powers. The first is acknowledging their role as the cause of problems. Economically, demographically, and ecologically, these economic giants are adding to the world's problems, politically they are involved in a series of conflicts. Their first task is to limit their own contribution to the overall damage and to engage in joint conflict management, as has already been described in the previous chapter. They need to transform themselves from being the main source of problems to being the leading problem solvers. Such a transformation would make them a positive example for others. The 'copycat effect,' in other words the tendency of smaller, weaker and younger players to imitate larger, stronger and more experienced players, has also been proven in international relations. This model function should not be underestimated; damaging though it is when the superpowers swing the ax in the forest, it can be just as beneficial when they display cooperative behavior for the common good. For, control achieved by emulation is one of the most economical instruments of all, because almost no resources are required.

In addition to setting a good example, the superpowers also have to demonstrate leadership – at least in the overall picture of things. Things are easier to regulate when they take the initiative, preferably in consultation with each other. Of course this does not preclude smaller countries with a strong sense of community (Canada and Sweden come to mind in this regard) from proceeding in individual issues. The more decisively and cooperatively the 'major countries' pull together in the right direction, the more quickly and smoothly solu-tions can be worked out for the serious problems, and the more easily initially antagonistic players can be convinced to enter into a mutually agreed solution. The superpowers have enormous resource potential. This puts them in a position to help others make their contribution to solving problems. Incidentally, this is also true for 'poorer' powers: China grants generous loans in Africa, and India is also independently active in development aid. Underdeveloped players primarily need administrative support, transfer of technology, capital, and training. 'Superpowers' are able to offer all these. Naturally, they reinforce their status by doing this, gain prestige, maintain good client relations – all of that is not harmful in itself, as long as it does not serve only the aggregation of power against other superpowers but instead contributes to solving mutual problems in a cooperative context. Their last important role is to help enforce regime rules against those who violate them. I discussed the most extreme case in chapter 5: dealing with disturbers of the peace. But the superpowers must also participate in encouraging others to adhere to rules such as those related to environmental policy. Their continual tendency to take obstreperous clients under their protective wing is harmful to global interests. It is to be hoped that the superpowers can agree to proceed in such conflicts 'without fear or favor.'

So that they can fulfill their roles as well as possible, conflicts among the 'great powers' must be contained to the greatest extent possible. The most suitable form in which this can take place is the 'concert' (chapter 5): a continuous round of consultations among the 'G-13,' i.e., the expanded group of G-8 states. 'Continuous consultations' means that the political directors of the foreign ministries should meet at least once a month, the ambassadors in the respective capital cities should meet once a week in order to be briefed by the host country about new foreign policy developments, and the UN ambassadors should also meet weekly. Specialists from the capital cities would convene to discuss individual issues. The relationship between the Security Council and the 'concert' would be decisive. The two bodies have different functions. For the 'concert of powers' it is mainly a matter of avoiding conflict among its members and clarifying positions regarding conflicts between other parties. The Security Council makes the decisions. The two institutions thus do not come into conflict with each other. On the contrary, as long as the extension of the Security Council in the direction of greater representativity is blocked, the 'concert' is a welcome transitional solution in order to allow all regions of the earth to participate through their most important countries in preparing decisions.

Non-governmental organizations

It may seem odd to many to discuss non-governmental organizations directly after the superpowers. However, as already suggested in the previous chapter, I consider them, to say it pointedly, to be the players in the international system which in the event of conflict would be in the best position to stand up to a superpower without provoking the riskiest political effects on the stability of world politics. NGOs are neither a trifling by-product of international politics nor are they the Holy Grail. In the 1980s and 1990s there was a tendency to misunderstand them as the bearer of world democracy. This has given way to a certain sobering assessment. It has been recognized that non-governmental organizations not only serve the public good but also their own organizational interests and sometimes the ego of individual leadership figures, that they sometimes all too will-ingly play the power game and give preference to spectacles that attract media attention rather than down-to-earth work. Some of them are not very democratically structured, their leaderships are elected (if at all) by nobody else but their members, and thus represent only these members, and they do not cancel out the North-South divide because the organizations from the 'north' are more numerous and better equipped.

Nevertheless, they have in the meantime become indispensable supplementary elements in the activities of the world of states. Many of these organizations are 'single-issue movements,' meaning that they are focused on one single 'public asset,' an element of the public good, and pursue this topic with maximum commitment. Perhaps the most important effect of these organizations is to get such topics onto the agenda of international politics in the first place. Would environmental policy be what it is today had it not been for the Club of Rome or Greenpeace? Would human rights policy be so prominent without Amnesty International or Human Rights Watch? Would the same be true for female genital mutilation were it not for the many women's movement organizations? Or for anti-personnel land mines without Medico International or the Red Cross? Certainly not!

Non-governmental organizations create a greater level of transparency for international events than do diplomats, whose preference is to carry on negotiations behind closed doors. This involves less a 'democratization of world politics' than an opportunity for the citizenry within democracies, in particular for members of parliament, to more closely monitor how governments conduct foreign policy: especially when agreements are to be concluded which solve problems and impose legal obligations on states. Their focus on one or just a few issues means that organizations are highly specialized. They operate at a level of expertise which exceeds that of representatives of countries – mostly diplomats and therefore generalists. NGOs are thus in a position to provide valuable specialist information to international processes of negotiation, which is why states are willing to allow them to take part as observers during such negotiations, to carry on exchange with NGOs in preparatory seminars or seminars run in parallel to negotiations, or to include their representatives in state delegations.

Through their input, NGOs have helped improve the quality of negotiations and their outcomes. Even the UN Security Council has come to appreciate the (informal) ongoing work contact with NGOs: in addition to the Arria meetings (see above), Security Council members and high-level UN civil servants regularly take part in meetings with the NGO Working Group on the Security Council, which has around 30 large NGOs as members.

Non-governmental organizations monitor the observance of rules by states and the behavior of multinational companies, and are far more strongly oriented towards values and objectives than these players. Thomas Risse and his associates have shown how the observance of human rights in countries with reluctant governments can be enhanced by the strategy of non-governmental organizations having representatives from the 'North' work closely together with local groups, with Western governments playing a supportive but not key role. The shift of human rights activism to the informal work of the NGOs refutes the accusation that world politics pursue Western cultural imperialism which results from the zeal of cosmopolitans to achieve their goals through the use of legal and political pressure. The fewer the number of political sanctions imposed by Western governments, the greater the relief of tension.

What can enable NGOs to bring a superpower to its senses if it violates international rules? The answer lies in the special type of power which NGOs possess. Unlike states, even in the case of well-off NGOs material resources are not the main issue. Their power lies in their 'mobilization capability,' a factor discovered by philosopher Hannah Arendt: the ability to gather many people behind the same project (states are also able to do this, but unlike NGOs they are able to rely more strongly on their considerable material resources). For instance they put the Ottawa Convention against anti-personnel landmines in place against the resistance of three permanent members of the Security Council, against Russia, China, and the United States, and also mobilized 'like-minded' states to back them.

So far the discussion has centered on dialog between the state and non-state level, in other words 'vertical communication.' But there is also horizontal communication between non-governmental organizations from various countries, regions and cultural groups. These contacts open up communication channels between societies and cultures. This is important because these elements of civil society often approach shared problems with initial opinions which differ widely. At the 1992 Earth Summit in Rio de Janeiro the visions of self-limitation held by Western environmental groups clashed with the development-oriented concerns of Third World participants. After this encounter, Western groups decided to integrate social aspects into their environmental policy demands as well. The 1994 Women's Conference in Beijing confronted feminist groups from the West with those from developing countries who called for improvement in the status of women, but at the same time for a 'more traditional' family-centered role for them. In each case it was decisive that those involved found common ground going beyond remaining differences in their values and demands, and focused on the shared values and demands, foremost the fight against violence to which women everywhere are subjected – an example of intercultural dialog in action.

The ability to mobilize people depends on the credibility NGOs have among the public. Credibility in turn demands of the

NGOs that they maintain a certain distance from the states. As much as they must exert their influence on the world of states and also use the resources of the states, they must also clearly remain immune to being taken over for the states' purposes. For in order to stay capable of mounting campaigns, they must always be able to credibly assert their own oppositional identity in the public eye. It is this 'mobilization capability,' which, if used deftly and energetically, could bring even a superpower to its knees. When the major multinational NGOs call for a boycott of Russian or Chinese or American products, this will have an effect. Millions of people will follow the call. The affected companies, employees, members of parliament will demand that their government revise its position (even in non-democratic states, incidentally). If the American government were to continue to thwart climate protection, a worldwide call to boycott American products would presumably be the only chance of forcing a change in policy. The NGOs should give affected companies the chance to 'buy their way out' of the embargo: by firmly committing to lowering their CO_2 emissions (or those of their products) by 2050, and to call upon their government to change their politics. The instrument of an NGO boycott must only be used very sparingly to target the 'worst offender.' The standard of 'equality before the law' cannot hold for the – always informal – campaigns of the NGOs because that would overstretch them. It can be assumed, however, that a campaign with severe economic consequences for one country would cause other violators to reconsider the unanticipated risks of such unlawful behavior. The advantage of such a punishment mechanism is that it limits the retaliatory and escalation risks resulting from setting up trade barriers between states. The risk of retaliation keeps many states from taking action against a superpower's behavior that violates rules; the risks of escalation include the potential for war. By contrast, no military intervention can be staged against NGOs; their actions cannot be attributed to a state, there is no powerful monopoly or military forces backing them, and a counter-boycott makes little sense.

Seen from the viewpoint of political ethics, is it not problematic to give NGOs such a role if they are not legitimized by anybody except their members? I do not think so. For – unlike states – the NGOs have no power to coerce anybody. Their 'mobilization capacity' only works if people voluntarily follow the call to take action. That makes every individual a referee on NGO policy. The success of the campaigns depends on how convincingly they reach the masses and affect their behavior; this response creates legitimacy for the exceptional case, and is also a precondition for success. Only if the outrage over the policy of a major power is worldwide or at least affects the consumers in large markets does the pressure and stress the boycotted state feels become extreme, because the boycott campaign has noticeable consequences. Only if NGOs themselves accept a code to resort to this last instrument only if the affected state disregards or blocks rules made by or desired by a vast majority of states can I detect no political-ethical dilemma. A campaign by NGOs in order to enforce an international principle of law against an offender would be a test of the degree to which a global society already exists today, and at the same time a contribution to building a world community. For, the 'compliance' with such a campaign, the extent to which the suggested boycott measure was followed beyond the borders of a country, region or cultural group, would be a symbol of community and a step towards creating such community.

In order to gain the power to act, NGOs must successfully increase their ability to coordinate. A coordination council of at least the major NGOs – cutting across the specialist areas they focus on – appears to be necessary for this. After the content of the earlier chapters, readers will not be surprised that I am arguing for such a coordination council to be set up interregionally and interculturally: developing countries must be represented on the council and have voting rights.

Panels of experts

Panels of experts which are appointed in part by states and their international organizations and partly by industry associations are exercising an increasing influence on global governance which should not be underestimated. Without the dedicated work of the Intergovernmental Panel on Climate Change (IPCC) and its reports, which have reverberated among the public like powerful blows, the stubborn Bush administration would not have shifted to the (still insufficient) position it has taken eventually.

These panels have two factors to thank for the effect they have: the aura of scientific competence and the worldwide diversity reflected in their members. Science still enjoys a special reputation among the public. This demands of scientists that they use their reputation responsibly. In addition, they must acquire the ability to convey their knowledge to a lay public so that it can be grasped and processed. This is difficult, but it can be done. Scientific results which contradict current political practice but take root in the public at large force governments to take notice and to increasingly have to justify policies which run counter to the prevalent view of the scientific community. A special panel of experts would be an ethics or cultural council as was envisaged in chapter 4: a group of educated representatives of the major cultural groups willing to carry on a dialog, who reflect on the ethical dimension while topic-based negotiations are being carried out, and then provide the results of their work as 'feedback' to the negotiating panels and to the transnational public. This work would serve the purpose of making transparent how the varying value systems can affect the systems of norms and rules which contribute to dealing with global problems. In addition, it would be the task of the ethics or cultural council to gradually create the building blocks for a universal concept of justice.

Commercial enterprise

Large corporations are important players in global politics. They possess formidable (economic) resources. With the help of these resources, corporations create hard facts which shape the underlying conditions of national government policy: corporate investment and trading activities influence the inner stability of societies and their states as well as the power relationships among them. They also have a direct influence on the decisions made by governments, houses of parliament, and international organizations, or at least try to.

In recent years it has been possible to observe an odd and contradictory development in the orientation of corporations which has serious consequences for our question – how favorable conditions for political regulation of global problems can be established. On the one hand there is the strict concentration on 'shareholder value' coupled with short-lived attention to quarterly results of companies; this trend works against our goal because the short-term nature of their outlook stands in opposition to sustainability, and the determined focus on the profit motive excludes all thought of the public good. On the other hand there is the opposite tendency to emphasize corporate ethics under the headings of 'corporate citizenship' and 'corporate social responsibility' which finds expression in the growing number of 'public-private partnerships' in which the partners commit themselves to balancing the legitimate inter-est of their corporations in being profitable with the interests of the general good. The most important institution in this context is the 'Global Compact' initiated by Kofi Annan; its ten principles set normative standards for appropriate behavior of companies in the private sector on questions related to human rights, employee rights, environmental protection and the fight against corruption. These principles manifest themselves in sec-tor-specific agreements among corporations and between them and other players which serve to limit the harmful impact of the economic sector on the level of violence in conflict situations. Included among these is the Kimberley Process to prevent traf-ficking of 'blood diamonds,' the Wolfsberg Principles which are intended to prevent money laundering, and the Durban Process for coltan mining (as diamonds do elsewhere in Africa, coltan fuels conflict in the Democratic Republic of Congo). The objec-tive of the Extractive Industries Transparency Initiative is to reveal the streams of payments in governments and business in the extractive sector. Companies have been more willing to dis-close information than states.

Acknowledging companies as political players requires choos-ing to give up the widely held negative prejudice against private enterprise. Just as is the case with states and non-governmental organizations, corporations are not to be judged 'good' or 'bad' from the start, but according to their practices. States and cor-porations must find ways which make it possible and easier for the latter to contribute to global social welfare while also staying profit-oriented; if they also make efforts going beyond this, all the better. Companies may sometimes be slow-witted and not comprehend that environmental compatibility is an impor-tant competitive factor of the future – the German automobile industry and energy sector are unfortunately glaring examples. Over the long term, a ruined environment is just as disadvantageous for commercial enterprise as is war or a trade war stoked up by cultural differences. If sustainable global governance wins out, this will provide the best conditions for development of private enterprise as a whole, and is thus clearly in its best interests. Of course – as with the superpowers – this calls for the strategic intelligence to keep long-term interests in mind when the lure of short-term profits beckons.

Where they do not recognize this interest, states must make rules, and civil society – as they do vis-à-vis the states – must keep a close eye on seeing that economic players also observe the norms of the Global Compact and other ethical guidelines such as the UN Draft Norms for Business and Human Rights, to which they have committed themselves. For it is often the case that carrying out good intentions is not subject to controls. Especially companies which manufacture brand-name products for the consumer market are extremely sensitive to negative campaigns, because these harm their chances on the market. Non-governmental organizations and rating agencies give companies a grade for their social-minded behavior, and these are already affecting the stock market decisions of some investors. This gives non-governmental organizations an effective lever for exerting 'subtle' pressure and, through 'blaming and shaming' to set unwilling companies on the path to an admirable stance on sustainability.

Summary

In this chapter I have provided a series of suggestions for action They are the answer to the question of how players and institutions in transnational and international relations can be 'arranged' so that the three potential obstacles to worldwide cooperation – diversity, disputes over justice, and war – are contained: only then will the path for jointly working on global problems be cleared. While making these suggestions, I have tried to find the middle way between daring vision and 'keeping my feet on the ground.' The suggestions made cannot be so revolutionary that their implementation is inconceivable. It is also just as true that one should not be so tied to the (clearly not all that convincing) practice of global governance today that this undesirable reality only propagates itself in the suggestions. That is why I have tried to find linkages in political reality, to start with today's status quo, but to develop the most promising approaches in such a way that a bridge can be built to a better and sustainable future for the institutional world order.

All things considered, prospects are not so bad. The institutional structure of world politics offers many opportunities for addressing the issues. With moderate corrections such as I have suggested its performance could be improved, its direction changed, involvement in negotiations and decision-making processes broadened, and the fairness of results increased. No earth-shaking institutional revolution is needed to improve the quality of global governance and thus create conditions under which the global problems of the world community could be attacked quickly and with lasting effect.

World politics is on the move and some of the movement – perhaps against the expectations of some readers – is going in the right direction. It is just that the steps being taken are too small. Above all, it has become apparent that global governance includes a wide variety of players; they each play a unique role. States and intergovernmental organizations still play the most important role, but they need other players in order to carry out the extensive tasks, because these can offset other functional weakness of state governments – such as their orientation towards a 'national interest' or the clumsiness of bureaucratic processes. Sustainable global governance reflects not only the diversity of regions and cultures but also the diversity of the players in today's world arena. To be sure – the players! If the core institutional requirements are already present, then they are clearly to blame for failing to achieve what is necessary. Especially the major powers are not living up to their leadership role; Western states are more interested in protecting their status and retaining what they have than governance aimed at preserving the existence of the world and humanity. Over and over again this chapter has stated that rational use of institutions and their reformation requires a new way of thinking on the part of the powerful. This may be dismissed as an idealistic appeal. In fact, it is an unshakeable statement of truth. And ultimately we normal citizens are called upon to play our part.

Much of what is written about global governance today has as its goal the foundation of a democratic world republic. Should I not be accused of having culpably neglected the topic of democracy – and therefore the most important element in good, sustainable global governance? For me it is a matter of setting priorities: when opportunities for implementing sustainable governance are sought in order to solve shared world problems as quickly as possible, the most important prerequisite is resolving violent conflicts and achieving inclusiveness, i.e., getting all the important players from outside Western culture to come aboard. This means that democratization cannot become the central vehicle of global governance. If it is a by-product, if global governance leads to non-democratic countries developing economically, ecologically, and socially, their society becoming more differentiated, better educated and more self-confident citizens demanding to be allowed to participate in the political process, and their rulers being forced to concede this bit by bit – all the better; we should support such a process, with equal measures of resolve and caution. But it should not be made a basic precondition for global cooperation. This would be a case of the best being the enemy of the good.

Have I made the state too strong? I have tried to show why global governance has better chances when stable and strong states cooperate with each other and why I believe that states are on average more robust and better able to take action than a substantial proportion of modern political analysts believes. In the last two chapters it has, however, become clear that global governance needs the assistance of other players. States are of central significance, but they are not in a position to carry the burden on their own. And for their own part, they need the external control of non-state players, international organizations, courts, and arbitration procedures, because in extreme cases unilateral sanctions imposed by states involve risks that are too great.

There are substantial hurdles on the pathway to solving global problems. The world is full of violent conflicts. There is dislike and mistrust between the members of different nations and cultures. Governments are short-term and oriented to (supposed) national interests. Power calculations obscure the view for appropriate options on what to do. Discrepancies in power and prosperity within and between nations are extremely large. In the one this sets off revolt against this inequality, in others efforts to preserve the status quo. Efforts to obtain one-sided advantages are accompanied by the attempt to avoid having to share the joint costs. Making collective goods available – and that is what solving our global problems is all about – is no trivial matter, precisely in the world of states, even if the great powers of the world will hopefully soon be better governed than in the recent past.

What will happen if we fail? It is easy to paint a black picture, but in this case it is appropriate for once. In this series of books there has been much talk of 'positive feedback'; processes that constantly and mutually reinforce one another. This exists not only in nature but in society and politics too. If the problems of population growth, energy, water, climate, and so on are not solved, more people will compete for fewer resources under worse conditions. The struggles for a share of the pie will escalate. This kind of struggle reinforces mobilization in support of one's own identity and vying for one's share against 'the others.' Under the banner of justice, people are taking up weapons in ever more regions, states and localities. War and anarchy are on the increase. A world which does not succeed in installing sustainable governance is doomed to regress into a world of conflict of all against all. And yet there is a silver lining on the horizon. The community of states has occasionally roused itself to sensible joint action. It agreed on the Montreal Protocol on Substances that Deplete the Ozone Layer, and then step by step made it more stringent. It enacted a ban on chemical weapons with strict control measures, and most states ratified it. In the much maligned World Trade Organisation it adopted rules to prevent the return of the raging trade wars of the 1930s, which contributed to the Second World War (a function of the WTO which its critics overlook). Through external pressure it helped the people in South Africa overthrow the racist apartheid regime. The Europeans have put behind them enmities that were regarded as unhealable. Overcoming conflicts is thus not prohibited by a 'law of nature.' It is possible when political good will, the resolve to act, and negotiating skill retain the upper hand.

The problems that our series of books has analyzed in detail and for which it has proposed solutions are concrete and well known. They can only be solved cooperatively. Certainly: that something is needed does not mean that it will be done. But a solution is in the long term interests of everybody involved. That is a place to begin, a strong argument on the side of those who have already gained insight into what is needed. Politicians are also capable of being convinced. The issues covered in this book could drive a person to resignation. All that is well and good, you may say, but am I not helpless in the broad sweep of world politics? Is it not the case that 'the people at the top' do what they want, and that means: mostly the wrong thing and, in any case, to further their own interests? Am I as an individual person not a helpless dust mote floating in the mighty stream of world events? Is there anything at all that I can do? The answer is: yes, there is! It is the resignation of the many that prevents rapid progress towards global governance. It is the courage of the few that carries it forward. Get informed. Read a good newspaper every day. Log on to the Internet and look for concepts such as 'Kyoto Protocol' or 'Security Council.' Being informed is the beginning of active life. Become involved in politics. Join a political party. Fight for the idea of sustainability there. Write a letter to your Member of Congress. Demand that he or she support sustainable governance. Attend election meetings if he or she does not do it. Criticize them in public. Write letters to the editor. Look for people with similar ideas with whom to join up. Become active for a sustainable corporate ethic at work. Suggest that your firm set up a non-profit foundation or, if one already exists, that it be better supported. If you are a teacher make it plain to your students that their future depends on the success of sustainability policy. Join a non-governmental organization. Arrange a partnership between your own church parish and a mosque in Jordan – or in Munich or Cologne. While still a student form a 'peer group' with your best friends. Promise each other that you will work for sustainability, no matter where; in politics, at college, at work, in non-governmental organizations. Hold regular meetings and report to each other. Encourage each other to carry on.

We enjoy the privilege of living in a democracy. We have a better chance of leading an active life that influences politics than people in dictatorships. The more of us who make use of this possibility, the greater the chance of moving world politics in the right direction. World politics begins with us, nowhere else. After his death, the Greek king Sisyphus was condemned by the gods to roll a huge boulder up a hill in the underworld. He did this over and over again; but every time just when he was nearly finished, the stone rolled down the hill again. Since antiquity, Sisyphus has been the symbol of hopeless effort in vain. Sisyphus was alone. If there had been enough friends with him – he would have done it.

AIDS – Acquired Immunodeficiency Syndrome is the result of an infection with the HI-virus (human immunodeficiency virus), which causes progressive destruction of the immune system.

ASEAN – Association of Southeast Asian Nations is an international organization of Southeast Asian nations with political, economic, and cultural goals.

ATTAC – Association for the Taxation of Financial Transactions for the Aid of Citizens is a worldwide NGO that is critical of globalization.

CIA – Central Intelligence Agency.

Communitarianism – Emerged above all from criticism of liberalism and the increasing individualization of modern pluralistic societies (loss of sense of community and devaluation of traditional lifestyles based on solidarity). A just order would require a return to and an adoption of common social values. This would only be possible – according to the communitarians – in a local framework, so that the largest imaginable community is the nation-state.

Corporate Citizenship – Systematically organized social engagement in and by corporations which have adopted a middle- and long-term strategy of responsible behavior and, over and above their business activities, see themselves as 'responsible citizens' who are active in the local civil society or take up ecological or cultural causes.

Corporate Social Responsibility – A concept of social responsibility of corporations with the goal of sustainable development based on the three pillars of economy, society and environment.

Cosmopolitanism – World citizenship, formation of a global society of human beings based on universal values shared by all.

Cultural fragmentation – The collapse of consensus about world-political values and conceptions of order as a result of the world-political changes summarized in the concept of globalization.

Deliberation – Public communication based on argumentation, with the goal of acknowledging and building up the abilities and competencies of participants as politically active citizens.

Diaspora – Dispersed immigrant communities which preserve common link to a homeland.

ECOSOC –Economic and Social Council of the United Nations.

EU – European Union.

Fundamentalism – A label for religious or ideological movements characterized by their unconditional, uncompromising adherence to missionary principles or articles of faith, which they represent with unconditional exclusivity, and whose goal is a return to the roots of 'their' religion or ideology.

G-8 – The Group of 8 is an international forum of the seven leading industrial nations (the US, Japan, Germany, France, Italy, Great Britain and Canada) plus Russia.

GA – The General Assembly of the United Nations.

Global Compact – Full title 'United Nations Global Compact' is a worldwide pact that was agreed upon between corporations and the United Nations with the aim of carrying out globalization in a more social and ecologically sustainable way.

Hegemony – Political, economic or social domination by one player (a collective or a state) in a national or international framework.

ICJ – The International Court of Justice is the highest court of the United Nations with its seat in The Hague (The Netherlands). Its function and responsibilities are laid down in the UN Charter and in the ICJ Statute.

Input legitimacy – Is based on the normative principle of the consent of the governed, so that according to this principle legitimacy derives from the consent of the governed.

International regime – A body of principles, norms, rules, and decision-making procedures which, on the basis of voluntary agreements of state, and to some extent also non-state players, regulate and restrict activities in a particular problem area by coordinating the behavior of the different players in accordance with their shared goals.

ICC – The International Criminal Court is a permanent international tribunal with the task of investigating the worst international crimes (genocide, crimes against humanity, war crimes) and bringing the people responsible to justice.

IPPC – *Intergovernmental Panel on Climate Change*.

Kyoto Protocol – A protocol to the international Framework Convention on Climate Change (UNFCCC) of the United Nations with the objective of protecting the global climate. The Kyoto Protocol sets the first binding target values for greenhouse gas emissions which are the primary cause of global warming.

NATO – North Atlantic Treaty Organization.

NGO – non-governmental organization

NPT – Treaty on the Non-Proliferation of Nuclear Weapons (or Non-Proliferation Treaty)

OECD – Organisation for Economic Cooperation and Development

Output legitimacy – based on the functional principle of usefulness, this concept means that an institution only obtains legitimation when the actions it takes conform to the requirements it is obliged to fulfill.

P-5 – The five permanent members of the United Nations Security Council: the United States, Russia, France, Great Britain, and China

Particularism – A striving for broad political, economic and cultural independence and representation of the interests of individual players, while placing less importance on overarching communities.

Pluralism – This concept describes multifaceted forms of order and world views; unlike totalitarian ideologies or particularism, pluralism recognizes existing varying interests and political positions, and views their individual implementation, representation and articulation as legitimate and desirable.

Public-Private Partnerships – Cooperation between the public sector and private enterprise.

Sovereignty – legal independence of a state from other states (internal sovereignty) as well as legal equality of all sovereign states (external sovereignty).

UNESCO – the United Nations Educational, Scientific and Cultural Organization.

Universalism principle – says that all members of a society are
    entitled to have the same rights.

Universality – the generalizability of scientific statements or
    cultural convictions (values) at a universal level.

UNO – the United Nations Organization.

WTO – the World Trade Organization.

Further Reading

Chapter 1

Beisheim, Marianne/Dreher, Sabine/Walter, Gregor/
Zangl, Bernhard/Zürn, Michael 1999: Im Zeitalter der
Globalisierung? Thesen und Daten zur gesellschaftlichen
und politischen Denationalisierung, Baden-Baden, Nomos

Brozus, Lars/Take, Ingo/Wolf, Klaus-Dieter 2003:
Vergesellschaftung des Weltregierens? Der Wandel nationaler
und internationaler politischer Steuerung unter dem Leitbild
der nachhaltigen Entwicklung, Opladen, Leske & Budrich

Stiftung Entwicklung und Frieden 2007: Globale Trends 2007,
Frankfurt a.M., Fischer

Walzer, Michael 2000: Just and Unjust Wars. A Model
Argument with Historical Illustrations, 3rd edition, New
York, Basic Books, 20

Rittberger, Volker 2006: Weltregieren: Was kann es leisten?
Was muss es leisten? in: Küng, Hans/Senghaas, Dieter
2003: Friedenspolitik. Ethische Grundlagen internationaler
Beziehungen, München/Zürich, Piper, 175–288

Zürn, Michael 2006: Global Governance, in: Schuppert,
Gunnar Folke (Ed.), Governance-Forschung. Vergewisserung
über Stand und Entwicklungslinien, 2nd edition, Baden-
Baden, Nomos, 121–146

Chapter 2

Münkler, Herfried 2007: Imperien, Reinbek, Rowohlt

Bollmann, Ralph 2006: Lob des Imperiums. Der Untergang
    Roms und die Zukunft des Westens, Berlin, Siedler

Brillmayer, Lea 1994: American Hegemony, Political Morality
    in a one-superpower world, New York

Daalder, Ivo/Goldgeier, James 2006: Global NATO, in Foreign
    Affairs 85 (5), 105–113

Slaughter, Ann Marie 2004: A New World Order, Princeton,
    Princeton University Press

Frum, David/Perle, Richard 2004: An End to Evil: How to Win
    the War on Terror, New York, Random House

Kuper, Andrew 2004: Democracy Beyond Borders, Justice and
    Representation in Global Institutions, Oxford, Oxford
    University Press

Held, David 1995: Democracy and the Global Order. From the
    Modern State to Cosmopolitan Governance, Cambridge,
    Polity Press

Höffe, Otfried 1999: Demokratie im Zeitalter der
    Globalisierung. München, Beck

Beck, Ulrich 2004: Der kosmopolitische Blick oder Krieg ist
    Frieden, Frankfurt a.M., Suhrkamp

Stiftung Entwicklung und Frieden 2006: Global Governance
    für Entwicklung und Frieden. Perspektiven nach einem
    Jahrzehnt, Bonn, Dietz

Zürn, Michael 1998: Regieren jenseits des Nationalstaats,
    Frankfurt a.M., Suhrkamp

Chapter 3

Meyer, Thomas 2002: Identitätspolitik. Vom Missbrauch
kultureller Unterschiede, Frankfurt a.M., Suhrkamp
Meyer, John W. 2004: Weltkultur. Wie die westlichen Prinzipien
die Welt durchdringen, Frankfurt a.M., Suhrkamp
Huntington, Samuel 1996, Der Kampf der Kulturen. The Clash
of Civilizations, München/Wien
Müller, Harald 1998: Das Zusammenleben der Kulturen. Ein
Gegenentwurf zu Huntington, Frankfurt a.M., Fischer
Taschenbuch Verlag
Senghaas, Dieter 1998: Zivilisation wider Willen, Frankfurt
a.M., Suhrkamp
Sen, Amartya 2006: Die Identitätsfalle. Warum es keinen Krieg
der Kulturen gibt, München, Beck
Walzer, Michael 1994: Thick and Thin: Moral Argument at
Home and Abroad, Notre Dame, University of Notre Dame
Press
Küng, Hans/Senghaas, Dieter 2003: Friedenspolitik. Ethische
Grundlagen internationaler Beziehungen, München/Zürich,
Piper

Chapter 4

Höffe, Otfried 1987: Politische Gerechtigkeit. Grundlegung
einer kritischen Philosophie von Recht und Staat, Frankfurt
a.M.
Forst, Rainer 1994: Kontexte der Gerechtigkeit. Philosophie
jenseits von Liberalismus und Kommunitarismus, Frankfurt
a.M., Suhrkamp

Albin, Cecilia 1996: Justice and Fairness in International
    Negotiations, Cambridge, Cambridge University Press
Rawls, John 2004: Justice as Fairness. A Restatement,
    Cambridge, MA, Belknapp Press
Habermas, Jürgen 1981: Theorie des kommunikativen
    Handelns, Vols I and II, Frankfurt a.M., Suhrkamp
Pogge, Thomas 2002: World Poverty and Human Rights,
    Cambridge, Polity
Sen, Amartya 1992: Inequality Reexamined, Oxford, Oxford
    University Press
Epiney, Astrid/Scheyli, Martin 2000: Umweltvölkerrecht, Bern
Chris Brown, Sovereignty, Rights and Justice, Cambridge,
    Polity Press
Alasdair MacIntyre, Whose Justice? Which Rationality?
    London 1988

Chapter 5

Vasquez, John A. 2000: What do we know about war?,
    Lanham, Rowman and Littlefield
Zürn, Michael/Zangl, Bernhard 2003: Frieden und Krieg.
    Sicherheit in der postnationalen Konstellation, Frankfurt
    a.M., Suhrkamp
Kaldor, Mary 1999: New and Old Wars. Organized Violence in
    a New Era, Stanford, Stanford University Press
Münkler, Herfried 2002: Die neuen Kriege, Reinbek, Rowohlt
Geis, Anna (Hrsg.) 2006: Den Krieg überdenken. Kriegsbegriffe
    und Kriegstheorien in der Kontroverse, Baden-Baden,
    Nomos

Czempiel, Ernst-Otto 1986: Friedensstrategien. Systemwandel durch Internationale Organisationen, Demokratisierung und Wirtschaft, Paderborn et al., Schöningh

Chapter 6

Byers, Michael/Nolte, Georg (Ed.) 2003: United States Hegemony and the Foundations of International Law, Cambridge

Rajagopal, Balakrishnan 2003: International Law from Below. Development, Social Movements and Third World Resistance, Cambridge, Cambridge University Press

Franck, Thomas M. 1995: Fairness in International Law and Institutions, Oxford, Clarendon Press

Fischer-Lescano, Andreas/Teubner, Gunther 2006: Regime-Kollisionen. Die Fragmentierung des internationalen Rechts, Frankfurt a.M., Suhrkamp

Koskenniemi, Marti 2006: From Aplology to Utopia: The Structure of International Legal Argument, Cambridge, Cambridge University Press

Morgenthau, Hans 1940: Positivism, Functionalism, and International Law, American Journal of International Law 34:2, 260–284

Zangl, Bernd/Zürn, Michael (Ed.) 2004: Verrechtlichung – ein Baustein für Global Governance, Bonn

List, Martin/Zangl, Bernhard 2003: Verrechtlichung internationaler Politik, in: Gunther Hellmann/Klaus Dieter Wolf/Michael Zürn (Ed.): Die neuen Internationalen Beziehungen: Forschungsstand und Perspektiven in Deutschland, Baden-Baden, 361–400

Abbot, Kenneth, W./Keohane, Robert O./Moravcsik, Andrew/ Slaughter, Anne-Marie/Snidal, Duncan 2000: The Concept of Legalization, International Organization 54:3, 401–419

Chapter 7

Czempiel, Ernst-Otto 1999: Kluge Macht. Außenpolitik für das 21. Jahrhundert, München, Beck

Beyerlin, Ulrich/Stoll, Peter-Tobias/Wolfrum, Rüdiger (Ed.) 2006: Ensuring Compliance with Multilateral Environmental Agreements, Leiden et al.

Brühl, Tanja et al. (Ed.) 2004: Unternehmen in der Weltpolitik. Politiknetzwerke, Unternehmensregeln und die Zukunft des Multilateralismus, Bonn, Dietz

High-level Panel on Threats, Challenges and Change, New York, United Nations 2004, http://www.un.org/secureworld/

Frantz, Christine/Martens, Kerstin 2006: Nichtregierungsorganisationen, Wiesbaden, VS

Glasius, Marlies/Kaldor, Mary/Anheier, Helmut (Ed.) 2001ff., Global Civil Society Yearbook, Oxford, Oxford University Press

Kaldor, Mary 2003: Global Civil Society: An Answer to War, Cambridge, Polity Press

Risse, Thomas/Ropp, Stephen C./Sikkink, Kathryn (Ed.) 1999: The Power of Human Rights: International Norms and Domestic Change, Cambridge, Cambridge University Press

Wolf, Klaus Dieter 2000: Die neue Staatsraison. Zwischenstaatliche Kooperation als Demokratieproblem in der Weltgesellschaft. Plädoyer für eine Entstaatlichung des Regierens jenseits des Staates, Baden-Baden, Nomos

Rittberger, Volker/Zangl, Bernhard 2006: International
    Organization. Policy, Politics and Policies, Houndmills,
    Palgrave Macmillan
Wolf, Klaus-Dieter 2005: Die UNO. Geschichte, Aufgaben,
    Perspektiven, München, Beck

327 MUL